Collins

# BTEC FIRST

# Business

Charlotte Bagley,
Andrew Dean,
Louise Stubbs, John Bevan

Published by Collins Education
An imprint of HarperCollins*Publishers*
77–85 Fulham Palace Road
Hammersmith
London
W6 8JB

Browse the complete Collins Education catalogue at
www.collinseducation.com

©HarperCollins*Publishers* Limited 2013

10 9 8 7 6 5 4 3 2 1

Petroc Learning Resources

ISBN 978-0-00-747979-5

Charlotte Bagley, John Bevan, Andrew Dean and Louise Stubbs assert their moral rights to be identified as the authors of this work.

Series editor Charlotte Bagley

All rights reserved. No part of this publication may be reproduced, stored in a retrieval system, or transmitted in any form or by any means, electronic, mechanical, photocopying, recording or otherwise, without the prior written permission of the Publisher or a licence permitting restricted copying in the United Kingdom issued by the Copyright Licensing Agency Ltd., 90 Tottenham Court Road, London W1T 4LP.

British Library Cataloguing in Publication Data

A Catalogue record for this publication is available from the British Library.

Project managed by Cambridge Editorial
Edited by Sue Ecob, Ros Horton and Sally Simmons
Picture research by Matthew Hammond
Design and typesetting by Jouve India Private Ltd.
Illustrations by Ann Paganuzzi
Cover design by Angela English
Printed and bound in Italy by Lego

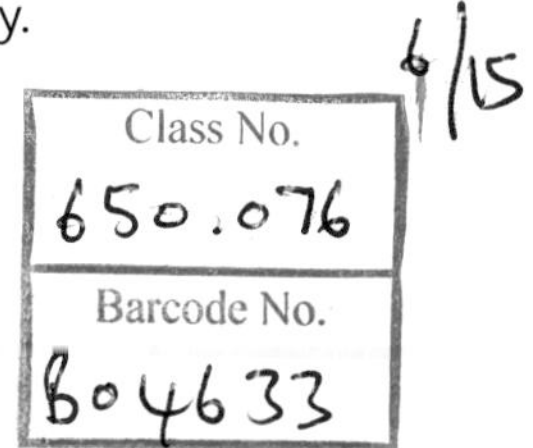


Every effort has been made to contact copyright holders but if any have been inadvertently overlooked, the publishers will be pleased to make the necessary arrangements at the first opportunity.

All Crown Copyright Material is produced with permission of the Controller, Office of Public Sector Information (OPSI)

# Contents

# Introduction

Welcome to the Edexcel BTEC Level 1/Level 2 First Award in Business student textbook.

This course book is written for students aiming to achieve the Next Generation Edexcel BTEC Level 1/Level 2 First Award in Business. In addition, the book gives the pointers you need in order to achieve a merit or distinction.

The skills and knowledge that you will learn while studying for your BTEC First Award in Business will allow you to progress to Level 3 courses or apprenticeships and enter the workplace in roles such as assistants in business administration, marketing finance, human resources, sales and customer service.

The Edexcel BTEC Level 1/Level 2 First Award in Business allows you to develop knowledge and understanding by applying skills in a work-related and vocational context. This book is focused on your need to gain your BTEC First Business qualification, and provides real-life, engaging, stimulating and up-to-date examples from the business world. The business world is ever-changing and, with the economic climate as it stands, it is an exciting time to learn about the subject. We hope that you enjoy the book as we have tried our best to establish all of your learning in the real world.

## How is the book organised?

The book consists of eight chapters, covering closely the first eight units of the Edexcel BTEC Level 1/Level 2 First Award in Business specification. This means that you can have confidence that all the topics and issues referred to in the course specification are in this book.

- Each unit matches the specifications for the Level 2 qualification. Each section provides you with a focused and manageable chunk of learning.

Overall, the chapters cover all of the learning and assessment requirements of the Level 2 Award qualification.

## How is assessment covered?

The Edexcel BTEC Level 1/Level 2 First Award in Business is assessed through coursework (internally assessed) and an externally assessed finance core unit (Unit 2). This will be assessed via an onscreen test. In order to achieve your Level 2 Award, you will need to provide evidence of your knowledge and understanding of business as well as displaying competence in various practical tasks. Units 1 and 2 are core units and are compulsory. They cover the content that employers value as essential. The remainder of the units (3–8) are specialist optional units that are sector specific.

Each unit of this book ends with a checklist of assessment criteria that you need to cover in order to gain either a pass, merit or distinction. This checklist will help you to keep track of your progress.

The suggested assessment tasks in each unit will help you gather the evidence you need for each unit. As for Unit 2 (externally assessed), there are practice questions covering all the topics to help you prepare for the external assessment. Your tutor or assessor will help you to plan your work so you can meet the overall assessment requirements of your target qualification.

We hope that you will find the material in this book accessible and interesting, and that it inspires you to pursue a stimulating career in business. Good luck with your course and your future career!

Charlotte Bagley, John Bevan, Andrew Dean and Louise Stubbs.

## Qualification information

The book has been written to cover the Level 2 Award in Business qualification.

The units that make up the Level 2 Award provide learners new to business with a solid awareness of issues and topics in the business world.

### Level 2 Award in Business

Learners aiming to achieve a Level 2 Award in Business must complete and pass the two core units (Units 1 and 2) plus a further two optional specialist units. Each unit should be taught over 30 guided learning hours. In order to pass this qualification, a total of 120 guided learning hours need to be completed.

| Unit number | Unit title | Guided learning hours | Type of unit/assessment |
|---|---|---|---|
| 1 | Enterprise in the business world | 30 | Core/internal |
| 2 | Finance for business | 30 | Core/external |
| 3 | Promoting a brand | 30 | Optional specialist/internal |
| 4 | Principles of customer service | 30 | Optional specialist/internal |
| 5 | Sales and personal selling | 30 | Optional specialist/internal |
| 6 | Introducing retail business | 30 | Optional specialist/internal |
| 7 | Providing business support | 30 | Optional specialist/internal |
| 8 | Recruitment, selection and employment | 30 | Optional specialist/internal |

# 1 Enterprise in the business world

## Learning aim A: Know how trends and the current business environment may impact on a business

- Topic A.1 Finding information: information is vital for a business to survive
- Topic A.2 Factors to consider in the current business environment: politics, the government and location
- Topic A.3 Trends affecting business: demographics, technology, the environment and ethical issues
- Topic A.4 Size of business and type: factors that affect the size of businesses and what help is out there for them

## Learning aim B: Plan an idea for a business

- Topic B.1 How business ideas can be successful: ideas can emerge from innovations that meet customer needs more effectively
- Topic B.2 Businesses ideas: researching the market to identify gaps and designing products to answer needs
- Topic B.3 Assessing the suitability of a business idea: business ideas need to be carefully assessed to minimise the risk of failure
- Topic B.4 Producing an initial plan for a business idea: initial plans must include the vision and the supporting evidence

## Learning aim C: Present a business model for a business start-up

- Topic C.1 Choice of format: a number of business formats need to be considered and selected before the business begins to trade
- Topic C.2 Sources of help and support in developing a new business: a wide range of support organisations can help with all aspects of running a business
- Topic C4. Business model: the selection of an appropriate business model is one of the most important decisions to be made and will include all aspects of the business's operation

# Finding information

## 2A.P1 Sources of information

Businesses need to understand the critical role information plays in many aspects of business. Information drives the way we communicate and make decisions. Managers in business spend a lot of time gathering information and processing it before communicating it to others within the business. Having the correct information at the right time allows managers to make the correct decisions about the business.

All businesses need information in order to find out what is going on in the business environment and guide their decision making. Sources of information come in a variety of forms. Printed material includes professional and trade journals and newspapers. Many businesses read national and local newspapers to review what is happening in the UK and local economies. Many businesses subscribe to **professional** and **trade journals** such as *The Grocer* for the retail trade.

Many businesses join **networking** organisations that can supply information to help support new businesses. An example is the Federation of Small Businesses (FSB) whose members can meet to discuss business issues.

Increasingly over the last few years, businesses receive information for the purposes of marketing, selling, distribution and paying for products and services. The development of Twitter, Facebook and other types of social media has allowed businesses to enhance and improve their information sources. Around three quarters of the world's top 100 companies have a Twitter account, posting company updates and offering customer service, deals and job information.

The information that a business uses must be up to date. This is known as **information currency**. Businesses must also take care to ensure that information is free from **bias**. If a confectionery retailer, such as Cadbury, wanted to find out more information about consumers' changing preferences for chocolate, it would have to ensure that it used market information from an unbiased source, such as **Mintel**. If one of its competitors, for example Nestlé, had written a report, it might be biased towards its own products.

Trying to decide whether a source of information is reliable can be quite difficult. Businesses must find out where the research has come from and whether the author is credible. They also need to check whether the information is up to date.

Your assessment criteria:

**2A.P1** Outline how the business environment can impact on a start-up business.

### Key terms

***Bias:*** *show prejudice for or against someone or something*

***Information currency:*** *how up to date the information is*

***Mintel:*** *a privately owned market research firm that provides market research reports on various different industries*

***Networking:*** *developing and maintaining contacts and personal connections with a variety of people who might be helpful to you*

***Professional journals:*** *contain information and articles for a particular profession, such as accountancy or law*

***Trade journals:*** *magazines aimed at people who work in a specific industry, such as retail or catering*

**Trade journals contain important information for businesses**

 **Discuss**

*In groups, discuss how reliable the following sources of information are likely to be.*

1. *A government report on skills levels of the workforce.*
2. *A published report by a major breakfast cereal manufacturer on the market for cereals.*
3. *A report on business finance from an organisation that does not operate within the business finance market.*

**Case study**

Sonny owns a small retail shop in a small town in West Sussex. He is getting increasingly concerned by the state of the economy and what impact this could have on his business. At the moment, his business is doing well. He has a steady and loyal customer base. He is looking to expand his business and perhaps buy other premises in another local town. However, he knows this will take a lot of research in order to make an informed decision.

1. Research and list the printed material sources that Sonny could use in order to find out the necessary information about the retail trade.
2. Research and list the networking organizations that Sonny could use in order to find out the necessary information about the retail trade.
3. Research and list any types of social media or technology sources that Sonny could use in order to find out the necessary information about the retail trade.

How could Sonny check the information currency of the sources that you have listed in your answers to questions 1–3?

# Factors to consider in the business environment

## 2A.P1 What factors to consider in the current business environment

The UK government can make political decisions that can either hinder or help a start-up business. For example, it could make a decision to force businesses to become more environmentally friendly. If a business is made to implement recycling and reduce its carbon footprint a lot of money needs to be invested in these schemes.

Political decisions can be made across a wide range of economic issues that businesses need to consider.

Taxation is where charges are placed on businesses and people to raise money for government expenditure. There is personal taxation, which can impact on the business in terms of how much money consumers have to spend on the business's products. If consumers have to pay more tax, they will not have so much money to spend. Businesses are also taxed. If businesses have to pay more tax they will make less profit as they will use the money they make to pay their tax bill.

Inflation is the general increase in prices, which means everything becomes more expensive to buy. When inflation is high people tend to save more and spend less, which in turn can create unemployment. If people stop spending, businesses suffer and have to lay off staff.

Unemployment can be good for businesses. There will be more people looking for jobs so the business has more individuals to select from. It can also be bad news for businesses as people will have less money to spend on products, which will cause the demand for them to fall.

Exchange rate is the price of one currency expressed in terms of another. If there is an increase in the value of the pound and a business imports products into this country then the imported products will be cheaper and more will be purchased. If the value of the pound increases and a business exports products and services abroad then these products will become more expensive to buy and demand from abroad will fall.

The cost of a loan is governed by the interest rate. Interest is expressed as a percentage and is added to the money someone borrows from a lender. Depending on the interest rate and the length of the loan, the business may have to pay back considerably more than the original amount borrowed. A fall in interest rates means it is cheaper to borrow money and businesses will be more likely to borrow in order to fund new

Your assessment criteria:

**2A.P1** Outline how the business environment can impact on a start-up business

### Key terms

***Exchange rate:*** *the price of one currency expressed in terms of another currency*

***Inflation:*** *the general increase in prices, which means everything becomes more expensive to buy*

***Loan:*** *a sum of money that is borrowed from a bank by a business and is paid back with interest*

***Taxation:*** *charges placed on businesses and people to raise money for government expenditure*

projects, such as opening a new store if they want to expand. A rise in interest rates will have the opposite effect.

At a local level, there are also important issues that a business must consider, such as location (its premises). Businesses usually need to be situated close to their suppliers so that they can replace stock as quickly as possible. They may wish to locate in a different area from their competitors so that there is less competition for their goods and services. For many businesses, such as retailers, it is also very important to locate near to their customers. Some businesses are dependent on having easy access to equipment for the ongoing operation of their businesses and they tend to locate near their equipment suppliers.

**Discuss**

*In groups, discuss the following issues.*

1. *What local factors may impact on the way a business operates in your area?*
2. *What sources of information would this local business need to use to guide its planning?*

**Unemployment affects the current business environment**

**Case study**

Darries Ltd is a new business that employs six staff making organically produced honey. Recent research has shown that honey has many health benefits and these have been reported in the national press. The government is proposing to increase the amount of tax that businesses have to pay.

1. What information source is mentioned in the case study? (2A.P1)
2. How does the tax increase impact on the business? (2A.P1)
3. What other national and local factors could affect the business? (2A.P1)

# The impact of changes to the current business environment

## 2A.M1 What is the impact?

When an **entrepreneur** wants to start a business, a business proposal is produced that describes what the business will do and how it will operate to answer customer needs and make a profit. This is known as a **business proposition**. The business proposition will clearly describe the different groups of customers it wants to target. For example, a leisure club may identify a clear distinction between daytime users, who are often young mothers with children, and older retired people, and evening users who like to keep fit after work. The leisure club has to tailor its facilities to cater for the needs of these different groups of customers. This may include providing crèche facilities during the day, and charging different rates at different times (prices tend to be higher in the evenings when demand is higher). There are many factors that can impact on these different **targeted groups** of customers. If unemployment rises, the group that goes in the evening, who have busy jobs and pay more, may become more cautious about spending their money on leisure activities. They may stop going or go less frequently due to fear of losing their jobs and a desire to save more money. The rising unemployment factor has therefore impacted on this group of customers and could in turn have a negative effect on the health and leisure club.

Your assessment criteria:

**2A.M1** Explain how changes in the current business environment are likely to impact on a start-up business

### Key terms

***Business proposition:*** *describes what the business will do and how it will operate to answer customer needs and make a profit*

***Entrepreneur:*** *a person who organises, operates and takes on the risk for a new business venture*

***Targeted groups:*** *customers with whom the business is trying to communicate to tell them about the benefits of their products or services*

**Factors in the environment impact on customers**

### Discuss

*Identify the possible target groups of customers for each of these propositions.*

1. *A business that repairs bicycles.*
2. *A business that operates a home cleaning service.*
3. *A business that arranges weddings.*

*What changes in the current business environment could impact on these businesses?*

**Case study**

Be Tan Safe is a start-up business that makes and sells organic suntan lotion. It is an internet-based company operating from the UK. It sources the aloe vera for its products from the Caribbean and has taken out a business loan to fund research into new products that help protect people from the sun. It has undertaken research and identified four different types of customers.

(a) Those customers who are scared of getting sunburn.

(b) Those who love being in the sun and understand sun protection factors.

(c) Those who like the sun but don't bother to protect themselves.

(d) Those who like a tan, use lotion but do not understand sun protection factors.

1. How will the changes in the current business environment impact on the business? Consider the economy, exchange rates and the cost of loans. (2A.M1)
2. What impact will these factors have on the different customers? (2A.M1)
3. What relevance do these factors have on the business proposition? (2A.M1)

**Discuss**

*Discuss with your family and friends the tax that they have to pay and how they would feel if that tax was increased.*

If the government imposes an increase in personal taxes, such as income tax, then more of customers' income will be used to pay for leisure activities such as going to the gym. The health and leisure club may therefore find that its customers stop renewing their membership and instead opt for cheaper forms of exercise such as going for a jog or buying an exercise DVD.

If the government were to impose an increase in business taxes, for example of corporation tax (the tax that companies have to pay on their profits), this would also have a negative effect on a business such as a health and leisure club. It would not make as much profit and would therefore not have as much money to invest in new equipment for the gym, putting on new classes or updating the crèche.

If inflation increases this generally means that consumers save more and spend less, so businesses like the health and leisure club may find they start losing customers who can no longer afford the membership fees.

If there was an increase in the value of the pound compared to other currencies it would mean that importing goods from abroad would be cheaper. This could have a positive effect for companies if they buy goods from other countries. If the health and leisure club wants to invest in the latest equipment for their gym, these machines may come from countries such as the USA and would therefore be cheaper to purchase.

If the health and leisure club is considering expanding its business, it will need money to do so. Taking out a loan from a bank could also have an impact on the business. If the interest rate is low, borrowing money is cheaper and it would therefore be desirable to borrow money to expand.

# Trends affecting business

## 2A.P2 Trends that affect businesses

A key aspect of successfully running a business is finding out about **trends** that could affect the **market**, which in turn will have an impact on the business in the future. For example, if house buyers are not being offered mortgages because of a credit crisis, the demand for new houses will decline and this will have a negative impact on construction businesses. There are four main types of trend that affect businesses:

- social – trends occurring within society
- technological – trends in the use and development of technology
- environmental – trends towards having greater concerns for the environment
- ethical – trends towards having a fairer and equal society

Your assessment criteria:

**2A.P2** Explain how current trends will impact on a start-up business

### Key terms

***Business start-up:*** *a new business that is just commencing trading*

***Carbon footprint:*** *refers to the amount of carbon dioxide ($CO_2$) a business emits*

***Demographics:*** *the most recent statistical characteristics of a population such as age, gender, etc.*

***Market:*** *where products and services are bought and sold*

***SMEs:*** *small and medium-sized enterprises*

***Trend:*** *general direction in which something tends to move*

**Figure 1.1 Trends that affect businesses**

| Trend | Example | Effect on businesses |
|---|---|---|
| Social | Population changes, for example increased life expectancy | Businesses are now catering for the growing elderly market. For example, pharmaceutical companies are developing more medicines for age-related illnesses. |
| | Households, for example more couples cohabiting | More houses being built for two or more people. |
| | Education, for example increasing achievements at GCSE | The minimum qualifications needed to get a job have been raised |
| | Labour market, for example increase in flexible working | Businesses offering a wider range of part-time jobs to fit in with people's changing lifestyles. |
| | Increasing travel for work, for example longer commutes to work | As jobs become more scarce, employees are having to look further afield for work and travelling times to work are increasing. |
| Technological | Increasing use of information technology | More businesses are advertising on the internet, using social media to post company updates and advertise jobs, etc. |
| | Telephony and web developments | Businesses are using more sophisticated electronic conferencing and e-commerce rather than expecting people to travel to a single place for meetings. |

| | | |
|---|---|---|
| Environmental | Increase in renewable energy | Businesses are now investing in solar energy equipment to become more energy efficient and save money in the long run. |
| | Increase in recycling | Businesses are using recyclable material in packaging. |
| Ethical (ethical concerns of potential customers) | Carbon footprint | Businesses now investing in equipment to reduce their carbon footprint. |
| | Sources of timber | Businesses are now using materials other than wood. |
| | Child labour | Businesses are now making sure that their suppliers are not using child labour. |
| | Inadequate pay | Businesses are now making sure that they buy from suppliers who pay their workers a fair wage. |
| | Animal welfare | Businesses are trying to ensure that materials they buy are not tested on animals. |
| | Values of an organisation and ethical codes | Many businesses now use or buy fair trade products. |
| | Contribution of business to the community | For example, businesses may sponsor the kit for a football team. This promotes the business to the local community and helps to fund local projects. |

**Case study**

The travel industry has been affected a great deal by some of these trends over the last few years:

- Rising oil prices
- Global recession
- Fewer people travelling by air
- Cuts in the number of flights
- More charges for checked luggage, meals, snacks and in-flight entertainment
- Fall in the number of hotel rooms and rental cars
- Decline in demand for meetings and conferences

1. How do these trends affect the travel industry? (2A.P2)
2. How should travel the travel industry respond? (2A.P2)
3. What opportunities might these trends provide? (2A.P2)

**Technology is having a huge impact on the way business is conducted**

### Types and sizes of businesses

Micro, small and medium-sized enterprises provide about 90 million jobs in the EU. Small and medium-sized enterprises are often referred to as **SMEs**.

**Figure 1.2 European Union classification of small and medium-sized enterprises**

| Enterprise category | Number of employees | Total sales |
|---|---|---|
| Large businesses | 250+ | Over £36.6m |
| Medium-sized | 50 to 249 | Up to £36.6m |
| Small | 10 to 49 | Up to £8.5m |
| Micro | 1 to 9 | Up to £1.7m |

Another way of classifying types of business is to categorise them as either **business start-ups**, which means that they are in the earlier stages of development, or existing businesses, which means they have been trading for some time.

## 2A.M2 Comparing trends

The world is a fast changing place where entrepreneurs can succeed by anticipating and responding to changing trends. They need to be constantly aware of how emerging trends will affect their business both now and in the future. The trend of people living longer is resulting in some businesses responding by producing products and services for the ageing population. For example, a business has recently developed a videogame device designed to help keep the minds of old people stimulated. Care homes are also becoming more popular as people are living longer and therefore they have to change their facilities in order to meet the growing demand. Where shared rooms and shared bathrooms used to be commonplace, these are being replaced with en-suite, individual rooms. The best way of gauging the effect of trends on a business is to compare how these trends can impact on a business that has just started trading.

In order to achieve 2A.M2, you will need to compare two trends that have affected a start-up business of your choice, or your own start-up business. This means describing what is similar and what is different about the two trends and their effects on the business. The effects on the business could be the development of new products, additional training for staff or the development of e-business, for example.

**Research**

*Research the changing social trends in the UK and try to estimate how these changes could impact on a business start-up.*

**Your assessment criteria:**

**2A.M2** Compare how two trends have impacted on a start-up business

**Case study**

Seward's is a start-up business that sells high-quality secondhand books from a small outlet in an affluent university town. Before the business started it had negotiated terms from a national secondhand book supplier as well as buying its stock from markets that specialise in used books. It had conducted research that indicated that there was significant demand within the town for secondhand quality books especially among the university students and staff.

When Seward's began trading, sales were disappointingly slow. It issued questionnaires and carried out focus groups in order to try and find out why the business was not generating the income that was planned. It found out that although customers felt they wanted a shop of this type, they were often too busy to go to the shop and would prefer to buy the books online. They also stated that the packaging material for the books at the till was not biodegradable or recyclable and many of the customers who were environmentally aware were put off by this part of the service offered.

This feedback prompted the owners who already had a website but no online ordering and delivery facility to introduce this as soon as possible and also to source new packaging that was far more environmentally friendly. The owners promoted these two developments to their potential customers and although they had incurred extra costs in introducing these new services, their sales increased by a third. This is a good example of how trends can impact on a start-up business and the importance of being able to respond positively to these changing trends.

1. Explain two trends that have affected Sewards.
2. Compare how the two trends have impacted on the business. (2A.M2)

**Changing trends cause businesses to respond**

**Research**

*Research a start-up business in your local area.*

*Compare how two trends have impacted on the start-up business.*

# Risks, opportunities and trends

## 2A.D1 Risks, opportunities and trends

Many individuals start their own business because they do not like working for someone else. However, the entrepreneur may soon find out that customers, competitors and suppliers can also be very demanding. Many start-up businesses have limited funds to buy things like furniture, fittings, equipment, supplies, operating space and transportation.

There is always the concern that the new business may not be able to generate sufficient revenue to pay all the costs. The owner of a business start-up must develop many skills including supervising, bookkeeping, accounting, selling, advertising, training and product knowledge.

For this assessment criterion you are asked to assess the current risks, opportunities and trends. Assess means to weigh up or judge the pros and cons of the current risks, opportunities and trends that may be affecting a business start-up.

### Current risks

An entrepreneur needs to make decisions and each one carries an element of risk. Entrepreneurs have the significant risk of losing a lot of money if things go wrong. Everything we do in life involves risk but risks can be minimised by setting goals and thinking through how they can be achieved.

### Current opportunities

Spotting business opportunities is essential for growth and survival. There are a number of ways of working out what are the best opportunities for a small business. One is to conduct an analysis of the strengths and weaknesses of the business, and the opportunities and threats it faces (a SWOT analysis). Opportunities can also be identified through market research to find out what customers want that is not currently being supplied.

### Current trends

Changes in social trends and demographics can impact on the demand for a business's products. In the UK, for example, the population has been ageing and this has impacted on demand for sheltered accommodation, pensions and medicines. The way people live their lives is constantly changing and businesses have to respond to these changing consumer needs.

Your assessment criteria:

**2A.D1** Assess the current risks, opportunities and trends in the business environment for a start-up business

**Key terms**

***Fair trade:*** *fair trade aims to help producers in developing countries maintain standards and have a fair price for their products*

***Market research:*** *gathering information about markets or customers*

***Revenue:*** *income that a company receives from its normal business activities*

***SWOT analysis:*** *examines a business's strengths, weaknesses, opportunities and threats*

There are also changing trends in technology. For example, more people have access to the internet. There is a considerable growth in internet shopping. The use of smart phone technology and web-based developments are revolutionising the way that businesses conduct their operations.

Finally, there are changing trends in environmental and ethical issues. The country is moving towards producing renewable energy resources and trying to encourage people and businesses to recycle their waste. People are also more concerned with ensuring that businesses conduct their operations ethically. Businesses are increasingly sourcing **fair trade** products and trying to be seen to contribute to their local communities.

All businesses need to identify trends that may have a positive or negative effect and plan to maximise the opportunities and minimise the risks the trends represent. If a business is fully aware of changing trends and has made plans accordingly, it may be in a better position to cope with these changes than its competitors.

**Discuss**

*In groups, discuss the current risks facing a local business of your choice.*

**Case study**

Ecotimes was established in 2007 as a green installation business. The two owners received local authority grants of £20 000. The rest of the start-up money came from their joint savings. In order to expand they have borrowed from banks at quite high interest rates and have found the increasing cost of diesel a major problem, causing distribution costs to escalate.

Both partners are engineers and have read that there is a growing demand for solar power equipment and its installation. More businesses and residential homes are looking for green solutions to their energy problems.

They also have plans to expand into Scotland where there is less competition for these services.

1. What risks exist for this business? (2A.D1)
2. What opportunities exist for this business? (2A.D1)
3. What trends can be identified from the case study? (2A.D1)

**Alternative sources of power are an opportunity for energy companies**

# How business ideas can be successful

## 2B.P3 Successful business ideas

There are many reasons why business ideas can be successful.

- Finding innovative solutions and meeting customer needs: businesses that have successful ideas tend to be able to find creative solutions. Innovation means the invention of better, more effective products and services. These businesses are able to keep ahead of the competition by developing innovative products and services that answer their customers' needs more effectively and fill a gap in the market.
- Identifying new needs: customers' needs are always changing and businesses need to be aware of these. New needs are always being found and staff have ongoing training and coaching in order to identify these developing needs. In some instances, established businesses mentor new start-up businesses to help them identify their customers' new needs. The Prince's Trust uses entrepreneurs from established businesses to mentor the owners of new businesses and help their business ideas become successful.
- Businesses can also use digital media such as social networking sites (for example, Facebook) in order to identify the new needs of their customers. By communicating with customers in this way, businesses receive feedback about what products to develop next.
- Continuing to meet established customer needs: businesses must continue to meet the needs of their customers and by identifying gaps in their current product offerings. For example, Apple is continually reviewing the needs of its customers and improving the iPhone in order to meet them.
- Being entrepreneurial, having a strong vision and seeing it through: being entrepreneurial means having a business idea that nobody else has had and having the vision to make it successful.
- Measures of success: successful businesses also tend to measure and evaluate their activity. They measure the financial performance of their ideas to see whether a profit or loss has been made. They measure the impact their ideas have, always trying to improve people's lives through their innovations. Finally, they measure how satisfied their customers are, as this will determine whether customers will return and purchase more.

Your assessment criteria:

**2B.P3** Describe, using relevant examples, the features of successful businesses

**Key terms**

***Digital media:*** *audio, video, and photo content that has been digitally compressed*

***Innovation:*** *the creation or invention of better, more effective products and services*

Figure 1.3 Examples of successful business ideas

| How business ideas can be successful | Examples |
|---|---|
| Finding innovative solutions | James Dyson pledges to create technology that is superior to his competitors. For example, the Dyson hand-held vacuum cleaner. |
| Meeting customer needs | Sony prides itself on products that fill a gap in the games market and are better than its competitors. For example, the PlayStation. |
| Identifying new needs | Many successful businesses believe social media are an important marketing tool for identifying new needs for their products and services. For example, when Microsoft launched Windows 7 to younger people it developed a programme with ReverbNation that allowed people to download free music tracks. |
| Continuing to meet established customer needs | Virgin has always endeavoured to continue to meet its existing customers' needs while being able to adapt, review and improve products and services. Virgin Airlines places great emphasis on its standard of customer service. |
| Being entrepreneurial | Many entrepreneurial ideas affect our daily lives. Tanya Budd invented the Hypo Hoist man overboard recovery system, a rescue device. Rose Grimond founded the company Orkney Rose to support traditional industries (farming, fishing and food production) on the Orkney Islands. Mark Zuckerberg had a vision of a social network that would allow people to keep up to date with what their friends were doing (Facebook). |
| Importance of a strong vision and seeing it through | The vision of Apple founder, Steve Jobs, was to see Apple products everywhere. Apple has become successful through constant innovation. |
| Measures of success | Tesco plc not only measures its financial performance but also the effects its business developments have on society, such as improved reputation, stronger customer loyalty and motivated staff. It also measures the level of customer satisfaction, in order to gain competitive advantage over its competitors. |

Successful business ideas can change the way we live

**Discuss**

*In groups, discuss two successful businesses in your area and make a list of the features that you think make them successful.*

# Features, strengths and weaknesses

## 2B.M3 Features, strengths and weaknesses

All businesses can be good at some of the activities they undertake and not so good at others. This is often referred to as strengths and weaknesses. All businesses are different and have features that are sometimes unique to that particular business or similar to other businesses. The best method for understanding the features, strengths and weaknesses of businesses is to compare these from one business to another. Compare means to examine and note the similarities and differences between two or more objects (in this case, businesses).

If we examine a business such as Tesco plc, we can see that its **financial performance** over the last ten years has been very good. Its key features are that it is a major retailer operating throughout the UK and in other countries and employs many thousands of people. These could be described as Tesco's strengths. Tesco believes that it in the future it needs to increase its sales of non-foods and to grow its retail services. Although these two developments are not weaknesses they are areas that have been identified by Tesco as requiring improvement.

If we compare Tesco's situation with another retailer, such as Peacocks, we can see that there are some similar features in that they both operate throughout the UK and are major retailers. Peacocks, however, is a clothing retailer whereas Tesco operates in a number of different retail markets. Peacocks' financial performance over the last few years has not been good as it has borrowed large amounts of money to finance the business and is paying huge amounts of interest, which is affecting its profit levels. Its strengths are its name in the high street and its relationship with its customers.

It can be seen from the comparison of Tesco and Peacocks that there are features which are similar and some that are quite different. Their strengths and weaknesses are also quite different from each other. All businesses will try to build on their strengths and introduce plans to overcome their weaknesses and turn them into strengths.

Your assessment criteria:

**2B.M3** Compare the features, strengths and weaknesses of two successful businesses

Key terms

***Financial performance:*** *how the business has managed its money and made a profit*

Discuss

*In groups, discuss the features, strengths and weaknesses of some businesses in your local town.*

**Case study**

Lowes is a small engineering firm based in the Midlands. It has shown good growth over the last few years and has won awards for the way it trains and develops its staff. It has first-class premises that are environmentally friendly and have a low carbon footprint. It does have a problem with the businesses it uses to deliver its products to customers and its computer system is outdated.

Peters is a business that manufactures wooden garden furniture and operates in the south of England. It is currently facing intense competition from other manufacturers and its sales are falling. Its products are of high quality and its prices are also high. Recently the wood Peters has been using has not been of the required standard and some major customers have stopped buying its products.

Discuss these two businesses.

1. Identify and describe the features of Lowes and Peters. (2B.P3)
2. Compare the features, strengths and weaknesses of Lowes and Peters. (2B.M3)

**Research**

*Research some large companies that are in the media at the moment and are in financial difficulty. Investigate their features, strengths and weaknesses.*

**Businesses need to be aware of their strengths and weaknesses**

# Business ideas

## 2B.P4 What business ideas have you got?

The table below describes the stages that successful businesses go through in developing their business ideas.

Your assessment criteria:

**2B.P4** Prepare a realistic plan for a business idea suitable for the local area

**Figure 1.4 Stages in developing business ideas**

| | |
|---|---|
| They research the market and identify gaps and opportunities. | Successful businesses are constantly conducting research to identify gaps and opportunities. The major electronic companies such as Sony, LG and Apple are good examples of businesses that follow this approach. For example, the development of the iPad 3 was based on the gap in the market for a tablet with a high-resolution screen. |
| They carefully select new products and services to develop. | These businesses spend a large amount of time selecting business ideas to develop and test and retest to ensure they will be successful. For example, Sky's new Formula 1 channel. |
| They **target customers** by age, location, interests and concerns. | Successful businesses are very good at communicating with their potential customers and are able to classify their customers based on similarities such as age, location, interests and concerns. For example, SAGA holidays target the over-50s. |
| They understand the difference between features and benefits. | A **feature** is something the product does. A **benefit** is how a feature improves the life of the customer. Promoting the benefits is far more important than promoting the features of a product. For example, oven manufacturers promote features such as safety and ease of use. |

### Case study

Joe wants to start an oven-cleaning business. He has decided on this idea as he has heard a number of his friends complaining about what a difficult job oven-cleaning is and how long it can take. He has looked on the internet and found that there is only one other business providing this service within a 50-mile radius of the town where he lives.

1. Discuss the suitability of Joe's business idea. (2B.P4)

### Key terms

***Benefit:*** *how a feature improves the life of a customer*

***Feature:*** *something that a product does, for example, cleans the carpet*

***Targeting customers:*** *identifying customers and communicating with them*

**Research is very important in the development of business ideas**

Business ideas that become successful products or services do not occur by accident. They are the result of deliberate plans that are developed over a number of stages. All successful businesses research the market and identify gaps or opportunities. The research should identify what the customers want in terms of the product benefits. This will then allow the business to select a product or service that will answer the needs of the customers more effectively.

The business will now have to communicate the benefits of the product or service to its customers. This is called targeting customers. Businesses will often group customers that have similar characteristics together as this makes targeting easier. Customers can be grouped together by their age, where they live (location) and their interests, such as hobbies and pastimes. They can also be grouped together by the concerns they may have over such issues such as the environment or the economy.

**Discuss**

*An entrepreneur has an idea for a device to detect when food has gone off when left in a fridge.*

*Discuss the stages that the entrepreneur should go through in developing this business idea.*

# Assessing the suitability of a business idea

## 2B.P4 How suitable is your idea?

All businesses need to find out whether their ideas are suitable and whether they will be successful. This is an important process as the business will not want to invest money developing something that customers do not want or like.

### Estimating resources required to develop ideas

All ideas cost money to put into place and therefore businesses have to estimate how much an idea is going to cost. Staff get paid for the hours they work and the jobs they complete. This is a cost to the business. If staff are working on the development of an idea it is a cost to the business. The development of the idea may require other people who have the skills and expertise needed to drive the project forward. The staff who are working on the idea may have to ignore other jobs they have to do in order to complete the development of the idea. These are additional costs. Other resources will be required, such as finance to support the development premises, materials and equipment to make products.

### Selecting the most appropriate idea

A business may have several ideas for possible products but will not have the resources to develop them all. A business will investigate the costs involved and the potential benefits of each product. It can then dismiss all the other ideas and concentrate on the idea that has the most potential.

### Likelihood of success or failure

The business will have to make an informed judgment about the likelihood of the idea becoming successful. Research will be conducted to make sure that it is a product or service that customers need and also to gauge the selling price that would be acceptable to customers. The business will have to find out how easy or difficult it will be for prospective customers to find out about and buy the product and estimate demand for the product. Most importantly, the business needs to predict how much profit the product will generate for the business. For example, Deano's is a café in a busy town. The owner's idea is to sell organic, fair trade coffee and tea. The owner researches whether her customers like the idea and the price they would be prepared to pay. From this information she can estimate the demand for these products and predict the possible profit.

Your assessment criteria:

**2B.P4** Prepare a realistic initial plan for a business idea suitable for the local area

**Key terms**

***Cash flow:*** *money flowing into and out of a business*

***Estimate:*** *making an approximation about something*

***Licences:*** *documents that give permission to operate a business or service that would otherwise not be allowed*

***Overdraft:*** *when money is withdrawn from a bank account, taking the available money below zero*

## Identification of major barriers for a start-up business

When a business is created there are large initial costs. These are known as start-up costs, for example, buying machinery and fitting out shops.

When a business starts up it also has to pay operating costs including wages and utility bills. These are payments made to others, so money is leaving the business. Money is also coming into the business from sales of its products. This movement of money coming in and out of the business is known as **cash flow**. Businesses need to manage their cashflow very carefully as there could be occasions when a very large amount of money has to leave the business (for example, buying a vehicle) but there may not be enough in the bank account to pay for it. In this situation the business may have to see the bank's business advisor and ask for an overdraft for a period of time.

Some new businesses require **licences** to enable them to operate, for example, taxi businesses. It is illegal to run some businesses without a licence. These licences are often very expensive and sometimes difficult to obtain. In some industries this can be a difficult barrier to overcome.

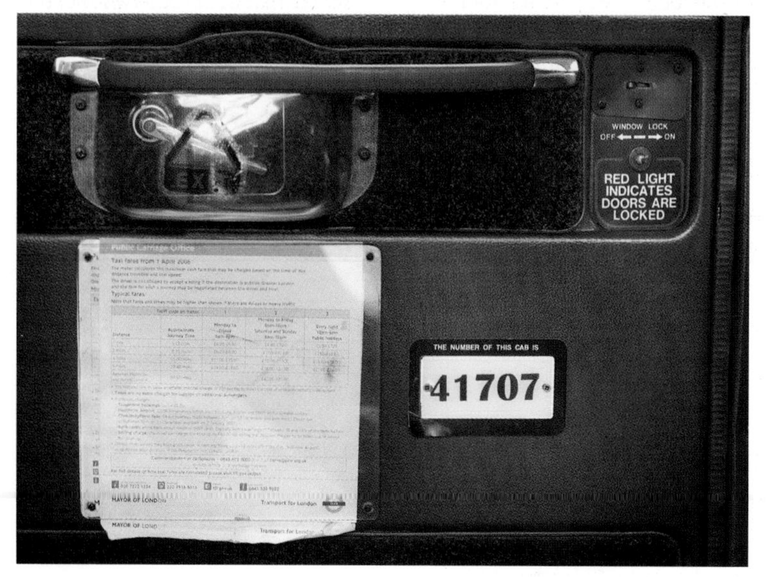


**Businesses have to consider many issues before selecting a business idea**

Trying to open a business that has lots of competition can pose a significant barrier. If there is lots of competition then customers have a large choice about whom to buy the product or service from. New businesses that open in very competitive markets tend to do a lot of promotion to show how much better their products are compared to their competitors.

### Discuss

*In groups, discuss any business ideas you may have that would be suitable for your local area. What have your friends said about your ideas? How could they be improved?*

# Producing an initial plan for a business idea

## 2B.P4 Producing an initial plan

### Initial business plans

A business idea could emerge from an entrepreneur's previous knowledge of a market in a local area. For example, an entrepreneur may know about catering and believe that there is no high-quality, reasonably priced restaurant currently operating in a nearby town. The entrepreneur could conduct research to find out if customers would welcome this type of restaurant and to identify the competition. If the research indicates that there is a demand, the entrepreneur should then begin to prepare an initial plan.

An **initial business plan** should include the following.

### A rationale, vision and concept for a realistic idea

A **rationale** is the reason why an idea is going to be successful and why it should be developed. If a business has invented a revolutionary method of cleaning the inside of a fridge using an environmentally friendly cleaning agent that no one else has, this would be the rationale for the business idea. Once the rationale for the business idea has been examined, the entrepreneur then has a **vision** and a **concept** of what the product will look like, its size and how it will be developed.

### Supporting evidence for the initial plan

When producing the initial plan, research needs to be conducted and evidence collected about the possible customers that the business will target. Market research will also identify possible **routes to market**. Routes to market means finding out how your target customers prefer to shop, for example in store, over the internet or through catalogues, etc.

Most businesses will have competitors and businesses need to devise ways of dealing with the threats that competitors present. For example, if you start a business selling computer accessories and there are other businesses in your area doing the same thing, you will need to think of ways of making customers come to you rather than your competitors. This could include lowering prices below the competitors' price or increasing advertising and promotion to persuade customers to buy from your business rather than the others. Very large businesses do this to fend off their competitors. For example, Asda's price guarantee means

Your assessment criteria:

**2B.P4** Prepare a realistic initial plan for a business idea suitable for the local area

**Key terms**

***Concept:*** *how a business idea will be developed*

***Implementation:*** *putting your idea into practice or making it happen*

***Initial business plans:*** *the outline of how the business is going to operate, including its concept and customers*

***Rationale:*** *justification for doing something*

***Routes to market:*** *finding out how your target customers prefer to shop*

***Vision:*** *an image of the desired future for a business or product*

it will refund the difference in price you have paid if you find items cheaper in a competing store.

The initial plan also needs to consider ideas of how the business will be financed. This may include securing a bank loan, using personal savings or issuing shares in the business to investors.

The way the idea will be implemented involves careful planning. Implementation means putting your idea into practice or making it happen. Implementation issues include when to start your business. Some businesses sell seasonal products (such as Easter eggs) and so it is important to consider when is best to open your business. The marketing of your products also needs to be considered. There is little point paying large sums of money for TV advertising if you are planning to sell your products in your school or college for example. Think about how your products will be distributed and what equipment you need for your business to operate. Will you have a store and distribute your products or will you offer a delivery service? Do you need extra staff in order to open and run your business successfully? If so, how many extra staff do you need and what will their roles be? The last element to consider is finance. You need to ensure that you can fund your business idea and consider where you will borrow money from in order to implement your idea. You will also need to consider how you will afford to pay the money back and what money you will live on.

For example, if you are going to open a new fast food take away, you will need to decide when you will open, who are going to be your suppliers, how are you going to tell customers about your business, what cooking equipment will be required and who is going to work for you.

**Discuss**

*In pairs, list as many of the local businesses in your area as you can. Looking at each one, discuss whether there would be a best time of year for you to open this business and why.*

**Some businesses sell seasonal products**

Poonam is considering starting a business making healthy sweet snacks for children. She plans to sell them initially in local markets. She completes an initial plan for her business idea.

**Design**

*Design an initial plan for your business idea, ensuring that you include the rationale for your idea and your evidence that it is going to work.*

**Figure 1.5 Poonam's initial business plan**

| Question | Answer |
|---|---|
| What is your rationale for the idea? | Being a mum, I have researched that there are not many sweet but healthy snacks for children. I plan to make healthy organic cakes and sweets. I have carried out a questionnaire among other mums at the local mother and toddler groups and have evidence that there is a gap in the market for these products. |
| What is the vision? | To sell sweet but healthy children's snacks in the local market initially, expanding to nurseries and playgroups within the first year. |
| What is the concept or idea? | Sweet, healthy, organic children's snacks. |
| Who are your possible customers? | Mums with young children. |
| How do the customers prefer to buy? | In person (not online). |
| What will be your routes to the market? | Establishing a stall in the local market initially, then to approach nurseries and play groups. |
| Who are your competitors? | Brands such as Organix and Hipp. |
| How will you deal with competitors? | These are big brands sold in supermarkets. I plan to stay local and make more appealing snacks such as cakes and sweets, which these competitors do not offer. |
| How will your business idea be financed? | I have borrowed money from my parents, which I have to pay back within a year. |
| How will the business idea be implemented? | I have a food hygiene certificate and have looked into the legal side of producing food. I meet all the requirements. I will package the food and rent a stand at my local market. I will then research the local nurseries and playgroups and offer to sell my products to them. |

**All business ideas need to produce an initial plan**

**Case study**

Chloe wants to start her own business making her own jams and selling these in local markets. She doesn't want to give up her daytime job until the business starts earning money. She cannot therefore dedicate much time to the business. She lives in a very small apartment that she shares with a friend who has no interest in Chloe's idea. She has little money to start the business and the markets where she hopes to sell the jams operate on weekdays at the same time as she is working in her full-time job.

1. What barriers is Chloe facing in starting her business? (2B.P4)
2. What is the likelihood of success with this business venture? (2B.P4)
3. Prepare an initial plan for Chloe's business idea. (2B.P4)

**Investigate**

*Talk to your family and friends who may have started their own business. Try to investigate what their initial business plan would have looked like.*

# Responding to market needs and the potential for success

## 2B.M4 Responding to market needs

Market needs are what customers want from a product or service within that particular market place. Businesses need to meet these needs in order to be successful. Market needs can also include an examination of the buying habits of customers and those who make purchasing decisions. This is done through constant market research to identify customers' changing requirements. Businesses respond by improving or developing products and services that answer the needs of their customers more effectively. For example, there was a market need a few years ago for mobile phones to be connected to the internet and perform the same functions as a computer. Mobile phone companies answered this market need by developing smart phones, which many people now use for both business and pleasure.

## 2B.D2 The potential for success

When the initial plan has been completed, it is important for the business owner to be able to prove that the business idea has the potential to be successful. The rationale for the business idea must be clear and related to detailed market research that proves there is a need for the idea in the market. The research process must also concentrate on competitors. Starting a business where there are lots of local competitors would be extremely risky. Success will depend on how the business enters the market and how it persuades customers to buy from the new business rather than from the competition.

The vision and concept need to confirm the potential for success. The vision needs to be realistic and the concept or idea must be economically viable. If the business needs to borrow money to start up, the borrowing needs to be justified by predicting the future income and profit levels that show how the money can be repaid.

Your assessment criteria:

**2B.M4** Explain how the initial plan for a business idea has the potential to respond to market needs

**2B.D2** Justify how the initial plan for a business idea has potential for success in relation to existing local businesses

**Key term**

***Market needs:*** *what customers require from products and services in a particular market place*

**Discuss**

*Tesco plc is a very large retail organisation where you can shop for anything from a packet of salt to a loan, all under one roof.*

*Discuss how you think Tesco is responding to market needs.*

*Are there any new ideas that you believe Tesco could implement to meet the needs of its customers better?*

**Case study**

An entrepreneur has a vision of setting up a high-quality, reasonably priced restaurant in the middle of the town. He has conducted research among potential customers and identified that there is no other similar restaurant operating there. Research shows that potential customers want fresh produce with high-quality meat used in all dishes. They would prefer the menu to offer mainly French and Italian dishes. People who live in the town are quite affluent, earning above average incomes.

1. Prepare the initial plan for the business, explaining how it is suitable for the local area. (2B.P4)
2. Explain how the initial plan is realistic for the local area.
3. Explain how the initial plan responds to market needs. (2B.M4)
4. How does the initial plan have potential for success in relation to existing local businesses? (2B.D2)

**Discuss**

*In groups, discuss how any local business you are familiar with uses strategies to entice customers to buy from them rather than competitors.*

**Success is dependent on how the business responds to market needs**

# Business models for a start-up business – sole traders and partnerships

## 2C.P5 What format to choose?

When starting a business, one of the most important decisions is the format the business will take. There are five main types of business format or ownership.

### Sole trader

A sole trader is a small business that is owned and controlled by one person, although employees may help with the day-to-day running of the business. There are 3.6 million sole traders in the UK, so they are very important to the UK economy. They are usually quite small businesses with relatively low sales. The owner has unlimited liability, which means he or she is responsible for the debts of the business. Sole traders operate in all areas of business, for example, florist, carpenter, plumber, etc.

Advantages of being a sole trader:

- Easy to set up – there are no forms or procedures.
- The owner can keep control of the business and make decisions without consulting others.
- Decisions can be made quickly.
- The owner keeps all the profits.
- The business is flexible – the owner can decide when to open, what stock to buy, and so on.

Disadvantages of being a sole trader:

- A sole trader has unlimited liability. This means the sole trader may be forced to sell personal possessions to cover any debts of the business.
- The business owner may have to work long hours and find it difficult to take holidays. The business may also have to close if the owner falls ill and there is no other staff. This could lead to debt piling up and loss of custom.
- It may be difficult to raise extra finance from a bank. The owner may also struggle with some aspects of the business if he or she does not have the necessary expertise, for example finance.

Your assessment criteria:

**2C.P5** Explain the reasons for the choice of format selected for a business start-up

**Key terms**

***Business format:*** *a way of owning and operating a business*

***Partnership:*** *a type of business owned by two or more individuals*

***Sole trader:*** *a type of business that is owned and controlled by one person and has unlimited liability*

***Unlimited liability:*** *the business owners may be forced to sell personal possessions to cover any debts of the business*

**Sole traders operate in all areas of business**

## Partnership

Partnerships are businesses that are owned by two or more individuals. Partnerships you may see locally include solicitors, dentists and doctors. However, many of today's best-known businesses started as partnerships, including Apple and Google.

Advantages of a partnership:

- There is shared responsibility for decision making and day-to-day running of the business.
- All profits are shared equally between the partners.
- If one partner has a specialism in one part of the business and another partner's expertise lies in another area, their strengths can complement each other.
- It is easier to take time off for holidays and sickness as the other partner can take responsibility.
- Partnerships are easy to set up.
- Partnerships are easy to expand by taking on more partners who will also bring extra capital into the business.

Disadvantages of a partnership:

- A partnership has unlimited liability meaning that if debt is created by one partner, all the other partners are personally liable for it.
- Partners may disagree on how the business should be run, which can make it difficult to progress.
- Arguments can arise over one partner's efforts compared with another's.
- Profits have to be shared between all the partners.

**Partnerships are important to the UK economy**

### Research

*Research examples of local partnerships and sole traders.*

# Business models for a start-up business – limited companies and social enterprises

## 2C.P5 Limited companies

Most companies start as a sole trader or partnership. When they want to expand they often find it hard to raise the necessary capital. They also have to accept that they have unlimited liability, which means every decision they make has added risks attached to it. The solution that many business owners find is to become a **limited liability** company. A **limited company** has its own legal identity, which allows entrepreneurs to keep their own assets and finances separate from the business itself. This means that people who have invested in the business (the shareholders) are only responsible for company debts up to the amount that they have invested.

There are two types of limited company.

### Private limited company (ltd)

A private limited company is often owned by friends and family and each owner becomes a shareholder in the business by buying shares. A share is a small piece of the business that can be bought by investing in the business. The shares are sold to a few people and cannot be sold to the public. Examples of limited companies include local builders but also larger organisations such as New Look. Each year, the shareholders meet at an Annual General Meeting (AGM) to discuss the business's progress over the last 12 months. It is easy to identify private limited companies as they always have 'ltd' after their name.

**Once a plc, New Look is now a private limited company**

Your assessment criteria:

**2C.P5** Explain the reasons for the choice of format selected for a business start-up

**Key terms**

***Limited companies (ltd):*** *a type of business whose liability is limited*

***Limited liability:*** *the owners of the business are only liable for the debt of the business according to their own levels of investment*

***Public limited companies (plc):*** *a type of business that sells its shares to the public and has limited liability*

***Social enterprise:*** *a business whose objectives are based on the public benefitting from their operations*

***Dividend:*** *payments made by a business to its shareholders*

Advantages of private limited companies:

- Limited liability – the company's shareholders can only lose the value of the shares they have bought, not their own possessions.
- A limited company is a separate legal entity from its owners. It can survive after the death of the shareholders.
- Ownership and control of the business are in the hands of the shareholders, who can control who buys shares.
- The business can raise more capital by selling more shares.

Disadvantages of private limited companies:

- They can be expensive to set up compared with a sole trader or partnership.
- Each year the business must produce a set of financial accounts to be checked by an independent accountant. This is sent to the Registrar of Companies and is available for the public to see.
- Profits have to be shared with the other shareholders.

## Public limited company (plc)

**Public limited companies** tend to be larger than private limited companies and their name always ends in 'plc'. They usually make large profits and employ large numbers of people. Public limited companies include Tesco, Google and Apple.

The major difference between a public and a private limited company is that the shares in a public limited company are bought by the general public and other organisations. The shares are bought and sold on the stock exchange at a particular price, which is listed in major newspapers and on the London Stock Exchange website. People buy shares in the hope that they will make a profit on the share price and receive an annual **dividend**. Since a plc can offer its shares to the public, it has more possibilities for investment than a private limited company.

Advantages of public limited companies:

- They are able to raise extra capital by selling more shares on the stock market.
- Limited liability – the shareholders only lose the value of the shares they have bought, not their own possessions.
- The business has its own legal identity.
- They may find it easier to borrow from banks as they are larger, well established and seen as less risky.

**Research**

*In pairs, research all the public limited companies in your area.*

**Limited liability reduces risk**

Disadvantages of public limited companies:

- They are expensive to set up as the legal side is very complicated.
- Profits have to be shared with all the shareholders.
- An annual report and accounts have to be drawn up and sent to all of the shareholders. It can also be seen by the competition.
- Some plcs can grow so large that they may become difficult to manage effectively.
- There is a risk that, in tough times, another firm can buy up your business cheaply by buying shares at a low price on the stock market.

## 2C.P5 Social enterprises

**Social enterprises** are businesses that trade for a social purpose. This means that they trade, that is sell goods and services, but reinvest some of their profit back into the business in order to fulfil their social mission. A social mission could be something like educating the poor or providing training for people with disabilities. There are benchmarks that outline what businesses have to do in order to be classed as a social enterprise. The Social Enterprise Mark criteria say that over 50 per cent of the business's income has to come from trading and over 50 per cent of any profits has to be invested in its social mission. Well-known examples of social enterprises are the Big Issue and the Eden Project.

Advantages of social enterprises:

- They help bring about positive changes to people and communities by reinvesting money into local communities and projects.
- They provide employment for local people.
- They have support from the government as they exist to improve the lives of local people.

Disadvantages of social enterprises:

- Sometimes perceived as taking jobs and services from the public sector as they provide employment in the local area and people may be more attracted to these jobs than to public sector jobs.
- They can struggle to survive financially as they rely on donations and have to reinvest parts of their profit back into the enterprise.

**Social Enterprise Mark logo**

**Research**

*Research examples of private and public limited companies and social enterprises.*

**The Big Issue is a social enterprise project**

**Case study**

The Eden Project in Cornwall is a great example of a social enterprise. It is the World's largest indoor rainforest, has stunning gardens, lays on arts and music events, runs social and environmental projects, creates huge learning projects for students and undertakes a lot of research into plant species and conservation.

1. Investigate what makes the Eden Project a social enterprise (2C.P5).
2. Research how the Eden Project's activities help to bring about positive change for the local communities (2C.P5).

**The Eden Project is a social enterprise project**

**Discuss**

*In groups, discuss any ideas that you have on starting a social enterprise in your local area. What would be the positive changes it could bring to the local community?*

# Sources of help and support in developing a new business

## 2C.P5 Sources of help and support in developing a new business

All new businesses at some stage or another will require help and support. There are many organisations and individuals that provide services to businesses. These are described below,

### Finance (bank manager)

When a new business is set up most people have to borrow money. Most new business owners go to their bank manager in order to get a business loan. The manager will have to be convinced that the loan will be a good investment and that the money will be put to good use in developing the business. Bank managers always want to see a detailed business plan of the business. This will include the projected profit that the bank loan will help achieve.

### Start-up capital

When a business is formed it incurs large costs, especially at the beginning. Selling shares in the business to family members is another option available to raise capital. The family members then own some of the business in return for investing money in it. There is also an organisation called the Prince's Trust that supports unemployed young people aged 18–30. The Trust helps them to work out if their business ideas are viable and whether self-employment is right for them. It can also help individuals with their finances by giving advice or offering low-interest loans. Many examples of how the Prince's Trust has helped young people can be found on the Princes Trust website (www.princes-trust.org.uk). The Prince's Trust helps young people to build their business ideas and provides them with a mentor who offers advice and new skills.

### Independent advice

Help and support can also be found independently from organisations that have been set up specifically to help business start-ups. www.gov.uk is the government's online resource for its services and essential information about the support and services the government provides for

**The Prince's Trust helps young people to start their own businesses**

Your assessment criteria:

**2C.P5** Explain the reasons for the choice of format selected for a business start-up

**Key terms**

***Business plan:*** *this is a plan for a business to look ahead, allocate resources, focus on key points and prepare for problems and opportunities*

***Chamber of Commerce:*** *this is a local organisation of businesses whose goal is to further the interests of businesses*

**Research**

*More help can come by learning what other similar businesses have done when faced with the same problems. Many businesses describe on their websites how they overcame problems and the help and support they received when starting up.*

businesses. www.gov.uk provides guidance on regulations, funding options and how to access government services and wider support.

## Support networks

The Chamber of Commerce is a local organisation whose aim is to further the interests of businesses. There are also trade associations, which are established and funded by businesses that operate in a specific industry, for example construction. There are also non-profit making organisations that support professions such as accountancy or law.
The business owner's family and friends form a very important support network. Apart from possibly investing in the business they can also offer advice and guidance or just a shoulder to cry on when times get difficult. Finally, there are a host of charities and voluntary organisations that can offer support and help to those starting a business, for example the Citizens Advice Bureau.

**Case study**

N-ergy Works is an organization whose pledge is to reduce reoffending rates among ex-offenders. It tries to obtain contracts from local authorities to remove graffiti and chewing gum from public areas and then employs suitable ex-offenders to deliver the contract. Research shows that if offenders leave prison and obtain employment their chances of reoffending are substantially reduced. It is a profit-making organisation but it reinvests 51 per cent of its profit in its social mission.

1. What type of business format is in place at N-ergy Works? (2C.P5)
2. Why do you think this format was chosen? (2C.P5)
3. Research other companies in the UK that reinvest some of their profits into their social mission.
4. Why do you think companies use some of their profits to 'do the right thing'?

**Research**

*Research how organisations such as the Chamber of Commerce, Prince's Trust and the Citizens Advice Bureau could help with the start-up of your new business.*

**Young offenders may be asked to clean up local areas**

# Business models

## 2C.P6 A business model

A **business model** describes how a business aims to generate **revenue** and make a profit from its operations. The model includes the components and functions of the business, as well as the revenues it generates and the expenses it incurs. The functions of a business include all the different departments and what they do to contribute to the operation of the business. A business model can be simple or very complex. A restaurant's business model is to make money by cooking and serving food to hungry customers. A website's business model might not be so clear, as there are many ways in which websites can generate revenue. Some make money by providing a free service and selling advertising to other companies, while others might sell a product or service directly to online customers. For example, Go Compare is an online insurance comparison website where each insurance company pays Go Compare a fixed introductory fee per sale.

### The components of a business model

The business model is a description of how all the business's activities come together to produce a strategy. A business model is made up of certain essential components.

- The results of researching the market to identify potential customers (either other businesses or individual consumers). This involves collecting information about what sort of people or other businesses may buy your products and should also include information on other businesses that offer similar products and services. Questionnaires can be used to gather customer views, either online or through interviews.
- An explanation and justification of whether a business decides to make or buy in products or services. Some businesses manufacture their own products and sell them on to customers. Other businesses buy ready-made products from a manufacturer and sell them to consumers. A manufacturing business may need to buy a component for its product from a supplier. If the supplier is unreliable the company may decide to make the component itself.
- The way in which the business delivers its products or services to its customers needs to be explored. Options include the internet, a **franchise** or direct sales. Increasingly people buy and receive products through the internet, for example computer software and music

Your assessment criteria:

**2C.P6** Present a realistic business model for a business start-up

**Key terms**

***Business model:*** *how a business aims to generate revenue and make a profit*

***Components of a business model:*** *the parts of the business's operation that can lead to generating revenue*

***Franchise:*** *a right granted to an individual or group to market a company's goods or services within a certain territory or location, for example McDonald's*

***Revenue:*** *income a business receives from its normal business activities*

***SMART objectives:*** *Specific, Measurable, Achievable, Realistic, Time-related*

***Stakeholders:*** *individuals or groups who have an interest in the business*

downloads. A franchise is where a business buys the right to market another business's goods or services. Some examples of popular franchises are McDonald's, Subway and Domino's Pizza. Direct sales are where a sales person sells you a product face-to-face, usually in your home, for example an insurance agent.

- The long-term visions or goals of the business have to be defined. Goals are the targets that the business sets, for example achieving an income of £120 000 within the first year of trading. The vision is the predicted image of the business or product at some point in the future. SMART objectives are set (Specific, Measurable, Achievable, Realistic and Time-related). These objectives need to be specific to a particular area, such as finance or operations. The objective also needs to be measurable, for example to achieve a 10 per cent increase. The business must also be capable of achieving a realistic objective. Finally, an objective must have a time limit. A good example of a SMART objective would be to increase sales by 5 per cent before December 2012. Setting a vision, goals and objectives is extremely important. It provides a focus for everyone in the business to work towards.
- Stakeholders and their influence on the business. The business model should describe any individual or group that has an interest in the business. A business can have many stakeholders such as the owners (shareholders), employees, customers, financiers, suppliers and the local community. Stakeholders are important as they can put pressure on a business if they feel it is not acting in their interests. For example, if the shareholders do not receive some of the profit in the form of a dividend because profits are too low, they can voice their displeasure and could even change the senior managers.
- Finances and costs for start-up need to be outlined. All businesses will need a certain amount of money to start the business and for its ongoing business needs. It would be impossible to start a business without any money as you need to purchase equipment and stock as well as buying or renting business premises.
- Providing evidence to justify why the idea will succeed. When a business idea has been accepted and a business plan drawn up, there must be supporting evidence to prove that the idea has a good chance of success. This evidence can be the result of research or even the plan itself.

**Discuss**

*Discuss in groups the possible business model for a business start-up that you are aware of that has just started operating locally.*

**Business models come in many forms**

# Realistic business models

## 2C.P6 Realistic business models

Consider your ideas for a start-up business that can be operated locally. The ideas need to be realistic and worthy of further consideration. This may involve some detailed market research to discover whether there are gaps in the market in the local business area. In order to do this you could create a questionnaire to ask local people, have a look at your local area and decide what is needed or interview people to get their opinions. Possible potential customers need to be identified. You also need to identify who are the main competitors for each of your business ideas.

Researching how you will manufacture your product will need to be explored and explained as part of your business model. For example, will you make your product yourself or buy it from a supplier? You will need to look into the costs needed to do this and whether you have the necessary skills if you decide to make the product yourself. If you decide to buy from a supplier, you will need to look at what products the supplier offers and whether they are cost effective. You also need to decide how the product or service will be distributed to customers. Research will have to be done to look at how your customers expect to receive the product. Will they buy it online or through a retail outlet? Which option will suit your potential customers best and be the most cost effective for you?

Financing your business also needs great consideration. Again, research will need to be done to decide what options are available to you. It is worth contacting one of your local banks to ask for advice, as well as looking online for advice from organisations such as www.gov.co.uk and the Prince's Trust.

Select the idea that has the greatest chance of success and clearly indicate why you have rejected the others. You will have to consider which business model is the most appropriate to take your business forward. You will also need to have evidence justifying which idea will be the most successful. This could be in the form of questionnaire and survey answers, leaflets and information from banks and other organisations and research about competitors. Business models have to be realistic if they are to have any chance of succeeding.

Your assessment criteria:

**2C.P6** Present a realistic business model for a business start-up

**Key term**

***Realistic:*** *something that is likely to happen*

**Research**

*Research all the components of your realistic business model for your business start-up. Complete the template in Figure 1.6 to help you generate your business model.*

**Figure 1.6 Business model template**

| Component of the business model | Answers to component question | How do these features enable your business idea to respond to market needs and be successful? |
|---|---|---|
| What are the results of researching the market to identify potential customers and competitors? | | |
| Is your business a product or a service? Describe it. | | |
| Is your product something that you are going to make yourself or buy ready-made and sell on? | | |
| How is your product or service going to be delivered to customers, for example internet only, franchise, direct sales? | | |
| What are your long-term visions or goals for the company? | | |
| What are your objectives? Are they SMART? | | |
| Who are your stakeholders and what influence do they have on your business? | | |
| What is the financial situation of your business, including start-up costs? | | |
| What evidence have you found to justify why the idea will succeed? | | |

**The selection of an appropriate business model is extremely important**

# Business models and formats

## 2C.M5 Realistic business models and appropriate formats

When you start your own business there are lots of decisions to be made. You have chosen the format for your business, but you need to explain how the format and the business model will enable your business to carry out its activities successfully. You will need to consider the potential success of your business in relation to your competitors in your local area. In order to do this you will need to research local competitors and explain how your business model meets the needs of the market compared to them. This must include how your business model has the necessary features and components to respond to these needs and therefore be successful. You will need to explain why you rejected other business ideas and models.

The business format you have chosen is vital as it can affect the financial risks you may face, the amount of tax you have to pay, the ownership and control of your business and the amount of administration you will need to carry out.

## 2C.D3 Realistic business models and formats supported by evidence

You now have to explain your chosen format and indicate how your research justifies the business idea. The business idea should have a vision of where you want the business to be in the future and this needs to be explained. You should describe the stages you have passed through from the original idea to the development of a plan for a business start-up. You must ensure you have selected one idea that others have not considered and one that responds creatively to market needs.

You now need to justify and evaluate the likelihood of developing the business idea successfully. This will involve discussing the pros and cons of the business idea. You will need to define what success is and use one or more sources of information, such as your business plan, to support judgments on whether the idea is likely to be successful, using comparisons to existing businesses.

Your assessment criteria:

**2C.M5** Present a realistic business model for a business, explaining how the format and business model will enable it to carry out its activities successfully

**2C.D3** Present a realistic business model for a business, explaining how the format and supporting evidence justifies the initial business idea

### Key terms

***Administration:*** *the paperwork that needs to be managed when running a business*

***Financial risks:*** *the risk a business takes by investing in business ideas*

***Ownership and control:*** *the people who own a business are not always in control of it (for example plcs) and this can sometimes cause conflict*

### Discuss

*Discuss a suitable format and business model for a carpenter who has just lost her job and wants to start a business making wooden cabinets.*

**A business's format and model can determine whether the business will be successful**

### Discuss

*Discuss, in groups, all the reasons why the chosen formats and business models of your business ideas will ensure success of your businesses.*

**Case study**

Lara and Terri are good friends and want to start a business cleaning residential homes. Their research indicates that affluent, busy home-owners would welcome this service and there is no competition in the area. They have a vision to make the business the best home cleaning business in the south west of England. They have one main business objective – to achieve £100 000 of sales in their first year of trading. They are borrowing £20 000 from the bank to start the business.

1. Present Lara and Terri's business model. (2C.P6)
2. Comment on how realistic their model is. (2C.P6)
3. Explain what business format they should select. (2C.M5)
4. Explain how the format and business model will enable them to carry out their activities successfully. (2C.M5)
5. Research on the internet for evidence about whether their business idea will be a success or not. (2C.D3)
6. Explain how the format and evidence you have found justifies the success of their business idea. (2C.D3)

# Assessment checklist

**To achieve level 1, my portfolio of evidence must show that I can:**

| Assessment criteria | Description | ✓ |
|---|---|---|
| 1A.1 | Identify factors of the business environment that can impact on a start up business | ☐ |
| 1A.2 | Identify current trends that may impact on a start-up business | ☐ |
| 1B.3 | Identify the features of successful businesses | ☐ |
| 1B.4 | Prepare an initial plan for a business idea for the local area | ☐ |
| 1C.5 | Outline the choice of format selected for a business start-up | ☐ |
| 1C.6 | Present, with guidance, a business model for a business start-up | ☐ |

**To achieve a pass grade, my portfolio of evidence must show that I can:**

| Assessment criteria | Description | ✓ |
|---|---|---|
| 2A.P1 | Outline how the business environment can impact on a start-up business | ☐ |
| 2A.P2 | Explain how current trends will impact on a start-up business | ☐ |
| 2B.P3 | Describe, using relevant examples, the features of successful businesses | ☐ |
| 2B.P4 | Prepare a realistic initial plan for a business idea suitable for the local area | ☐ |
| 2C.P5 | Explain the reasons for the choice of format selected for a business start-up | ☐ |
| 2C.P6 | Present a realistic business model for a business start-up | ☐ |

**To achieve a merit grade, my portfolio of evidence must show that I can:**

| Assessment criteria | Description | ✓ |
|---|---|---|
| 2A.M1 | Explain how changes in the current business environment are likely to impact on a start-up business | ☐ |
| 2A.M2 | Compare how two trends have impacted on a start-up business | ☐ |
| 2B.M3 | Compare the features, strengths and weaknesses of two successful businesses | ☐ |
| 2B.M4 | Explain how the initial plan for a business idea has the potential to respond to market needs | ☐ |
| 2C.M5 | Present a realistic business model for a business, explaining how the format and business model will enable it to carry out its activities successfully | ☐ |

**To achieve a distinction grade, my portfolio of evidence must show that I can:**

| Assessment criteria | Description | ✓ |
|---|---|---|
| 2A.D1 | Assess the current risks, opportunities and trends in the business environment for a start-up business | ☐ |
| 2B.D2 | Justify how the initial plan for a business idea has potential for success in relation to existing local businesses | ☐ |
| 2C.D3 | Present a realistic business model for a business, explaining how the format and supporting evidence justifies the initial business idea | ☐ |

# 2 | Finance for business

## Learning aim A: Understand the costs involved in business and how businesses make money

- Topic A.1 Understand the costs involved in business: in this section the start-up and running costs of a business are explored
- Topic A.2 Understand how businesses make a profit: all businesses need to make money to finance the running of the business and make a profit

## Learning aim B: Understand how businesses plan for success

- Topic B.1 Understand the planning tools businesses use to predict when they will start making a profit: break even is important in allowing a business to find out when it has made enough money to cover its costs
- Topic B.2 Understand the tools businesses use to plan for success: budgeting and cash flow forecasting are important activities in the business planning process

## Learning aim C: Understand how businesses measure success and identify areas for improvement

- Topic C.1 Understand how businesses measure success: businesses measure success by making a profit and by looking at financial statements
- Topic C.2 Understand how businesses can be more successful: a business can become more successful by taking action to improve based on their analysis of financial statements

# Understand the costs involved in business

## A.1 Understand the costs involved in business

A business has many costs. Some of these are spent to get the business off the ground (start-up costs) and some have to be paid throughout the business's lifetime (operating costs).

**Figure 2.1 The costs of start-up and ongoing operating costs for a new travel store business.**

| Start-up costs | Operating costs |
|---|---|
| Office equipment (desks, pens, computers, etc.) | Salaries |
| Deposit for the lease of the office | Utility bills |
| Sales and marketing literature | Interest and repayment on start-up cost borrowing |
| Website construction | Banking services |
| Trade association memberships | Professional indemnity insurance |
| Software | Sales and marketing literature production and postage |
| Legal costs | Marketing campaign spend |

### Start-up costs

When a business starts up, money needs to be raised to allow the business to start trading. However, these are one off costs and never have to be paid again.

The key decisions at the start up of a business are:

- How much money does the business need?
- When does the business need the money?
- How much money does it need straight away and how much does it need at some points in the future? (Long-, medium- and short-term finances.)
- Does the owner of the business have any security to offer to raise a bank loan, for example the owner's house?

### Key terms

***Costs:*** *what a business spends its money on, such as wages and materials*

***Fixed costs:*** *costs that stay the same irrespective of any increase in production*

***Investment:*** *putting money into something with the expectation of a gain*

***Security:*** *assets that the business owner pledges to the bank in order to receive a business loan*

***Variable costs:*** *these are costs that can change as output varies*

### Discuss

*Discuss with a partner the likely start-up and operating costs for a small flower shop.*

- Is the owner willing to give up some of the ownership of the business to somebody else in return for their investment in the form of money?
- If the business borrows money, is the interest rate acceptable?

## Operating (running) costs

These costs are faced every week for the lifetime of the business. If the business is going through difficult times, the operating costs may force the company to go out of business.

There are two types of operating cost.

1. Fixed costs are costs that stay the same irrespective of any increase in production. For example, following the Christmas period, Tumble's toy factory sales dropped and so production fell too. However, the rent on the factory still had to be paid, regardless of how many toys the business made. Rent is a fixed cost and will not change in relation to output produced. Other examples of fixed costs include advertising, staff salaries, heating, lighting and insurance. Fixed costs are also known as indirect costs.
2. Variable costs are costs that can change as output varies.

For example, Tumble's toy factory has seen a slump in sales and production following the Christmas period. However, it has not had to buy as much material to make the toys as these are variable costs and depend on output. If, however, Tumble's was to make more toys, for example in preparation for the Easter period, the variable costs would increase. The business would have to buy more plastic and glue to make the toys. Variable costs are known as direct costs because they are linked directly to the activities of the business.

**Fixed costs include the rent for premises**

**Discuss**

*Talk to a family member or a friend who has started and owns their own business. Discuss what their direct and indirect costs are.*

# Direct, indirect and total costs

## A.1 Direct and indirect costs

Costs can also be categorised in another way. For example, there are two sorts of costs for a car sales business. Costs that are directly related to the selling of cars, such as the cost of the vehicle to the business, are **direct costs**. Conversely, **indirect costs** are costs that have to be paid whether a car is sold or not, for example rent of the car showroom.

### Total costs

Business owners tend to worry most about **total costs**. These are the sum of all of the costs of the business.

They are calculated by adding together the fixed costs and the variable costs:

- total costs = fixed costs + variable costs

To work out total costs you need to:

- multiply the variable cost per unit by the number made/sold
- add that total to the fixed costs

For example, if a bicycle business sold 500 bikes per week with variable costs of £250 per unit (that is per bike) and £1000 of fixed costs, the total costs would be:

- £200 x 500 = £100 000
- £100 000 + £1000 = £101 000

### Key terms

***Direct costs:*** *costs that are directly related to the production process*

***Indirect costs:*** *costs that cannot be directly related to the production process*

***Total costs:*** *fixed costs + variable costs (or direct costs + indirect costs)*

**Chocolate bars are made in large quantities**

### Investigate

*A chocolate bar manufacturer has fixed costs of £000 per month. It sells chocolate bars at 50 pence each. It is going to make 50 000 bars. The variable costs of producing each bar are 25p each. What are the total costs for making 50 000 bars?*

**Case study**

Majid owns a small manufacturing business that makes sports bags. He is trying to analyse his annual costs. He knows that he pays £18 000 to rent the premises, management salaries are £100 000 and insurance is £15 000. The wages of those producing the bags are £200 000 and the cost of the materials for the bags is £150 000.

1. Explain Majid's fixed costs.
2. Explain Majid's variable costs.
3. Calculate Majid's total costs.

 **Discuss**

*Talk to a family member or a friend who has started and owns their own business. Discuss what their direct and indirect costs are.*

**Business owners worry most about total costs**

# A.2 Understand how businesses make a profit

## A.2 Understand how businesses make a profit

All businesses need to make money not only to make a profit and make the business successful but also to ensure they can pay for all the other expenses that are required to keep the business operating such as wages, stock, electricity, etc.

### Revenue

All businesses need revenue. Revenue refers to how the business makes money from what it sells, whether it makes goods or provides services. For example, a bicycle business may receive revenue from the sale of bicycles but it may also receive income from selling some of the land that it owns to another business. Revenue can therefore come from a number of sources not just the money a business receives for selling its products.

**Key terms**

***Revenue:*** *all the money coming into the business (the income) from selling its goods and services*

***Sources of revenue:*** *the various ways in which a business can receive income*

**Revenue is the number of bicycles sold multiplied by the selling price**

The revenue of a business can be calculated by multiplying the price that a customer pays for each unit by the number of units that the business sells:

- revenue = number of sales x price per unit

If a bicycle business sells bicycles for £500 per unit (per bike) and sells 1000 units, the total revenue for that month would be:

- £500 x 1000 = £500 000

Before a business can make a profit it first has to sell enough products to cover all its costs, both variable and fixed. Only when it has generated enough revenue to cover all its costs can it start making a profit. Revenue is all the money that comes into the business. Profit is when more than enough revenue has been received to cover all the costs. Once all the costs have been covered by the revenue, a profit is generated from this point onwards.

## Sources of revenue for a business

Revenue means the money received from sales of goods or services. When a business sells goods to its customers or provides a service, such as car repairs or hairdressing, it receives payment. This is only one way that a business can receive revenue. There are many other ways for a company to receive revenue.

- It may have lots of money available in its bank account and decide to invest this money either in a high interest bank account or perhaps in another business.
- It could also receive revenue by receiving a discount from other businesses to which it owes money. Some suppliers will offer discounts for buying a large quantity or for paying the bill on time.
- The business may own land, buildings and equipment that it no longer needs. It could sell these to provide another source of revenue.

**Investigate**

*Which one of the following is a source of revenue for a business?*

*costs*

*loan repayments*

*sales*

*utility bills*

**Investigate**

*A business sells 2500 bicycles at £150 each.*

*What is its revenue?*

*£37 500*

*£375 000*

*£3 750 000*

# A.2 How businesses have to spend money

## A.2: Expenditure and overheads

All businesses have to spend money to keep the business going and succeed. This is called expenditure. Expenditure can be described as cash spent in order to generate sales. For example, a small business sells greetings cards to retailers and operates from a distribution warehouse. Every week it has to buy cards from card manufacturers. It also has to pay the wages of the eight staff who work in the warehouse and pay for heating, lighting and fuel for its delivery vans. These are all examples of expenditure. If these things were not bought or paid for the business would very quickly grind to a halt. Expenditure is essential for any business to operate.

Overheads are a type of expenditure that is not directly related to making or producing a product. Typical examples of overhead expenditure are rent, insurance and professional fees, for example legal fees. All of these have to be paid whether a business produces very little or a lot during a trading period. Overheads are another term for indirect costs.

### Types of expenditure

Expenditure or payments that a business has to make can be for a variety of activities. Some of the more important are listed below.

- utility bills (water, gas and electricity)
- telephone bills
- general maintenance costs (of equipment and machinery)
- insurance (insuring the business)
- wages and salaries
- fuel (petrol and diesel for the business's vehicles)
- stock (the cost of buying raw material or ready-to-sell products)
- professional fees (for example for an accountant or lawyer)
- loan repayments
- advertising and marketing
- travel and entertainment (travelling, for example to visit customers or taking customers out for a meal)
- tax

**Key terms**

***Expenditure:*** *the money that a business pays out*

***Overheads:*** *the everyday running costs of a business*

**Discuss**

*Which two of the following are overheads for a business? Explain your reasons.*

*income*

*cash sales*

*wages*

*utilities*

*interest earned*

*tax rebate*

## Revenue and expenditure

Businesses must know how much money is coming in (revenue) and going out (expenditure), before it can work out whether it has made a profit or a loss.

All businesses, even social enterprises, need to make a profit. There are very few organisations that can operate without making a profit such as the NHS.

Profit is the money made when you take the money you have paid out of the business (expenditure) away from the money that you have coming into the business (the revenue). Profit is very important to businesses as it shows the financial return that entrepreneurs have achieved for their efforts.

- profit = revenue is more than expenditure
- loss = expenditure is more than revenue
- profit = revenue – expenditure

For example, Paula owns a small business selling cuddly children's toys. Her revenue for the year is £35 000 and her total expenditure for the year is £19 500.

To find out if Paula has made a profit we need to take away Paula's expenditure from her revenue.

£35 000 – £19 500 = £15 500.

Paula's business is therefore making a profit.

**Discuss**

*Toni owns a small restaurant and her profit last year was £15 000. Her total expenditure was £35 000. What was her revenue?*

**Case study**

Jaya Sharma owns a business making woollen scarves. Last year she sold £75 000 of scarves to clothing retailers. The cost of manufacturing the scarves was £45 000 and the costs not associated with the manufacturing process were £50 000.

1. Which costs are overhead costs?
2. What is Jaya's revenue for last year?
3. What is Jaya's profit or loss?

**Some costs are associated with making scarves and some are not**

# B.1 Planning for success

## B.1 Understanding the planning tools businesses use to predict when they will start making a profit

All businesses need to plan to ensure that the business survives and becomes successful. They need to be able to identify when they start making a profit, set targets to enable them to monitor performance and forecast when money will be coming into the business and when it will be going out of the business. If costs are greater than revenues the business will not make a profit and could cease to trade.

## B.1 Costs, revenue and breaking even

Breaking even is when a business has made enough money through product sales to cover the cost of making the product. The **break-even point** is the point at which the volume of sales or revenues exactly equals total expenses. There is no profit or loss. The break-even point tells the business what level of **output** is required before the business can make a profit.

The break-even point can be calculated by using a formula:

$$\text{break-even} = \frac{\text{fixed costs}}{\text{selling price per unit} - \text{variable cost per unit}}$$

RVD Ltd is a business that manufactures ballpoint pens. It has fixed costs of £60 000. Its variable costs are raw materials and assembly line workers' wages. The variable costs have been calculated to be 80p per unit (per pen). The pens are sold at £2 each.

From this information, we can calculate the break-even point for RVD Ltd.

- fixed costs = £60 000
- selling price per unit = £2.00
- variable cost per unit = £0.80

$$\text{break-even} = \frac{60\ 000}{2.00 - 0.80}$$

$$= 50\ 000 \text{ pens}$$

RVD Ltd has to produce and sell 50 000 pens in order to cover its total expenses, fixed and variable. At this level of sales, it will make no profit. It will just break even.

### Key terms

***Break-even point:*** *the sales level at which revenue and costs are equal*

***Output:*** *the amount of product that is produced*

***Margin of safety:*** *the comfort zone between actual sales and break-even point*

**A company has to sell a lot of product just to break even**

## A company has to sell a lot of product just to break even

There are many examples of businesses that fail to reach a break-even point and fail. Even professional football clubs have to break even or make a profit to survive. Glasgow Rangers had problems recently as its expenditure was far greater than its revenues, resulting in an inability to break even and make a profit.

**Even football clubs need to manage break-even**

## Break-even point and margin of safety

A business needs to work out what volume of sales it needs to achieve in order to cover its costs. This is known as the break-even point. The key to breaking even is to work out the variable costs made from the sale of each unit.

For example, Rachel sells ladies' clothing in an upmarket boutique in Balham. Her dresses sell for £15 and she has variable costs per unit (per dress) of £11. Her fixed costs are £20 000. She has calculated that she needs to sell 5000 units (dresses) in order to break even.

The **margin of safety** is the difference between the number of units planned or actual sales and the number of units at the break-even point.

If Rachel plans to sell 7000 units (dresses), then the margin of safety would be:

margin of safety = number of units planned to be sold or actual sales (break-even units)

= 7000 – 5000

= 2000

Rachel will be able to sell 2000 fewer dresses than she plans before she is in danger of making a loss.

**Research**

*Research businesses that have recently had problems making a profit and breaking even.*

# B.1 How to present information graphically on a break-even chart

## B.1 Break-even charts

Break-even charts are a useful way of showing the break-even point and looking at the profit and losses made for different levels of output.

David has set up a business to produce sport vests with printed designs on the front. The fixed cost of premises and printers is £3000. The variable cost per sports vest is £5. The printed sports vests sell for £25 each.

Key terms

***Break-even chart:*** *a graph showing the break-even point and the profit and loss at different levels of output*

**Businesses must understand their break-even point and the profit and loss at different levels of output**

**Figure 2.2 Sales versus costs**

| Sales volumes of T-shirts (no. of T-shirts sold) | Variable costs (£) (@ £5 per T-shirt) (£5 × no. of sales) | Fixed costs (£) | Total costs (£) (Fixed costs + variable costs) | Sales revenue (@ £25 per T-shirt) (£25 × sales volumes) |
|---|---|---|---|---|
| 50 | 250 | 3000 | 3250 | 1250 |
| 100 | 500 | 3000 | 3500 | 2500 |
| 150 | 750 | 3000 | 3750 | 3750 |
| 200 | 1000 | 3000 | 4000 | 5000 |
| 250 | 1250 | 3000 | 4250 | 6250 |

**Figure 2.3 (a–h)**

(a) You first need to name the vertical axis Costs/Sales revenues (£)

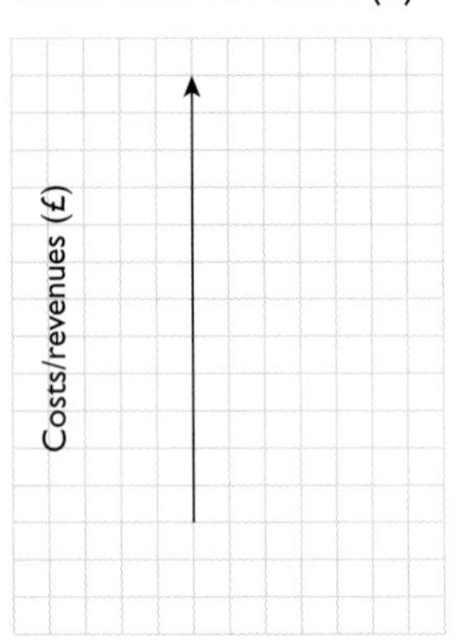


(b) Name the horizontal axis 'No. of T-shirts sold'.

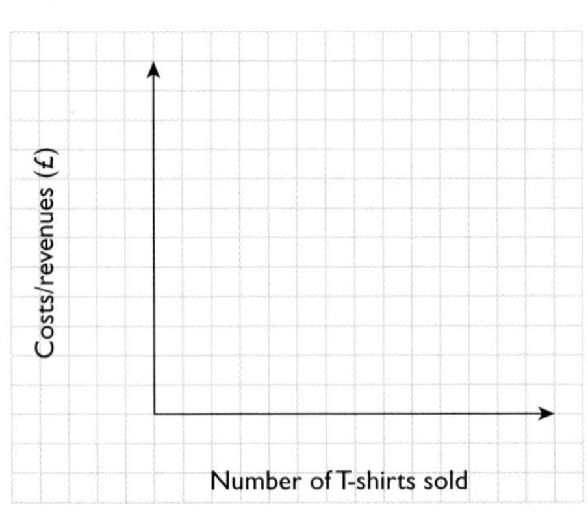

(c) Decide the scales that you want to use by looking at the sales volumes figures and the sales revenues figures that are given.

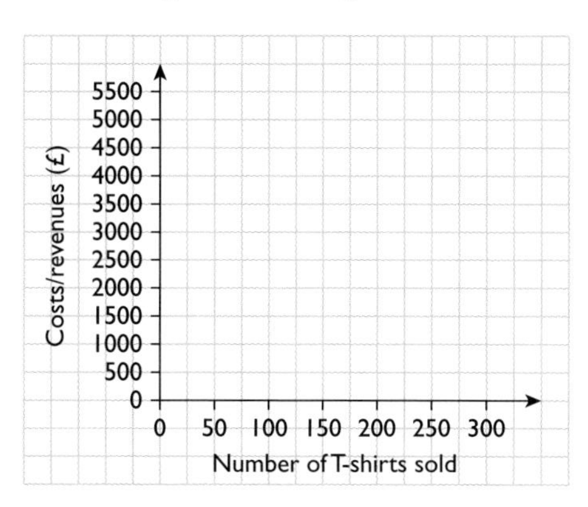


(d) Plot any two points from the sales revenue data for the sales revenue line and then draw a straight line for sales revenue.

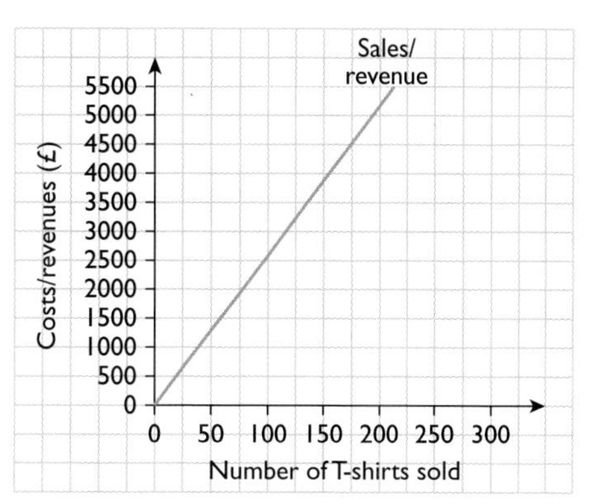


(e) Draw a horizontal line for total fixed costs starting at the point on the vertical axis at the level of costs.

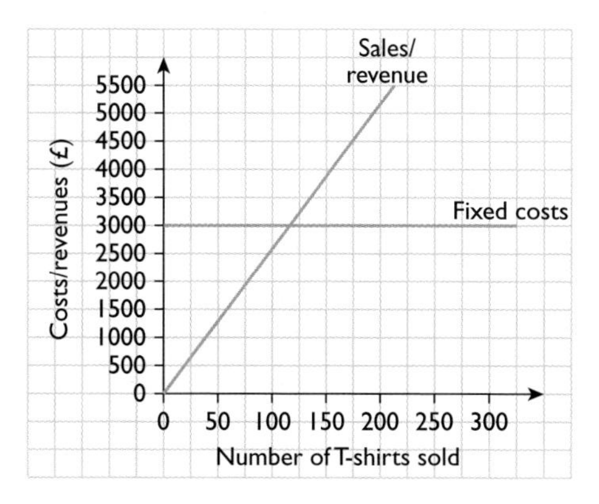


(f) Draw the total costs line. Total costs are fixed costs plus variable costs. Draw the straight line starting at the same point as the fixed costs started and then through the two plotted points.

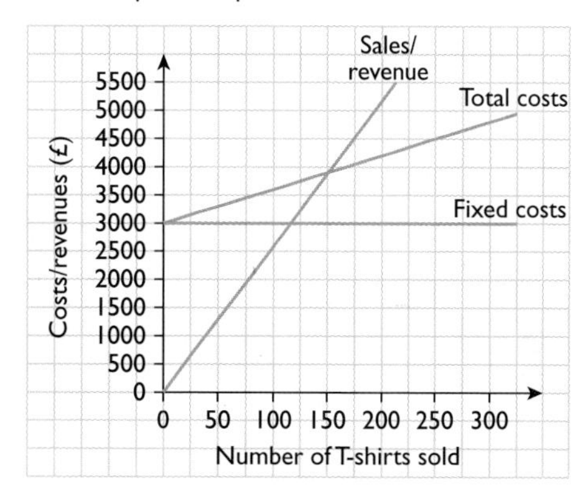


(g) The point at which the sales revenue crosses the total costs line is the break-even point. The gap between the total costs line and sales revenue line after the breakeven point is the level of profit. The area below the total costs line is where the business is making a loss.

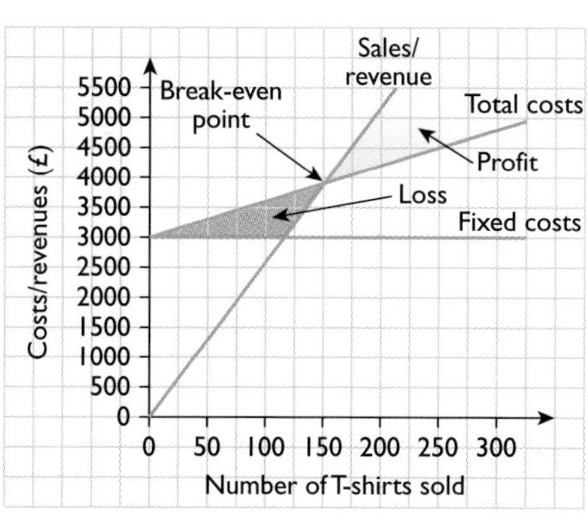


(h) The diagram below shows the margin of safety for David's business when his output is 250 sports vests.

If David sells 250 sport vests, the margin of safety is 250 – 150 = 100. This means he could sell up to 100 fewer sports vests before he starts to lose money.

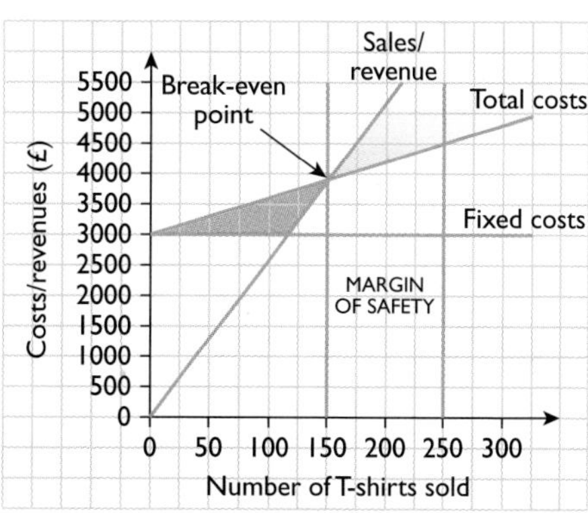

# B.1 The importance of break-even analysis

## B.1 Break-even and its use for planning for success

**Break-even analysis** is a valuable tool when planning for success. It is very important for a business to understand where its break-even point is positioned as every unit sold above the break-even point adds to profit. Finding the break-even point helps the business work out whether the forecast sales will be high enough to produce a profit and whether further investment in the product should be considered.

The break-even point can be calculated quickly so managers can see the margin of safety and take action to cut costs or increase sales if they need to expand it. The break-even point also allows the business to forecast how variations in sales will affect costs, revenue and profits. Any variations in price and costs will affect how much the business needs to sell.

**Key term**

***Break-even analysis:*** *finding the point at which revenue equals cost*

### Risks to the business of not completing a break-even analysis

If a business does not complete a break-even analysis it will not be able to predict when it will start making a profit. It will be unable to measure profit and loss at different levels of production and sales. It will not be able to predict the effect of changes in price on sales.

Without conducting a break-even analysis the business has no idea if the decisions made on prices and costs are going to generate a profit. This could cause the business significant financial problems.

**Discuss**

*In groups, discuss the problems that may arise if a business does not complete a break-even analysis.*

### The effect on the break-even point if sales or costs change

The break-even point will change if any of the other figures (fixed costs, variable costs or selling price) used to calculate the breakeven is altered.

The formula for break-even is:

$$\text{break-even} = \frac{\text{fixed costs}}{\text{selling price per unit} - \text{variable cost per unit}}$$

For example, Mugs'n'Mugs Ltd manufactures decorated mugs.

The fixed cost of producing 100 000 decorated mugs is £30 000 each year.

**The break-even point will change if sales or costs change**

The variable cost per unit (per mug) is £2.20 materials, £4 labour, and 80p overheads. Therefore the total variable cost is £7 per unit.

The selling price for each mug is £12.

The break-even will be:

$$\frac{£30\,000}{(£12 - £7)} = 6000 \text{ units.}$$

Mugs'n'Mugs Ltd has to sell 6000 mugs at £12 each before the business will start to make a profit.

The owner of the building that Mugs'n'Mugs Ltd uses for manufacturing has raised the rent by £10 000. This means that fixed costs have risen to £40 000.

The break-even is now:

$$\frac{£40\,000}{(£12 - £7)} = 8000 \text{ units.}$$

The business now has to make and sell an extra 2000 mugs just to break even. If they are unable to do this the business will make a loss and get into difficulty.

If the variable costs fall to £6 per unit, due to a reduction of the number of staff required on the production line, with fixed costs at £30 000 and a selling price still at £12, the break-even will change again:

$$\frac{£30\,000}{(£12 - £6)} = 5000 \text{ units}$$

In this case a fall in variable costs has caused the break-even to fall to 5000 units. The reduction in the variable costs per mug will have a positive impact on the business. It now only has to make and sell 5000 mugs to break even.

The business decides to lower the selling price to £11 because its competitors are reducing their prices. The £30 000 fixed costs and £7 variable costs per mug stay the same, but the break-even changes again:

$$\frac{£30\,000}{(£11 - £7)} = 7500 \text{ units}$$

The break-even has risen because of the reduction in the selling price. This has a significant impact on the business as it has to make and sell an additional 1500 mugs in order to break even.

### Investigate

*A wrist watch manufacturer sells its watches for £12 and has variable costs of £7 per watch. It has fixed costs of £30 000.*

*Calculate the break-even.*

*Explain the impact on the business if the selling price is reduced to £10 and the variable cost per watch increases to £7.20.*

## The value of break-even to businesses

When businesses are planning for success, break-even has many advantages. Businesses can use it to indicate how changes to fixed costs, variable costs and revenues can affect levels of profit and the break-even point.

Break-even's most important use, however, is that it can show the lowest level of production or sales that is required to prevent a loss. It also allows the business to forecast how changes to sales will affect costs, revenues and profits. Businesses can use break-even to help persuade a bank or other lender to give them a loan. It is also particularly useful if a business is considering whether or not to launch a new product. If the break-even shows that the business would have to sell an enormous quantity of the new product to break even, then the business would probably decide not to go ahead with the launch.

### Investigate

*Select three correct reasons why a business should produce a break-even chart.*

*(a) to find out the level of sales to cover costs*

*(b) to identify cash flow shortages over a period*

*(c) to enable a profit and loss to be produced*

*(d) to show the bank in order to obtain a loan*

*(e) to show shareholders how well the business is performing*

*(f) to identify items for the balance sheet*

*(g) to identify how much profit will be made from the launch of a new product*

**Case study (B1)**

A business makes small dog kennels that sell for £30 each. It has variable costs per unit of £22.The business has fixed costs of £40 000.

Its break-even is therefore $\frac{£40\,000}{(£30 - £22)} = 5000$ units.

The business plans to sell 15 000 units.

1. Draw a break-even chart to show the break-even point.
2. Calculate the margin of safety.

Any new business has to incur lots of costs in setting up the business before any customers 'walk through the door' and start paying for its goods or services. The first few months and maybe even years of many businesses mean that they will have lots of debts. Whether the business will be a success or not will depend on whether it can pay these debts.

The Eurotunnel faced many problems when it initially opened. However, its variable costs were not one of them as they are relatively small; the cost of operating the tunnel now it is built is very low. The fixed costs of the Eurotunnel include admin costs, advertising, insurance and interest payments.

The Eurotunnel encountered mounting construction costs and this has been the main problem in trying to pay back its debts. The interest payments on these debts have been Eurotunnel's biggest problem as It was not making enough revenue to cover them. Its revenue is created from passengers using the Eurotunnel and therefore the only way to increase it is to get more passengers and increase prices. Eurotunnel has restructured its debts to make them more manageable; however, it is a company that will never break even. This has happened because of the huge costs incurred in building the tunnel and the fact that it cannot be used for anything else!

**Effective planning of production and sales increases chances of success**

# B.2 Budgeting for success

## B.2 Understand the tools businesses use to plan for success

Many highly paid celebrities including Kerry Katona, Meatloaf, MC Hammer, Mike Tyson and Sarah Ferguson (Duchess of York) have all ended up bankrupt. They were earning plenty of money, yet never managed what they earned effectively. This is why it is so important for businesses, like people, to manage their income and spending, in business terms, their revenue and expenditure.

### The purpose of budgeting

For a business to manage its revenue and expenditure effectively, it needs to start budgeting. This means the business has to plan what funds are going to be allocated to each department within a business. For example, a business may decide that for next year it can spend £50 000 on advertising. This allows managers to look at what has actually been spent on advertising and compare it to the budgeted figure. Budgeting therefore allows people who manage the business to control overspending and take corrective action.

Expenditure budgets predict what the business's total costs will be for the year. In an expenditure budget the business will list all the purchases and other costs it will make, for example buying stock, equipment, software, machinery and so on. An expenditure budget includes everything the business will buy or spend over the coming year. The table below is an extract from an expenditure budget for a small manufacturing business.

**Figure 2.4 Expenditure budget for RN Engineering Ltd**

| Expenditure (costs) | Budgeted costs (£) | Actual costs (£) |
|---|---|---|
| Wages | £720 000 | £850 000 |
| Rent | £120 000 | £120 000 |
| Other costs | £60 000 | £55 000 |

Revenue budgets forecast the amount of money that will come into the business as revenue. The business needs to predict how much it will sell and at what price. Managers use sales figures from previous years, as well as information from market research, to estimate this. They must also take into consideration their competitors, promotional plans and other relevant factors. For example, a retail convenience store will

**Key terms**

***Budgeting:*** *a list of all planned expenses (outflows) and revenues (inflows). A plan for saving, borrowing and spending*

***Budgetary control:*** *comparing actual financial results with budgeted financial results and the actions taken to correct any differences*

***Expenditure budgets:*** *prediction of total costs for the year*

***Revenue budgets:*** *prediction of how much money will come into the business*

***Variances:*** *differences between actual and budgeted figures*

**We must all manage our finances**

use a revenue budget to forecast future sales for each product that is in the store. The table below shows the revenue budget for a typical convenience store.

**Figure 2.5 Revenue budget for Ali's convenience store**

| Product group | Budgeted sales (£) | Actual sales (£) |
|---|---|---|
| Confectionery | 120 000 | 122 000 |
| Tobacco | 300 000 | 301 000 |
| Soft drinks | 140 000 | 138 000 |
| Newspapers and stationery | 95 0000 | 95 000 |
| Snacks and crisps | 132 000 | 130 000 |

## Budgeting and budgetary control

**Budgetary control** is when a manager compares actual results with the budgeted figures. If there are differences (**variances**) the manager can take action to try and ensure the actual figures come nearer to the budgeted figure.

For example, in the revenue budget below, the business estimated that sales in January would be £128 000. The actual sales for January were only £123 000. Figures in brackets indicate negative variance.

**Figure 2.6 Actual vs budgeted sales for a three-month period**

| Month | Actual sales | Budget sales | Variance |
|---|---|---|---|
| January | £123 000 | £128 000 | (£5000) |
| February | £147 000 | £147 500 | (£500) |
| March | £148 000 | £147 000 | £1000 |

The manager will investigate why the sales figure is lower than expected. This could be as the result of competitor activity. Or perhaps suppliers did not deliver enough stock and sales were lost? The manager could then consider activities that could ensure these sales are recovered in the following months. For example, the price of the products could be reduced for a short while or advertising could be increased to boost sales.

# B.2 Cash flow forecasting

## B.2 Cash flow forecasting

Cash flow forecasts show the amount of money that the business expects to come in and flow out over a period of time in the future. Managers can use cash flow forecasts to make sure they always have enough money to pay suppliers and employees. They can predict when they will be short of cash and arrange a loan or overdraft to ensure the business doesn't find itself in trouble.

Businesses must have enough money to meet their debts as they fall due. Businesses need to pay money out for fixed assets such as buildings and vehicles as well as covering operating costs. A cash flow forecast therefore predicts the net cash flows of the business over a period in the future. The forecast estimates the cash inflows into the bank account and outflows out of it.

### Sources of inflows and outflows

Cash inflows are monies received by a business as a result of its operating activities.

Examples of cash inflows could include:

- Sales – revenue from selling goods and services to customers.
- Capital – a one-off injection of cash that comes from the owner investing in the business, for example when the business is starting up, the buying of machinery and equipment.
- Loans – when a business first takes out a loan, this injection of cash is an inflow. (The paying of the interest on the loan after this will be an outflow.)
- Regular and irregular inflows – some inflows, such as weekly sales, will be regular, whereas some will be irregular, that is they only happen now and again, for example selling machinery.

Businesses must consider when cash inflows are likely to happen. Knowing that there will be plenty of sales for a toy manufacturer in the lead up to Christmas is little help as they struggle to survive in January and February. It is important that customers pay businesses on time, as otherwise they will be starved of cash and may not survive.

Cash outflows are monies paid out by a business as a result of its operating, investment and financing activities.

**Key terms**

***Cash flow forecasts:*** *These show the amount of money that the business expects to come into and go out of the business over a period of time*

***Inflows:*** *Money coming into the business*

***Outflows:*** *Money going out of the business*

Cash outflows could include:

- Purchases – stock and raw materials have to be purchased regularly.
- Wages and bills – staff wages and electricity, water, gas and phone bills all need to be paid regularly.
- Loan repayments –the interest on any loans taken out. These have to be paid regularly.
- Regular and irregular outflows – regular outflows include paying the interest on a loan or paying your suppliers on certain days of every month. Irregular outflows include any repairs that may arise in a shop or the cost of replacing equipment. Irregular outflows, although they do not occur very often, should be planned for so that the business does not face a cash flow crisis.

Like cash inflows, the timing of cash outflows is also very important to the survival of a business. If a big bill has to be paid in two months' time, the business should do all it can to delay paying out a lot of cash this month and next month.

## The impact of timings of inflows and outflows

There will usually be a delay between money going out and money coming in so it is very important that there is always enough money available to pay suppliers and wages. Businesses try to improve their cash flow by trying to persuade customers to pay sooner. This will get money into their account more quickly. They may also chase their debts more firmly or order less stock. In addition, when a business starts up, money flowing into the business also includes the capital (money) that the owner decides to invest in the business in the first place in order to set it up. This is recognised on the cash flow forecast as the 'opening balance'.

For example, a new business starts up selling computers and accessories with a loan of £36 000 and £10 000 of the owner's money (opening balance).

**Cash flow helps the business plan**

**Discuss**

*Talk to a family member or a friend who has started and owns their own business. Discuss what their cash inflows and outflows are.*

It expects to sell:

- £10 000 of goods in January
- £70 000 in February
- £70 000 in March
- £70 000 in April

All customers receive a one-month credit period (items bought in one month are paid for in the following month).

Wages and rent will cost £30 000 each month and advertising costs are expected to be:

- £10 000 in January
- £16 000 in February
- £4000 in March
- £4000 in April

The closing balance at the end of December is £6000.

Step 1. The first step is to identify the inflows (the sales from January to April and the start-up loan). The money for the £10 000 of sales in January will be received in February as customers have one month's credit. February's sales income is received in March, and so on. The loan of £36 000 is also entered as other cash in for January. The cash in then needs to be totalled for each month:

**Figure 2.7 Cash flow chart (inflows)**

| | Item | January | February | March | April |
|---|---|---|---|---|---|
| Cash in (inflows) | Sales revenue | | 10 000 | 70 000 | 70 000 |
| | Other cash in | 36 000 | | | |
| | Total cash in | 36 000 | 10 000 | 70 000 | 70 000 |

Step 2. The next step is to identify the outflows (wages and rent at £30 000 each month and the advertising costs). These are then totalled for each month:

**Investigate**

*Make a list of all of your cash inflows and outflows for the last six months.*

**Figure 2.8 Cash flow chart (outflows)**

| | Item | January | February | March | April |
|---|---|---|---|---|---|
| Cash in (inflows) | Sales revenue | | 10 000 | 150 000 | 70 000 |
| | Other cash in | 36 000 | | | |
| | Total cash in | 36 000 | 10 000 | 150 000 | 70 000 |
| Cash out (outflows) | Wages and rent | 30 000 | 30 000 | 30 000 | 30 000 |
| | Advertising | 10 000 | 16 000 | 4000 | 4000 |
| | Total costs | 40 000 | 46 000 | 34 000 | 34 000 |

Step 3. You now have to put the net monthly cash flows into the cash flow chart.

The net cash flow is the total cash in for the month less the total cash out. This part of the cash flow forecast also contains the opening balance in the bank account at the start of January (£10 000). This is the owner's money, which was put into the account in January.

The closing balance for January is the opening balance less the net cash flow which is £10 000 – £4000 = £6000.

The closing balance for January becomes the opening balance for February and so on.

*Using the cash flow example below, complete the cash flow for the next four months (May to August). Sales revenue is £50 000 each month, wages and rent are £30 000 each month and advertising is £5000 each month.*

**Figure 2.9 Cash flow chart (closing balance)**

| | Item | January | February | March | April |
|---|---|---|---|---|---|
| Cash in (inflows) | Sales revenue | | 10 000 | 70 000 | 70 000 |
| | Other cash in | 36 000 | | | |
| | Total cash in | 36 000 | 10 000 | 70 000 | 70 000 |
| Cash out (outflows) | Wages and rent | 30 000 | 30 000 | 30 000 | 30 000 |
| | Advertising | 10 000 | 16 000 | 4000 | 4000 |
| | Total costs | 40,000 | 46 000 | 34 000 | 34 000 |
| Net monthly cash flows | Net cash flow | –4000 | –36 000 | 36 000 | 36 000 |
| | Opening balance | 10 000 | 6000 | –30 000 | 6000 |
| | Closing balance | 6000 | –30 000 | 6000 | 42 000 |

## B.2 Cash flow forecasting

Businesses can use cash flow forecasts to make sure they always have enough cash to pay suppliers and employees. This allows businesses to predict when they will be short of cash and arrange a loan or overdraft in time. Businesses can also show their cash flow forecasts to banks to try and get a loan for a new venture. This might be launching a new product, investing in new equipment or expanding or reducing various parts of the business.

A cash flow is particularly useful when a business is going to introduce new products or services. There will be costs that have to be paid for some time to finance new equipment and raw materials before the new products are sold to customers and generate revenue. The cash flow will indicate whether the extra costs required will result in a negative balance for a few months. This may mean a loan or overdraft is needed until the new products begin to sell and generate revenue to cover costs.

Similarly, the business may want to expand or reduce its activities. Perhaps one of its products or services is not generating enough profit from its sales and the business has to decide whether to continue to produce and sell it. The manager can use the cash flow forecast to see what will happen to cash flow if the business stops producing and selling a product. Again, this may require a loan or overdraft to cover the period where income falls.

The business may want to invest in new resources (for example new machinery) to produce products more efficiently and reduce staff costs. The cash flow forecast will indicate when the cost of purchasing the new machinery will occur and its effect on the business's cash flow. It will also show how the new efficient machinery will reduce costs in future months.

Without a cash flow forecast, a business cannot be sure that it has enough cash to pay suppliers and employees. If these people are not paid they will stop working and delivering. Without a cash flow forecast a business will have no idea when it may run short of cash and will not have arranged a loan or overdraft for those periods. A business is taking a huge risk if it doesn't complete a cash flow forecast. Lack of financial planning could lead to the business closing.

**Key terms**

***Deficit:*** *money that is left after all outflows have been deducted from the previous balance and inflows added (negative value)*

***Surplus:*** *the money that is left after all outflows have been deducted from the previous balance and inflows added (positive value)*

## Completing cash flow forecasts and dealing with surpluses and deficits

A manager in charge of cash flow has to balance the cash coming into the business with the cash going out. The danger is that demands for cash, from the landlord, employees or the tax office, will arrive before the business receives the cash it is owed. More often than not, cash inflows seem to lag behind cash outflows, which can leave the business short of money. If cash flow is not monitored properly and action taken when necessary, the business may find itself in trouble. If cash flow is carefully monitored, the business should be able to forecast how much cash will be available at any given time, and plan its business activities to ensure there is always cash to meet upcoming payments.

A cash flow forecast contains anticipated cash inflows, anticipated cash outflows, a cash flow bottom line highlighting potential **surpluses** that could be reinvested or deposited and **deficits** that must be covered with loans or the owner's money.

**Discuss**

*Talk to a family member or a friend who has started and owns their own business. Discuss how important cash flow forecasting is to them and their success/survival.*

**All businesses need cash to pay suppliers and employees**

**Figure 2.10 Cash flow forecast**

| | Item | January | February | March | April |
|---|---|---|---|---|---|
| Cash in | Sales revenue | | 10 000 | 70 000 | 70 000 |
| | Other cash in | 36 000 | | | |
| | Total cash in | 36 000 | 10 000 | 70 000 | 70 000 |
| Cash out | Wages and rent | 30 000 | 30 000 | 30 000 | 30 000 |
| | Advertising | 10 000 | 16 000 | 4 000 | 4 000 |
| | Total costs | 40 000 | 46 000 | 34 000 | 34 000 |
| Net monthly cash flows | Net cash flow | –4000 | –36 000 | 36 000 | 36 000 |
| | Opening balance | 10 000 | 6000 | –30 000 | 6000 |
| | Closing balance | 6000 | –30 000 | 6000 | 42 000 |

Above is a cash flow forecast for a computer repair shop.

In February, there is only £10 000 of sales flowing into the business. This results in a negative net cash flow for that month, which means the closing balance is –£30 000.

This negative net cash flow is known as a deficit.

The business should have anticipated this and arranged a short-term loan or overdraft from the bank to cover this trading period.

Without arranging a short-term loan or overdraft the business will not have been able to pay all the costs and the business might not be able to pay the staff's wages.

Simon runs a chain of card and gift shops all over the country. His cash flow forecast for the first four months of the year is shown in Figure 2.11. In March it is predicted that there will be a very high revenue figure (£150 000) due to Easter and Mother's Day. The business will have a lot of money in its bank account at this time. This is known as a surplus and is far more than is needed for the monthly expenditure of the business.

Simon has decided to allow this money to work for him and generate more revenue. He has taken financial advice and has two options. He can either deposit some of this money in a high interest-earning account or reinvest the money in the business to expand.

**Gifts and cards will sell different amounts at different times of the year**

**Figure 2.11 Simon's cash flow forecast for the first quarter**

| | Item | January | February | March | April |
|---|---|---|---|---|---|
| Cash in | Sales revenue | | 10 000 | 150 000 | 70 000 |
| | Other cash in | 36 000 | | | |
| | Total cash in | 36 000 | 10 000 | 150 000 | 70 000 |
| Cash out | Wages and rent | 30 000 | 30 000 | 30 000 | 30 000 |
| | Advertising | 10 000 | 16 000 | 4000 | 4000 |
| | Total costs | 40 000 | 46 000 | 34 000 | 34 000 |
| | Net cash flow | –4000 | –36 000 | 116 000 | 36 000 |
| Net monthly cash flows | Opening balance | 10 000 | 6000 | –30 000 | 86 000 |
| | Closing balance | 6000 | –30,000 | 86 000 | 122 000 |

**Case study**

Ryan Williams owns a small manufacturing business and is trying to prepare a cash flow forecast for the first three months of the year.

His opening balance is £5000 at the beginning of January. The business will receive inflows of £55 000 sales each month and in February there will be a £20 000 bank loan credited to the business account.

The business will also have the following outflows each month: £25 000 wages, £300 insurance and £5000 fuel and other expenses. In February, a lorry has to be bought for £70 000.

1. Produce a cash flow forecast for the first three months of the year.
2. What should the business do about any months that show a deficit balance?
3. Explain the importance of cash flow forecasting for businesses such as Ryan's.

# C.1 Understand how businesses measure success

## C.1 Making a profit

All businesses need to make a profit. Even businesses that are social enterprises such as The Big Issue need to make a profit in order to reinvest money in their charitable causes. There are only a few businesses, such as the police and fire service, that can survive operating at a loss.

There are two types of profit: gross profit and net profit.

### Cost of sales

The cost of sales is the cost of producing the product, otherwise known as the total variable costs. These can include:

- the cost of your stock
- components/raw materials to make your product
- labour to produce the product
- machine hire
- small tools.

Rowan's Books is a small bookshop where the average price of a book is £15 and the number of books sold is 10 000 per year.

The turnover is therefore: 10 000 x £15 = £150 000.

The cost of sales is the cost of buying the books for resale in the shop. The bookshop buys in 10 000 books at an average cost of £7 each.

The cost of sales is therefore: 10 000 x £7 = £70 000

### What is gross profit?

Gross profit is the money made from selling a product (revenue) after the cost of producing the product (cost of sales) has been deducted. It is calculated as sales minus all costs directly related to those sales, such as manufacturing, raw materials, stock, labour and marketing.

The gross profit tells you how much money a business would have made if it didn't pay any other expenses such as salaries, income taxes and utilities.

gross profit = revenue – cost of sales (variable costs)

In the example of Rowan's Books:

- revenue = £150 000
- cost of sales = £70 000
- gross profit (= revenue – cost of sales) = £80 000

### Key terms

***Cost of sales:*** *the cost of obtaining or creating a product*

***Gross profit:*** *the money made from selling a product after the cost of producing the product has been deducted*

***Net profit:*** *the money made from selling a product after all costs have been deducted*

### Investigate

*Which of the following best describes cost of sales?*

*(a) The expense incurred in building a factory to manufacture products*

*(b) The expense incurred in buying delivery vehicles and drivers*

*(c) The expense incurred in manufacturing, creating or selling a product*

*(d) The expense incurred in employing company representatives to sell*

As well as the cost of sales, a business will also have to pay overhead costs. These costs cannot be directly related to each unit of output made or sold (in the example of Rowan's Books, the purchase of books from suppliers). Overheads are also referred to as to expenses, and include items such as heating, lighting, administration, insurance and advertising.

When gross profit is positive it means that there is gross profit from which overheads can be deducted to leave a positive net profit. The larger a positive gross profit, the greater the chance of achieving a positive net profit after the overhead is subtracted. It is possible to achieve a large gross profit but still produce a negative net profit if expenses are very high.

## Net profit

Net profit is what is left after all the operating costs have been paid. It is calculated by subtracting the total expenditure from the gross profit.

net profit = gross profit – expenditure

Rowan's Books' gross profit (see below) looks quite good at £80 000 but when the expenses are deducted they are greater than the gross profit, which means the business is making a loss.

| | |
|---|---|
| Turnover | £150 000 |
| Cost of sales | £70 000 |
| **Gross profit** | 150 000 – 70 000 = **£80 000** |
| Less expenses: | |
| Heating and lighting | £2500 |
| Insurance | £4000 |
| Advertising | £8000 |
| Administrative expenses | £7000 |
| Wages | £60 000 |
| Total expenses | **£81 500** |
| **Net profit** | **£80 000 – £81 500** |
| | **= –£1500** |

The net profit is used to pay tax and to help the business grow in years to come. A limited company will also share some of its profits with shareholders (dividends) as long as it has made a positive net profit. A negative net profit means there will be no dividends paid as the business is making a loss.

### Investigate

*Which two of the following are ways of improving a business's gross profit?*

*(a) Sell the business to a competitor*

*(b) Reduce the business's costs*

*(c) Reduce the business's turnover*

*(d) Reduce productivity*

*(e) Reduce business efficiency*

*(f) Increase productivity*

### Case study (C1)

Michael owns a newsagent shop and would like to find out what his gross and net profit are. His sales revenue for the year is £130 000 and his cost of sales is £60 000. His expenses are wages £40 000, advertising £5000, administration £6000 and heating and lighting £6000.

1. What is Michael's gross profit?
2. What is Michael's net profit?

**Gross and net profit determine the success of the business**

# C.1 Measuring success

## C.1 Measuring success by looking at financial statements

Financial statements record the financial activities and resources of a business, sometimes required by law, including:

- an income statement (profit and loss account)
- a statement of financial position (balance sheet).

### Income statement (profit and loss account)

The income statement is a record of the trading of a business over a specific period, usually one year. It shows the profit or loss made by the business.

#### Trading account

A profit and loss account starts with the trading account, which shows the profit made by a firm. The main income is from sales. To earn those sales a firm has to spend money either on making goods or on buying them from other firms to sell.

Apart from new firms, most businesses start their year with stock left over from the year before. These goods are opening stock. During the year the firm buys new supplies. The goods a firm sells during the year consist of the opening stock plus the purchases. The figure that results is the cost of the goods sold in that year.

The value of the closing stock is found by adding up all the goods left at the end of the year and multiplying them by the price at which they were bought. Adding up the stock is called stocktaking. The closing stock from one financial year is the opening stock for the next.

Cost of goods sold = opening stock + purchases – closing stock

The trading account can be shown as a separate account or, as in the example for Haycraft Limited (Figure 2.12), it can be combined with the profit and loss account.

**Key terms**

***Balance sheet:*** *a statement of the total assets and liabilities of an organisation*

***Income statement:*** *a record of the trading of a business over a specific period*

***Opening stock:*** *the amount of stock held by a business at the start of a new financial year*

***Purchases:*** *the buying of stock needed by a business in order to produce sales*

***Trading account:*** *this shows the gross profit (sales or revenue – cost of sales)*

***Stocktaking:*** *the total amount of stock owned by a business at the end of a trading year*

## Profit and loss account

The trading account only shows the cost of the goods actually bought and sold by a business to find the gross profit. In order to make that gross profit, a firm has many other costs that have to be met. These are the general expenses of running the business. They include rent, utility bills and wages. The costs of these expenses are listed in the profit and loss account. The total of these costs is taken away from the gross profit to find the net profit for the year. The net profit is the profit made by the business as a whole before taxes have been paid.

**Figure 2.12 Trading Profit and Loss Account for Haycraft Limited for the year ended December 2013**

| | | £0 | £0 |
|---|---|---|---|
| Sales | | | 758 |
| *Less:* | | | |
| Opening stock on 1 January 2012 | | 98 | |
| Purchases | | 385 | |
| | | 483 | |
| Closing stock on 31 December 2012 | | 118 | |
| **Cost of goods sold** | | | **365** |
| **Gross Profit** | | | **393** |
| Wages and salaries | | 123 | |
| Heating and lighting | | 34 | |
| Rent | 39 | | |
| *Add rent due:* | 13 | 52 | |
| Rates | | 16 | |
| Telephone | | 11 | |
| Advertising | | 18 | |
| Insurance | 14 | | |
| *Less paid in advance* | 2 | 12 | |
| Administration | | 22 | |
| Bad debts | | 9 | |
| Depreciation | | | |
| *Furniture and fittings at 10%* | 8 | | |
| *Machinery at 12%* | 23 | | |
| *Vehicles at 20%* | 15 | 46 | 343 |
| **Net Profit** | | | **50** |

The profit and loss account includes only expenses for the year in question. Any expenses paid in advance, such as insurance, have to be taken away (Figure 2.12.). Any money that is owed, like rent, also has to be added into the account.

## What happens to net profit?

The way net profit is divided up is shown in an appropriation account at the end of the profit and loss account. Before deciding how to use net profit, limited companies must pay corporation tax, which is taken away from net profit to show the net profit after tax. Partnerships and sole traders do not have to pay corporation tax.

**A profit and loss account tells you the financial performance over a period of time**

### Research

*Johns Computers Ltd has the following information as at 31 July 2012.*

*Sales £249 000*

*Cost of sales £193 000*

*Wages £20 000*

*Rent and rates £5000*

*Telephone £500*

*Advertising £5000*

*Transport £12 000*

*Heating and lighting £3500*

*Tax £5000*

*Produce a profit and loss account for Johns Computers as at 31 July 2012.*

# C.1 Understand how businesses measure success

## C.1 Statement of financial position (balance sheet)

From time to time every business needs to know what it is worth, what it owns and what it owes to others. This information is shown in a balance sheet. Every limited company must by law draw up a balance sheet at the end of its financial year and send a copy to the Registrar of Companies.

The balance sheet shows a business's:

- assets – what the business owns and the resources used in the business
- liabilities – what the business owes to other people or firms
- capital – what the business owes to its owners

A balance sheet must always balance according to the formula:

- assets = liabilities + capital

The value of each item may change, but the two sides of the formula must always be equal. Someone must own the assets of a business.

For example, if a firm buys an asset for £50 000 and pays a deposit of £25 000 but owes the supplier £25 000, it will have assets of £50 000, liabilities of £25 000 and capital of £25 000. When it pays the rest of the money to the supplier, the firm has assets of £50 000, no liabilities and capital of £50 000.

There are several ways of setting out a balance sheet. A typical example will look like the balance sheet for Haycraft Limited shown on page 81.

Strictly speaking a balance sheet is not an account. It is a summary of the balances in the firm's accounts at a certain date. It is only accurate on that date, so that the heading is always 'as at' the date. There are some rules about the way a balance sheet should be set out.

- The fixed assets should be shown first, followed by the current assets.
- Current assets mainly consist of stock, debtors, cash in the bank and cash held in the business, and should be stated in that order.
- It is usual to deduct current liabilities from current assets to show working capital.
- The net assets employed will be equal to the capital employed in the business.

 **Key terms**

***Assets:*** *what the business owns, including cash in the bank*

***Balance sheet:*** *this is a statement of the total assets and liabilities of an organisation on a particular date*

***Creditors:*** *the people or businesses to whom the business owes money*

***Debtors:*** *the people or businesses who owe the business money*

***Depreciation:*** *the loss in value of fixed assets over time*

***Liabilities:*** *the money the business owes*

***Working capital:*** *the funds needed to pay for the day-to-day running of a business*

Everything that a business owns, and that has a money value, is part of the assets. A business cannot exist unless it has assets. The assets are the resources used in the business. There are two types of asset.

### Fixed assets

These assets have a long life. They are likely to appear in the balance sheet over more than one year. Examples include premises, machinery, vehicles, office furniture and equipment. Fixed assets are only sold when they come to the end of their useful life.

Fixed assets can be shown in the balance sheet as two different figures:

- They are shown 'at cost', which is the price at which they were bought.
- They are also shown 'at net value', also called the 'book value'. This is the value of the assets 'at cost' less depreciation. Fixed assets, other than premises, are worth less as time goes by. This loss in value is called **depreciation**. The net value is shown so that the balance sheet gives a true value of the fixed assets.

### Current assets

The value of these assets changes all the time. For example, every time goods are sold the stock goes down. Cash sales increase cash, credit sales increase the number of **debtors**. When a debtor pays a bill the money in the bank or in cash rises. When a firm pays its bills the money in the bank falls.

Current assets are liquid assets. They can be turned into cash very easily. Cash (which includes money in the bank) is the most liquid asset. It is followed by debtors and stock, in that order. Current assets are always shown in the balance sheet in the reverse order of liquidity. How quickly and easily a firm can change its assets into cash determines its liquidity. An aeroplane manufacturer has a lower liquidity than a bread manufacturer. Liquidity is important because it affects a firm's cash flow and its ability to pay its short-term debts.

### Liabilities

The liabilities are what a firm owes to individuals or other firms. There are two main types of liability:

- Current liabilities are the short-term debts of the firm that have to be paid within one year. They are mostly trade **creditors**, that is, other businesses to which the firm owes money. Like current assets the figure changes all the time, as goods are bought on credit and debts are paid. A bank overdraft is also included because it changes as money is put into and taken out of the current account.
- Long-term liabilities are debts that are not paid for more than one year. They are mainly bank loans and mortgages. They are sometimes called the loan capital of a business.

## Capital

When a business is set up, money is used to buy or rent premises, stock, tools, equipment and all the other things needed to run the business. These are the business's assets. The assets all have a value and are equal to the firm's capital minus any debts (liabilities).

The capital is equal to what the business owes its owners. If the business is closed, all the assets are sold. Part of the money is used to pay off the business's debts. What is left over belongs to the owners and equals the firm's capital.

## Working capital

The funds needed to pay for the day-to-day running of a business are called its **working capital**. The formula for calculating the working capital is:

- working capital = current assets – current liabilities

Working capital is important to a business:

- It is used to pay the everyday costs of running the business, such as wages, bills and expenses such as phone, gas and electricity bills, and stock.
- It is a measure of a business's liquidity. If working capital is too low a business will have a cash flow problem and will not be able to pay its bills on time. If working capital is very low a business may become insolvent and have to close.
- Working capital should not be too large. It should be enough to cover all the current liabilities with a little to spare, in case of emergencies. If it is greater than this, resources that could be used for other purposes are being wasted.

## Reserves

Profits that are not paid to the shareholders are kept in the business. These retained profits are built up in the company's reserves, often for several years. Since the reserves are made up of profits that have not been paid to shareholders, they are shown as part of shareholders' funds in the balance sheet. The reserves are normally invested. Reserves are an important way of financing a company's expansion.

**Figure 2.13 Balance sheet for Haycraft Ltd as at 31 December 2012**

| | At cost £000 | | Net value £000 |
|---|---|---|---|
| **Fixed assets** | | | |
| Premises | 250 | | 250 |
| Fixtures and fittings | 98 | | 80 |
| Machinery | 250 | | 190 |
| Vehicles | 88 | | 75 |
| | 686 | | 595 |
| **Current assets** | | | |
| Stock | 84 | | |
| Debtors | 88 | | |
| Bank | 77 | | |
| Cash | 23 | 272 | |
| ***Less* current liabilities** | | | |
| Bank overdraft | 47 | | |
| Dividends proposed | 40 | | |
| Creditors | 75 | 162 | |
| **Working capital** | | | 100 |
| | | | 695 |
| ***Less*** long-term liabilities | | | |
| Bank loan | 20 | | |
| Mortgage | 100 | | 120 |
| **Net assets employed** | | | 575 |
| **Financed by** | | | |
| *Issued capital* | | | |
| 500 000 £1 shares | 500 | | |
| General reserves | 63 | | |
| Profit and loss account | 12 | 75 | |
| **Shareholders' funds** | | | 575 |
| **Capital employed** | | | 575 |

## Investigate

*The following figures are taken from a rock studio's business accounts as at 30 June 2012. Fixed assets are £500 000. Non-current assets are valued at £260 000, current assets at £694 500, current liabilities at £375 000 and non-current liabilities at £134 000. The business is financed by £50 000 share capital and £395 500 retained profit.*

*Produce a balance sheet as at 30 June 2012.*

**All businesses have assets and liabilities – even the music industry**

# C.2 Understand how businesses can be more successful

## C.2 Identify ways in which a business can increase profits

There are two main ways for a business to improve its gross profit. First, it can increase its prices. Second, it can lower the cost of producing its goods. An increase in prices can make sales drop. If sales drop too far, the business may not generate enough gross profit to cover operating expenses. Price rises to increase gross profit need to be considered very carefully to ensure that demand for the product will continue.

The second method of increasing gross profit is to lower the variable costs of producing goods. This can be done by reducing the cost of materials or making the product more efficiently. The more material you buy from a supplier, the more likely the supplier is to offer discounts. Another way to reduce material costs is to find a cheaper supplier. However, you might sacrifice quality if the materials are not as good.

Whether you are starting a manufacturing, wholesaling, retailing or service business, you should always be on the look out for ways to deliver your product or service more efficiently. However, you must also balance efficiency and quality.

### Analysis of financial statements for a small business

By analysing financial statements, it is possible to identify the financial strengths and weaknesses of the business by establishing relationships between the items on the balance sheet and the profit and loss account.

A balance sheet can tell you how much the business is worth. This can only ever be a general figure, showing the underlying value of the funds in the business at that particular time. It is most useful when it is used to compare with previous years.

This balance sheet (Figure 2.14) shows how much one business is worth. You can see that working capital (net assets) has increased in 2012. This means that the business has more cash, and assets that can be easily turned into cash, to pay its day-to-day debts. This is very important for the business as it must make sure that it collects money quickly to get cash to pay its liabilities.

By comparing this year's balance sheet with the previous year's it is possible to pick out **trends** in the business's finances. The retained profit is increasing year on year, which shows the business is growing. The business has increased its borrowings with an increased loan but overall it has substantially reduced its total liabilities due to having fewer creditors to whom it owes money and by reducing its overdraft.

**Key term**

***Trends:*** *recognising trends in finances can help businesses adapt their behaviour*

**Investigate**

*Which two of the following methods can make a business more profitable?*

*(a) Increasing the number of staff*

*(b) Purchasing more expensive raw materials*

*(c) Reducing costs*

*(d) Reducing quality of products*

*(e) Increasing selling price*

*(f) Reducing delivery times to customers*

**Figure 2.14 Balance sheet comparisons over a two-year period**

| | 2012 | 2011 |
|---|---|---|
| | £ | £ |
| Fixed assets | | |
| Property | 24 000 | 28 000 |
| Plant and machinery | 20 000 | 24 000 |
| Vehicles | 12 000 | 18 000 |
| Office equipment | 6000 | 8000 |
| Total fixed assets | 62 000 | 78 000 |
| Current assets | | |
| Stock | 16 000 | 12 000 |
| Debtors | 4000 | 8000 |
| Cash | 2000 | 1000 |
| Total current assets | 22 000 | 21 000 |
| Total assets | 84 000 | 99 000 |
| Current liabilities | | |
| Creditors | 6000 | 26 000 |
| Overdraft | 8000 | 16 000 |
| Loan | 3000 | 1000 |
| Total liabilities | 17 000 | 52 000 |
| Net assets (total assets *less* total liabilities) | 67 000 | 47 000 |
| Represented by | | |
| Capital | 40 000 | 40 000 |
| Retained profit | 27 000 | 7000 |
| **Total** | 67 000 | 47 000 |

**Financial statements can help a business improve performance**

### Investigate

*Which of the following activities can identify ways of making a business more successful by increasing profits?*

(a) *Analysing financial information in the media*

(b) *Analysing financial information about competitors*

(c) *Analysing the business's bank statements*

Profit and loss accounts usually contain the previous year's data as well as this year's to compare what has changed. This is useful for spotting trends in revenue, costs and profit and helps the business to assess its financial position. In this example for Ferdinand Clothing Ltd (Figure 2.15), sales (revenue) have increased this year, as have gross and net profit, so the business appears to be going in the right direction. Some of the costs are rising, which needs to be monitored, but this has been offset by the rise in revenue.

**Figure 2.15 Profit and loss account comparisons over a two-year period for Ferdinand Clothing Ltd**

| **Income statement** | **2012** | **2011** |
|---|---|---|
| **Year ended 31 March** | **£** | **£** |
| Revenue | 10 725 | 9890 |
| Cost of sales | 6732 | 6340 |
| Gross profit | 3993 | 3550 |
| Distribution costs | 1605 | 1493 |
| Administration costs | 1090 | 952 |
| Net profit | 1298 | 1105 |
| Finance costs | 78 | 60 |
| Profit before tax | 1220 | 1045 |
| Tax expense | 373 | 290 |
| Dividends | 847 | 755 |

**Case study (C2)**

The following information has been extracted from the business accounts of a sole trader, Gemma Leigh, for her first two years of trading, which ended on the 31 December 2011.

**Figure 2.16 Gemma Leigh's business accounts**

| | 2012 | 2011 |
|---|---|---|
| | £ | £ |
| Cost of goods sold | 88 400 | 132 600 |
| Sales | 125 890 | 188 835 |
| Rates | 4850 | 7275 |
| Heating and lighting | 2120 | 3180 |
| Wages and salaries | 10 350 | 15 525 |
| Office equipment | 8500 | 12 750 |
| Vehicles | 10 750 | 16 125 |
| Debtors | 3950 | 5925 |
| Money in the bank | 4225 | 6338 |
| Cash | 95 | 143 |
| Creditors | 1750 | 2625 |
| Tax to be paid | 450 | 675 |
| Capital at start of year | 20 000 | 30 000 |
| Drawings for year | 8900 | 13 350 |

1. Prepare a balance sheet and a trading profit and loss account for Gemma Leigh for both years.
2. What conclusions and trends can you draw from comparing the financial statements?

**Discuss**

*Discuss, in groups, the importance to businesses of producing a trading profit and loss account and a balance sheet.*

# 3 Promoting a brand

## Learning aim A: Explore the use of branding and the promotional mix in business

- Topic A.1 The importance of branding to businesses: what a brand is and what benefits can be gained from branding
- Topic A.2 Promotion in business: why businesses promote themselves using the 4Ps of the marketing mix
- Topic A.3 Elements of the promotional mix and their purposes: the ways in which a business can promote itself are examined, focusing on their purpose
- Topic A.4 Promotional activities in business: how a business identifies its customers and uses promotional activities

## Learning aim B: Develop and promote a brand for a business

- Topic B.1 Branding methods and techniques: planning effective brand ideas, including the use of celebrities, logos and straplines
- Topic B.2 Promoting a brand: by designing an appropriate promotional mix, businesses can promote their products using different types of media

Cola
DRINK COCA-COLA IN BOTTLES 5¢
Phone
89
¡Espumante! ¡Deliciosa! ¡Refresc

# The importance of branding to businesses

## 2A.P1 What is a brand?

Branding started off as a way of telling the difference between farmers' cattle but is now a multibillion-pound industry in which businesses try to show their products in a positive way. Quite simply, if customers recognise and respond to a **brand**, the business does well.

### Becoming a brand

Think of the most popular businesses in the world. Do you think of Apple? Google? These have unique branding, setting them aside from other competitors. For Apple, the use of its symbol confirms customer interest, whereas Google uses its name. It may also take the form of a **legal instrument**, such as a patent or copyright, personality, vision or image.

A brand is very important to a business as it can alter the perception of a customer, increasing sales and loyalty. This will mean that customers are more likely to buy other products made by that brand, so businesses use branding to develop this trust and loyalty. A good example of this was the new Android system developed by Google, which has developed a very successful brand image. Designing a strategy on how best to use different aspects of a brand will help improve its chance of success.

Your assessment criteria:

**2A.P1** Explain how branding is used in two businesses

### Key terms

***Brand:*** *a design, symbol or name that allows the customer to associate or identify a business's goods or services*

***Brand personality:*** *the human characteristics of a brand that are portrayed to the customer*

***Legal instrument:*** *a legal document or asset that helps design a brand, such as the patent Dyson holds on cyclone technology*

***Value added:*** *the difference between the production and sale costs of a product or service*

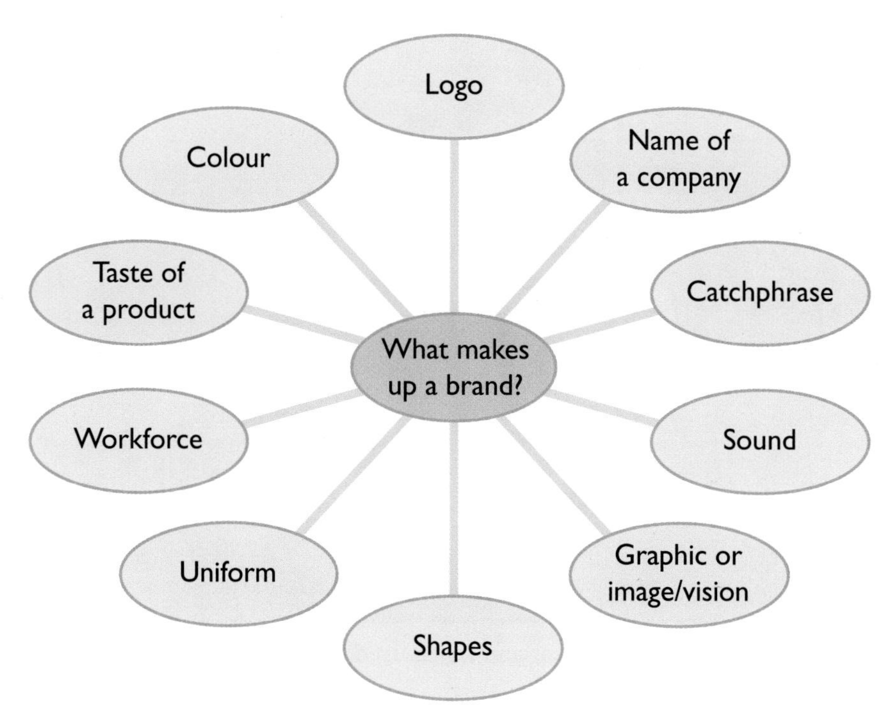


**Figure 3.1 What makes up a brand?**

## Brand personality

It is important for a business to angle itself correctly. In other words, its personality should match that of the customers it is trying to reach. Apple has reinvented itself into a younger, more innovative company. However, companies such as Saga and Werther's Original have a more mature **brand personality**. This helps create an image of what the customer should expect from the company and its product. Brand personality can be generated by simple things such as staff uniform, and more sophisticated things, like adverts and product range.

### Discuss

*Discuss in pairs a brand that demonstrates the following brand personalities:*

*1. trustworthy*

*2. mature*

*3. fun*

*4. athletic*

*5. cheeky*

*Explain your thoughts.*

### Research

*Using your research skills, try to find out the highest value brand. What has helped this brand become so well known?*

**Werther's Original specifically target older customers by creating a more mature brand image**

**Coca-Cola has a clear brand through the colour scheme, font and words used in its labels. Even in Arabic, it's clear.**

## Adding value

According to www.brandz.com, in 2010, Google was the world's most valuable brand coming in at $114 260 000 million. If you were to buy a new t-shirt, you would decide on an amount that you were willing to pay for it. However, by adding a brand name or logo to the t-shirt, this amount may increase. This is **value added**. This may be because the brand is more trustworthy, fashionable or reliable.

## The undeniable benefits of branding

A successful brand will continue to increase revenues as more customers turn to its products. By using the right promotion techniques, businesses can create global brands. In 2011, Facebook helped to raise the profile and image of thousands of businesses; some of the most successful were Converse trainers and Oreo cookies. It also offers the makers of these products multiple marketing opportunities, linking them in with other products in the range. For example, Apple's success with the iPod has helped sales of the iPhone and iPad.

 **Discuss**

*In pairs, start by discussing how brands can add value to their products. Now try and highlight the factor you think helps them the most. This could be customer service or just the logo.*

A successful brand also improves the image of a company, making it more sought after and valuable. Successful branding can communicate real quality. The use of sponsorship and celebrity endorsement can help brands become worth millions overnight. For example, Dr Dre's 'Beats' headphones are now a hugely valuable brand.

However, not all branding works; in 2004, Coca-Cola released its new pure bottled water product. This was supposed to be natural water, purified using NASA technology. However, it turned out to be taken from the mains tap, using the same process as many other producers. This was a branding disaster for Coke. In the end, they pulled all stock off the shelves!

**Design**

*Design your own logo or slogan for a well-known company.*

**Converse – bankrupt in 2001 but now a modern-day success story**

**Research**

*Using your research skills, identify a product that adds large amounts of value along the production process. Can you find out the exact added value?*

**Case study: 2A.P1**

Edward has recently set up his own brewery. His new home brew, named 'Millerners' was a non-alcoholic drink aimed at those who do not wish to drink alcohol when in pubs. His new brew was released in early 2012, creating a fairly large following.

In June 2012, he faced a crisis. With a product range now developed, he was struggling to keep his product in the local pubs. His price was identified as too high, and customers were starting to say that the brand had lost its focus.

1. Why is added value such a difficult area to get right?
2. Why is brand recognition so important in the drinks industry?
3. How could Edward improve his brand recognition?

# Comparing brands

## 2A.P1 How to use branding

The use of branding is crucial for success. Even the best products need to be nurtured and developed as a brand, attracting customers, and developing trust and loyalty. Businesses will use different techniques to inform customers of their brand.

### Google

Google was started in 1998 by two university students and is now the world's largest search engine. Today, the Google homepage receives over 2 billion hits per day worldwide. The brand is now a global monster, with the word itself representing the brand. The use of simple colours and easy-to-read font has made it very easy for customers to relate to and trust it. The brand itself is based on reliability and ease of use. The customers can see Google's vision; information at everyone's fingertips.

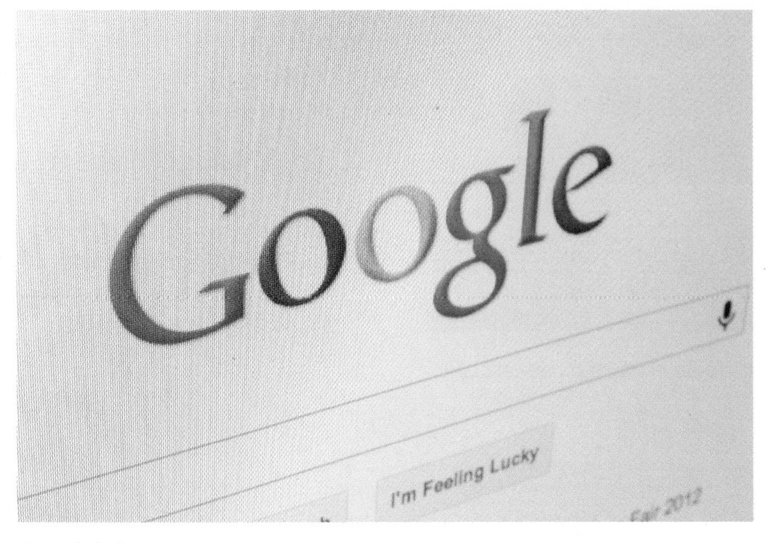


**Google's home page**

### Abercrombie & Fitch

Abercrombie & Fitch has recently defended its brand against counterfeiters and unwanted celebrity users. In August 2011, the company was reported to have offered the cast of *Jersey Shore* a 'substantial amount' not to wear its brand, as it feared the show would damage its image.

Abercrombie & Fitch has built its brand around the casual luxury idea, with a range of hoodies, t-shirts and other everyday items. Today, it

Your assessment criteria:

**2A.P1** Explain how branding is used in two businesses

**2A.M1** Compare the use of brand promotion in two businesses

**Key term**

***Brand promotion:*** *the way in which a business informs the customer about their brand*

**Discuss**

*Discuss other companies who focus on their name as their main tool for branding.*

has over 300 stores worldwide. The luxury materials and store layouts work well with the simple and clean finish. Abercrombie also uses the brands Hollister and Gilly Hicks to grow sales. The main tools used by Abercrombie & Fitch are its photography and in-store models, which have led to problems with its staffing policy.

## 2A.M1 How do they compare?

For 2A.M1 in this unit, you should compare the use of **brand promotion** in two businesses. Comparing Google to Abercrombie & Fitch will highlight plenty of differences, but this may not be the same for firms operating in similar industries.

The key branding tool used by Google is the Catull typeface or font on its homepage and logo. This has helped shape Google into one of the world's most recognised brands. However, even this has changed, most recently in 2010, when the shadow around the letters was reduced. Google worked hard on the simple layout to create the perception that it is the best product on the market. The logo, colour scheme and font of the company name have become a successful brand promotion.

Similarly, Abercrombie & Fitch uses its brand name to put across the ethos and image of the company and also to create a perception of luxury for the customer. Both firms use branding successfully to promote quality and trust, and offer a range of products. Abercrombie and Fitch, however, also use uniform and staff image to help boost their brand promotion. As they sell their products, they also allow the customer to experience the atmosphere of the store.

### Design

*Design your own brand for a new firm that makes sports shoes. You should create the business name, as well as the product names. You should think about branding at all times. How will you brand your product? How will this be different to your competitors?*

**Abercrombie & Fitch**

**Case study**

Moma! (www.momafoods.co.uk) is a new healthy breakfast snack brand. Founded by Tom Mercer in London, it now serves thousands of people each day all over the capital. It is also available on BA and Virgin flights, as well as in Selfridges. Operating in a market dominated by larger brands such as Kelloggs, Innocent and General Mills, Moma! has been working hard on its product and branding. Research Moma! foods and answer the following questions:

1. Explain how Moma! has used branding to enhance sales. (2A.P1)
2. Compare Moma! foods' branding methods with those used by Kelloggs. (2A.M1)
3. How could Moma! foods improve its branding? Give examples where possible. (2A.M1)

### Research

*Research how Innocent smoothies and Moma! breakfasts compare in their branding.*

*What are the similarities and the differences?*

# Promotion in business

## 2A.P2 Mix it up!

The marketing mix is made up of four parts: Product, Price, Place and Promotion – the 4Ps. Businesses use this to help plan the marketing of their brand. The 4Ps are crucial for promoting a brand.

### Why do businesses need to promote themselves?

Even the best product needs some sort of promotion to capture sales. Without promotion, customers would not even be aware of the existence of the product or business. One of the most powerful promotional tools is word of mouth. Imagine your friend tells you about a new phone or film; you are more likely to buy it because of this tip-off. Without promotion, a business will lose out to its competitors and struggle to generate any revenue. A business will need to consider all aspects of the marketing mix.

### Product

The key aspect here for a business is: 'Do I have a product that people want and will pay for?'

This starts with research and development, before a product is actually produced. In this stage, the business will try to determine what customers want, and develop something that is better than anything already out there. Apple spent a long time developing the iPod, making sure it was better than anything already released. Apple also offers a service alongside the product: iTunes. These combine to form Apple's product. A product must link to the brand. If Mercedes produced a low-quality, cheaper car, it could damage the company's high-end image.

**Apple shop selling a range of Apple products**

### Price

Price is the amount of money consumers pay to acquire the product. Pricing is crucial in establishing the brand and promoting the product

Your assessment criteria:

**2A.P2** Assess the marketing mix for a selected branded product

**Key terms**

***Marketing mix:*** *the tactics a business uses to enhance its product or brand and determine its unique selling point*

***Research and development:*** *creative and scientific work undertaken in order to improve, develop or create new ideas and products*

***Revenue:*** *income received by the business from its day-to-day activities*

**Research**

*Using your research skills, choose one of the large supermarkets and visit its online shop. What do you notice about its prices? Why does it use these pricing strategies?*

in an effective way. For brands such as Sky, Tesco and Ford, pricing is a pivotal part of the brand. They need to get their pricing right or risk losing their identity. There are different types of pricing a business can use. Many of these link in well with a company's branding.

**Figure 3.2 Different types of pricing**

| | |
|---|---|
| Penetration pricing | The selling of a product at a lower price than competitors to gain market share. The opposite of this is skimming, going in high and then reducing the price later on. This is often undertaken by new entrants into the confectionery and drinks market. |
| Psychological pricing | Using prices that are more likely to attract customers; for example, £1.99 instead of £2.00. This is commonly used in supermarkets. |
| Cost-plus pricing | This takes the costs of making the product, and then adds a mark-up based upon what the market will pay. Many businesses will use this method, especially smaller ones that have to focus on covering their costs. |
| Destroyer pricing | Setting a price so low it puts competitors out of business. Larger companies who try to dominate a market will often use this; petrol companies, for example. |

## Place

Place describes where and how the consumer can obtain the product. Where a business sells and promotes the product is very important. Selling the new *Call of Duty* PlayStation game in specific retailers allows the product to be accessed by the relevant target market. Sony would also only advertise it where it thought that market might see it. Getting customers to come to the place of sale is very important. However, too many customers can turn up! Apple stopped selling its iPhone 4S in China due to the size and behaviour of crowds outside its shop in Beijing. Place no longer has to be a physical location. Consumers can buy many products over the telephone, via the internet or through their TV remote control. Companies have to choose carefully the best method to ensure consumers can find their product in an appropriate place when they decide to make a purchase.

*Which well-known brands have used these pricing strategies?*

**Pricing labels**

*Which aspect of the marketing mix is the most important? Why?*

## 2A.P2 Why is promotion so important?

It does not matter how good a product is; if promotion is not well planned and accurate then customers will not know about it and there will be no sales. Customers will lack information on the price, what the product is and where to buy it. Understanding why promotion is so important is crucial for a business.

### Promotion

Once the other aspects of the marketing mix are determined, the business must choose the most appropriate type of promotion. This will need to be chosen carefully as it is often the most crucial part of the marketing mix and needs to match all of the other elements. This is an important decision that businesses face, and is often decided by the **promotion budget** set for each business. The larger the business, the higher its promotion budget will be. There are a number of techniques businesses can use to promote themselves and their products; these will be looked at on pages 98–99.

**A magazine advert for a phone**

Your assessment criteria:

**2A.P2** Assess the marketing mix for a selected branded product

**Key term**

**Promotion budget:** *the amount of money that can be spent on promotion*

**Promotion of products in a supermarket**

**Design**

*Design a new promotion campaign for Apples 5S iPhone. This could include a TV, magazine or radio promotion.*

## The importance of promotion

Without promotion, customers simply would not know about a product. A business can design the best product, in the best place and for the best price, but without promotion, it will not reach its customers. Businesses like Apple and Dyson rely heavily on a mixture of promotion techniques that get their products into the homes of millions of people worldwide. Tesco prides itself on being seen on all forms of promotion. If you open a newspaper, you will find numerous Tesco adverts that highlight key deals and offers in store. With the introduction of the Tesco bank, additional promotion is needed.

Could you imagine companies like Sony, Tesco, Warner Brothers or Cadbury existing as we know them without a large amount of promotion? This is also the case for smaller businesses. Despite smaller budgets, it is just as important for smaller businesses to promote themselves as they struggle to gain market share and a customer base. Promotion can bring new customers to the businesses, increase loyalty and maintain market share.

During poor economic conditions, such as recession, it can become even more important to promote the business. This is because fewer customers may be spending on the business's products and it must therefore attract those who do spend. Often, businesses cut back on their promotional budgets as a way of saving money. However, with fewer customers coming through the door, this can work in a negative way.

### Discuss

*In pairs, decide on your favourite product. This can be anything you like! Now, discuss the promotional activities that went into it. Think about all the forms of promotion, not just advertising.*

### Research

*Research into a company of your choice. How does it promote itself?*

**Case study**

In January 2012, Sainsbury's saw a 2.1 per cent increase in like-for-like sales on the year before. With a 20 per cent increase in online sales, it started to put even more pressure on Tesco. One of the bestselling brands for Sainsbury's was the Celebrations chocolate tins and boxes. With its combination of Mars products such as Galaxy and Maltesers, Celebrations has become a popular product in the UK. Its branding has helped it catch up with the favourites, Roses and Quality Street.

1. Discuss the pricing methods used by Sainsbury's. (2A.P2)
2. Which part of the marketing mix is most important to the success of Celebrations? (2A.P2)
3. How does Mars promote Celebrations? (2A.P2)
4. Identify an example for each part of the marketing mix for Celebrations. (2A.P2)

# Elements of the promotional mix and their purposes

## 2A.P3 What is the promotional mix?

By identifying the elements of the promotional mix, a business can make sure all of these are focused on the brand. Different brands have a slightly different focus. All brands are different and some require different promotional mixes depending on their industry and target customer. Some may argue that sofa retailers such as DFS over-use cut-price sales, seeming to continue them all year round.

### Advertising

Advertising is often the most common form of promotion. This tends to be used by nearly all businesses, although the scale and cost differ greatly. The idea for all types of advertising is to inform the customer and persuade them to choose that specific product. There are many different methods a business can choose from to advertise their product or service.

**The message:** First the business must decide what it wants to put across to the customer

↓

**The medium:** Then it must choose how it wants to deliver that message

**Figure 3.3 The advertising message and medium**

**One method of advertising**

Your assessment criteria:

**2A.P3** Identify elements of the promotional mix used for a selected branded product

**Key terms**

***Advertising:*** *any paid-for space used to communicate ideas or products to potential customers in the prime media*

***Direct mail:*** *this is contact direct from a business to a customer – post, email or phone calls*

***Press releases:*** *articles or information given to newspapers, magazines or other press institutions about the business or product*

***Sales promotion:*** *marketing communication aimed at increasing sales of a product for a limited time*

**Research**

*Go on the following websites and note down the adverts that appear. Are they relevant to the site?*

1. *www.skysports.com*
2. *www.amazon.co.uk*
3. *www.dailymail.co.uk*

*Why do you think these adverts appear on these sites?*

**Figure 3.4 Different methods of advertising**

| | |
|---|---|
| Moving image | This could be at the opening of a television programme (Harveys advertise before *Coronation Street*) or at the start of a DVD or film at the cinema. This is a direct way to advertise as you target the market you want. |
| Print | This could be pages in newspapers or magazines that are specifically linked to the product (for example clothing ranges in *Vogue*). Billboard posters are seen by a large number of people. They often have to be simple and easy to read, showing the product in use. This may also include **direct mail** to the customer, or **press releases**. |
| Ambient | Using the sides of taxis and buses can help promote the business and its products. Divine chocolate has one London taxi with its advert on to help boost the profile of the company, while others may do large advertising campaigns. On a smaller scale, for example, pens and other stationery can be used. |
| Digital | The growth of the internet means that there is now a lot of advertising online. This could be a banner (permanent advert on a webpage) or a pop-up (advert that appears when triggered or when a web page is opened). The use of blogs (personal files recorded online) and podcasts (recorded audio files) is also common. SMS text messages are also used to send adverts or messages direct to a customer's phone.<br><br>Facebook is a good example of social networking advertising. Next time you are on your page, have a look at the adverts that appear. Are they relevant to you? |
| Audio | The use of radio is still common as an advertising medium. This is usually chosen by businesses advertising a service or event as customers don't need to see the product, and is often used for local rather than national advertising. Podcasts can also be used, as can public address systems – common at large events such as festivals. |
| Video | With the growth of sites like YouTube, many businesses advertise using video. |

## Sales promotion

Have you heard of a Tesco Clubcard? Or BOGOF deals in supermarkets? These loyalty cards and buyer incentives are a form of **sales promotion**. The purpose of these is to increase the sales of certain products and attract customers. Over Christmas 2011, supermarkets were offering a range of sales promotions: money-back vouchers, extra loyalty points, coupons and competitions. This helped Sainsbury's increase its sales, while Tesco saw a drop. Asda offered to give customers the value of the difference if it was not cheaper than other supermarkets.

### Design

*Design a new newspaper advert for a product of your choice. It could be a computer game, phone or something more simple, like fruit, pens or a film.*

### Discuss

*For the businesses below, discuss with your partner which type of advertising medium would be most suitable:*

1. *A new take-away selling handmade pizzas.*
2. *Sony's new flat screen television with a built-in Blu-ray player.*
3. *Olympic Games calendar.*

*Explain your answers.*

## 2A.P3 What is the promotional mix?

Your assessment criteria:

**2A.P3** Describe the purpose of elements of the promotional mix used for a selected branded product

Personal selling is a common form of creating sales through promotion. By speaking to customers directly, many businesses can increase their sales. Public relations is another technique used by business. This is often favoured as it is free! However, each brand has its own unique best mix of these methods.

### Personal selling

**Personal selling** involves interaction between a customer and a salesperson for the purpose of closing a sale. This may be over the phone, face-to-face or via email, but it is normally used to sell complicated products such as greenhouses, insurance or car finance, which need explanation and advice. It is often used for products that have a great deal of variation so that customers can be talked through any changes they require. Some businesses may also use web conferencing and video to sell abroad, often on a large scale.

Often, this form of promotion is very difficult and can result in a large amount of time being put in to produce sales. Many people do not like being approached at home or on the phone to be sold a product or service, as this invades their privacy. Businesses also have to be careful as personal selling can damage reputations. If a business becomes known for pestering new or existing customers with visits or phone calls then it is likely to struggle to keep its customers.

**Door-to-door salesperson**

**Key terms**

***Direct marketing:*** *targeted marketing towards customers who have requested or established a relationship with the brand*

***Personal selling:*** *a sales person selling directly to a customer*

***Public relations (PR):*** *a free way to advertise through the creation of media articles and reviews*

**Design**

*Have a go at personal selling!*

*Design a role-play in which you try to sell a product of your choice to your partner.*

*Remember, the customer should know about the product, its benefits and why they should buy it.*

## Public relations (PR)

**Public relations (PR)** is often the best form of advertising. It can gain a huge amount of publicity for a business or product at no cost. This involves placing an article, press release, review or news story in some form of media. The most common is through magazines and newspapers, both on and offline. You will have seen these on a daily basis with reviews being written in magazines or online for video games, films and phones. Public relations can also be done through exhibitions. For example, the Ideal Home Exhibition allows businesses to show off their products to thousands of customers for a very small cost. Sponsorship is also a form of PR, allowing a business to associate with an event, team or person. Businesses may have to pay for this but not in all situations. Barcelona football club chose not to have a sponsor on their shirts for many years until recently. They decided to help promote children's charity UNICEF and now show this on their shirts despite not receiving any money in return.

### Research

*Research a brand of your choice. How has it used PR in its promotional mix?*

*Try to find two articles online that show the use of PR.*

### Discuss

*To what extent do you think direct sales work? In pairs, think about the arguments for and against this method. Be ready to tell the class your ideas.*

## Direct marketing

By developing an individual relationship with a customer, a business can target the customer and gain continuous sales. When customers sign up for a membership, more information or updates, a business can send them mail, catalogues or magazines directly. Businesses may also use direct mail to their customers, and continue to send catalogues in the hope that they generate sales. Clothing retailers often use magazines to promote their new ranges, sending them directly to customers. They may also follow these up with direct telemarketing phone calls. **Direct marketing** can often be regarded in a negative way as invasive and irritating. Customers may not want to be sent lots of mail, or be pestered on the phone, and this may damage a business's image. Businesses tend to ask their customers if they can pass on their details to other companies that may interest the customer. This reduces the anger and damage direct marketing can cause.

Sales catalogue

## 2A.M2, 2A.D1 The importance of the promotional mix

### Selecting an appropriate promotional mix

It is vital that a business selects the appropriate promotional mix for its brands. If the products are not promoted in the appropriate way, customers may be put off the product. Advertising provides the basis of the promotional mix for many larger firms. Depending on its size, a business may choose to advertise in many different ways. If the wrong form of promotion is chosen, the business may put its financial health at risk, miss out on potential customers and gain negative attention from the media. The business must also link the promotional medium to the product. For example, Coca-Cola would not use SMS texts or radio broadcasts to advertise its new flavour. This would not help promote its products as customers would want to see or try them. The use of sales promotions would also need to be looked at carefully. Using offers, vouchers or price promotions would lead to a short-term loss, but with the hope of creating a loyal customer base in the future. If a business uses too many sales promotions, it could lose money. The business must also decide whether it needs to use personal selling and direct marketing. Both of these techniques can produce a negative image if used inappropriately.

### Evaluating the effectiveness of the promotional mix

When judging a promotional mix, you must look at the entire mix that has been used. It may be more difficult to judge whether certain parts have been effective or not. For example, Apple's use of PR to introduce its new iPad often receives negative attention but, at the same time, this raises awareness of the product and will help to increase long-term sales. A business will also find it difficult to judge the effectiveness of its promotional mix if there are a range of products.

To judge the effectiveness of the promotional mix, you could ask these questions:

- Has the product generated a profit?
- Have the targeted customers heard of the product?
- Have sales been more than predicted, or for previous products?
- Which aspects of the promotional mix worked particularly well?

Your assessment criteria:

**2A.M2** Explain the importance of selecting an appropriate promotional mix for a selected brand

**2A.D1** Evaluate the effectiveness of the promotional mix for a selected branded product

**Discuss**

*In pairs, pick one of the following promotional campaigns:*

- *Coca-Cola Christmas promotion: 'Holidays are coming'*
- *Apples' iPad Mini*
- *A recent film release*

*What has gone well for this campaign Can you pick on any key points?*

*Has there been anything that needed improving or didn't work very well?*

Most promotional mixes could be improved if done again. In 2006, Nintendo launched the Wii into the console market. The interest was so high that they sold out in days and production had to be stepped up to keep up with demand. Nintendo later admitted that they overspent on advertising as word of mouth and PR generated enough sales. They also admitted getting the price wrong – it was too cheap!

Many businesses, like Apple, try to use similar promotional activities so they build their brand image up through consistency. Making sure the mix is correct will help a business meet its financial objectives and continue to grow.

**The Nintendo Wii campaign could have been done better**

**Case study**

Mindshare is a global media company whose clients include Google, Facebook and Nike. Richard, an Account Director, is in charge of making sure the promotional mix for Nike is specific, well thought out and delivered to a high specification. The firm specialises in online advertising, developing PR campaigns and online sales promotions for its customers. In 2011, its Nike campaign saw a market share increase of 2 per cent, resulting in a £23 million increase in UK profits.

1. Describe how Nike uses advertising to increase sales. (2A.P3)
2. What is the purpose of the sales promotions created by Mindshare for its customer Nike? (2A.P3)
3. Discuss why PR is so valuable for brands such as Nike and Facebook? (2A.M2)
4. How effective has the Nike campaign been? (2A.D1)

# Promotional activities in business

## 2B.P4 How to select the target market

Identifying the correct target market will allow the business to see its brand successfully. Sell its brand successfully. Pitching the product to the correct audience will increase sales and make it easier to generate word of mouth interest. However, businesses will also sell to other businesses, so creating successful communication and marketing for both may be necessary.

### Types of market

When a business sells a product to a consumer, it acts in a different way from when it sells to another business. A business is always trying to find out information about its customers – why they buy the products they do, how often they buy, and much more. If a business sells a product to a business it will act in a different way.

When you download a track from iTunes, you are acting as a customer. Apple will try and make this process as easy as possible, hoping to keep its customers. It will ask for feedback, altering its products, processes and website accordingly. This is called B2C marketing.

However, Apple will have a different relationship with Sony BMG or EMI. These are the record companies that produce the records iTunes sells. This is B2B marketing. These record companies will work with Apple to make sure they gain as much exposure on the website as possible, suggesting improvements to the website and looking at new ways Apple could sell their products.

**iTunes logo**

Your assessment criteria:

**2B.P4** Use branding methods and techniques to recommend a brand personality and a target market for a brand.

**Key terms**

***Business to Business (B2B):*** *transactions between two businesses*

***Business to Consumer (B2C):*** *transactions between a business and a customer*

***Target market:*** *the customers a business wishes to sell to*

***Word of mouth:*** *when customers tell their friends and family about a product or service*

**Research and discuss**

*For the following products, research and discuss what the target market segment/segments will be:*

1. *Blue ray player*
2. *New Audi TT*
3. *'The Real Easter Egg' company Easter eggs.*

### How to identify the customer

When a business develops a product, it must decide who its target market will be. It can break up the market into smaller segments to help with this. Figure 3.5 shows some of the segments it could focus on. For example:

- Online dating websites are aimed at single people of both genders who do a variety of jobs.
- Apple aimed its iPad at younger professionals who were busy and on the go. The iPad would allow them to keep in contact with their workplace and friends.

**The latest tablet computer**

**Market segments**

- **Age** – Is it a product aimed at teenagers?
- **Family status** – Is it aimed at single people?
- **Gender** – Will both males and females buy the product?
- **Income** – Is it targeted at the very richest customers?
- **Occupation** – What does the ideal customer do for a job?
- **Ethnic groups** – Can everyone eat it? E.g. halal meat
- **Lifestyle** – Is the product aimed at very busy professionals?
- **Attitudes** – How do people feel about a product or industry?

**Figure 3.5 Identifying the target market**

Once a business decides its target market and how it segments the market, it will set objectives to achieve. These will give the business and staff targets to achieve in order for their promotional activities to be a success. These can be seen as the steps a business needs to take to achieve its aim, as shown in Figure 3.6.

The objectives have to be SMART: Specific, Measurable, Achievable, Realistic, and Time-related.

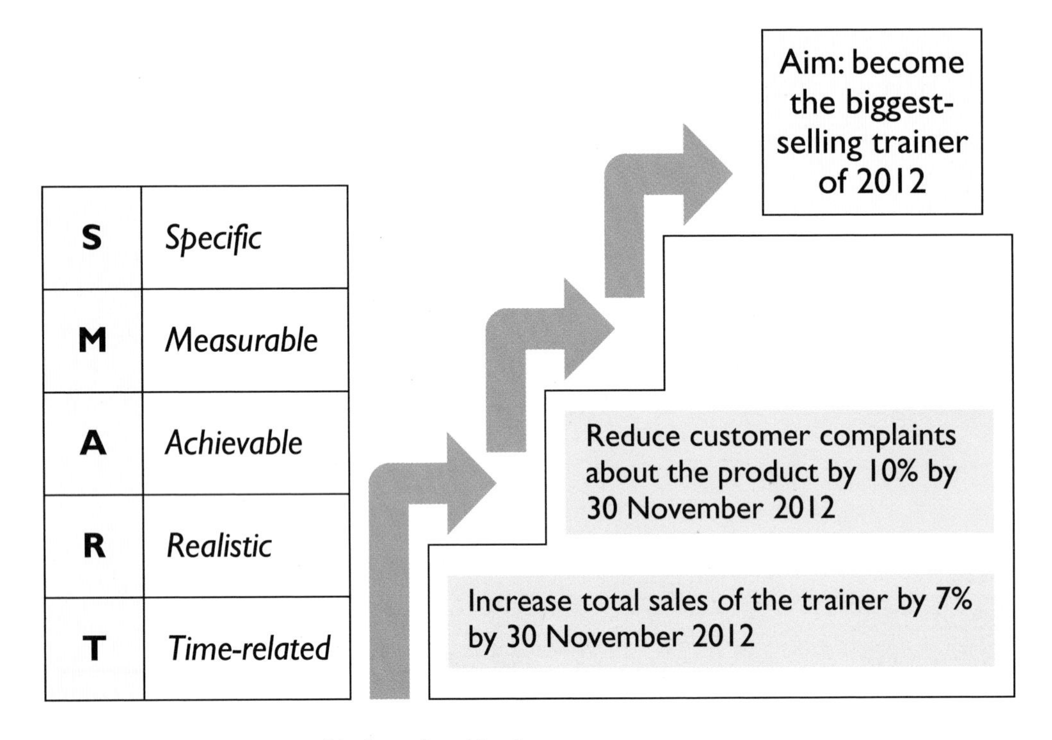


**Figure 3.6 SMART steps to achieving sales objectives**

The promotional mix that is used has to be appropriate to the business. It must focus on its budgets, workforce skills and products. If the business overspends or designs a poor advertising campaign it could put the business's future in jeopardy. Selecting the right promotional mix will result in increased revenues through sales, brand recognition, larger market share and higher customer awareness. It must also make sure it is focused on the correct target market so that the promotional mix works. For example, the placing of adverts must reflect the interests of the target customers. However, the business must continue to maintain and improve its promotional mix. It can do this by gaining feedback from its target market. To do this it will use the AIDA model to achieve the sale and then some feedback research to improve its service.

**Design**

*Design some SMART objectives for the following aims:*

- *Local Chinese take away wants to increase its customer base*
- *Sky Sports wants to increase its sales next year*
- *Apple wants to design the next must-have TV*

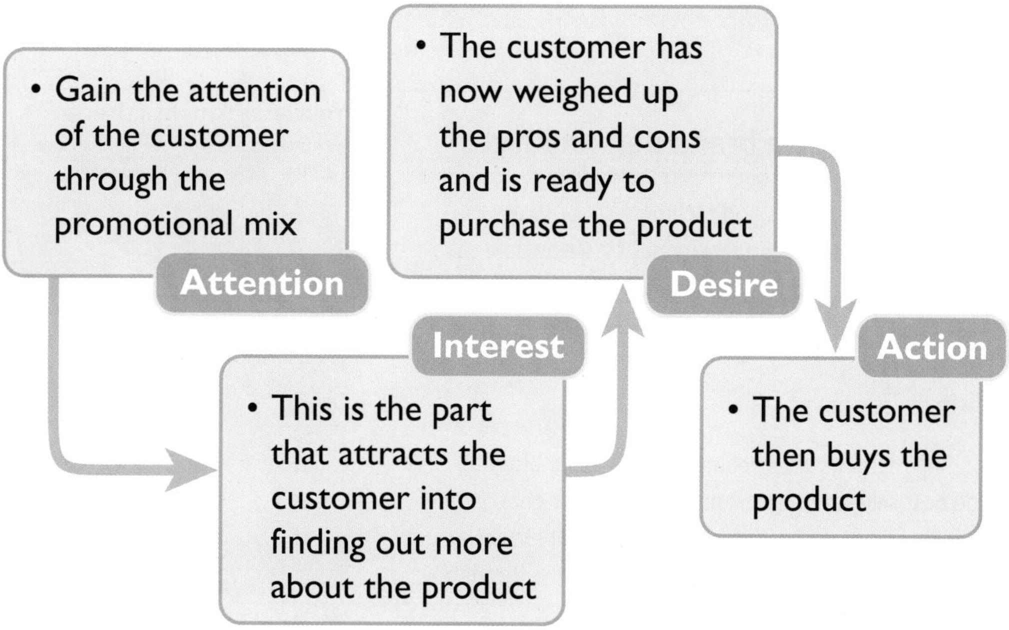

**Attention**
- Gain the attention of the customer through the promotional mix

**Interest**
- This is the part that attracts the customer into finding out more about the product

**Desire**
- The customer has now weighed up the pros and cons and is ready to purchase the product

**Action**
- The customer then buys the product

**Figure 3.7 The AIDA model**

**Case study**

In the last two years, Dave has seen his ballet school grow from strength to strength. The business now employs nine part-time staff and is close to generating £100 000 profit this year. When asked why his business is so successful, Dave answers, 'I set clear aims and objectives. The staff all know them, even the students.' The business even sets out the aims and objectives for the customers to see. The objectives Dave sets are SMART. This means he and his staff can judge whether they have been achieved or not.

1. Why should aims and objectives be shared with staff and other stakeholders?
2. Outline two reasons why objectives need to be timed.
3. Discuss why objectives need to be SMART.

**Investigate**

*You may have already thought about your future career. Set three SMART objectives that will help you achieve this aim.*

# Branding methods and techniques

## 2B.P4 How to determine a brand personality

By identifying the appropriate methods and techniques a business wants to use, it can then develop its **brand personality**. Being able to recognise the correct personality and target market will help guarantee success for the brand.

### Effective branding

Effective use of branding methods and techniques will help a product become a worldwide best seller. If you look at your favourite chocolate bar or games console, they have all been branded successfully. Whether this is the use of a logo, a new **celebrity endorsement** or just through word of mouth, they are most probably global brands.

Coca-Cola is the world's most recognised brand. Its association with Father Christmas leading its Christmas adverts, and with over 1.7 billion servings of Coke sold every day, has led many to praise its branding methods and techniques. Coke Zero's new **strapline**, 'beacon of possibilities' has added to the already strong brand, which uses word of mouth, social networking and multimedia to boost its brand image.

When a firm plans to create a new brand or revitalise an existing brand, it has to plan its ideas. Using these branding methods and techniques, a firm would then need to work through the rest of its plan, taking into account all the ideas in Figure 3.8 to produce an effective brand.

**A well-known confectionery brand**

Your assessment criteria:

**2B.P4** Use branding methods and techniques to recommend a brand personality and a target market for a brand

**2B.M3** Explain how branding methods and techniques were used to recommend a brand personality and a target market for a brand

### Key terms

***Brand objectives:*** *the targets or goals the brand is looking to achieve*

***Brand personality:*** *how the brand is perceived using human characteristics*

***Celebrity endorsement:*** *using well-known figures to promote the brand: for example, David Beckham and Adidas*

***Strapline:*** *a sentence the business wants to be remembered by, which links to the brand*

### Discuss

*In October 2012, Chanel No 5 used Brad Pitt as its first ever male model for its new branding leading up to Christmas. Why do you think it did this? What were the benefits?*

**Figure 3.8 Planning an effective brand**

**Type of brand** – First, the business must decide whether it is trying to create a brand for a commodity or concept. This will determine which method or technique the business will use. If the brand is based on a commodity, it may favour focusing on celebrity endorsement and product recognition through packaging and logo design.

**Considerations** – Next, the business must consider the different groups of customers it may have. For example, the brand may be rejected by some religions or nationalities. It should also consider race, children, people with disabilities and any environmental issues.

**Brand personality** – This is an important part of deciding on a brand. If the target market and brand personality are not closely linked, the brand will fail. The customer's perceptions of the brand must be taken into account and the personality tailored if needed. It is important that the customer's needs and wants are shown in the brand personality.

**Brand objectives** – Before the brand is launched, its objectives must be set. These are the targets the brand is trying to achieve. They may be based on sales, recognition or market share. The business should ask itself: What do we want from this brand? What do we want people to say about our brand? Objectives may include:
- Being recognised in the market
- Increasing sales of the product range
- Gaining market position

**Target market** – The target market is then chosen. Using the different market segments, a business must decide who it is aiming its brand at. For example Ryanair focuses on lower income groups, Moma! foods on busy professionals in London and Powerade on the young athlete.

### Discuss

*Discuss the brand objectives for the following brands:*

*1. Monster.co.uk*

*2. Orange*

*3. Nicorette*

*4. Blu-ray*

### Research

*Research a brand of your choice. For this brand identify its brand personality, target market and the considerations it would have taken into account.*

### Case study

In February 2012, Nestlé introduced a new range of Kit Kit Chunky. It produced four new flavours aimed at improving its brand image and sales figures. To enhance the customer uptake Nestlé announced that one flavour would be kept in production, and that voting would be done on the social media site, Facebook. The new flavours were in response to claims the Kit Kat brand was declining.

1. Describe the brand personality for a Kit Kat Chunky. (2B.P4)
2. What brand objectives would have been set for the new flavours? (2B.P4)
3. Who is the target market for the new Kit Kats? (2B.M3)

# Promoting a brand

## 2B.P5 Planning the mix

Being able to choose a successful promotion campaign is often contracted out to firms who specialise in this area. Brands such as Nike, Google and Facebook all use outside companies to help develop their brand. These companies do, however, have to justify the campaigns they develop, being held accountable based upon the results the campaigns deliver.

Businesses work very hard creating a brand that is attractive to their customers. The next step in their promotional campaign is to promote their brand image. They do this by using a variety of media types. They can use:

- social media sites (for example, Facebook)
- television
- radio
- newspapers and magazines.

All of these media types allow a brand to grow and improve its image. Many brands link to good causes, such as charities, natural disasters or individual organisations. This helps boost the brand image and increases publicity, as well as doing something good!

The growth of Facebook has helped businesses of all sizes increase communication with their customers. Facebook has allowed small businesses the chance to target specific customers and increase their market share. With many potential customers using their phones and laptops as a key tool for communication, the importance of online and social advertising has grown.

However, at times, social media can have a damaging effect on a business's brand. Waitrose tried to harness the power of social media by launching a promotional campaign on Twitter using '#Ishopatwaitrosebecause'. The aim was for its customers to help promote the business and expand its global reach. This was not the case. Customers started to write comments highlighting the expensive product range and posh clientele. Opinion is divided as to whether this was a PR nightmare or publicity triumph but it shows the strength social media can have.

Your assessment criteria:

**2B.P5** Plan a promotional campaign for a brand

**Key terms:**

***Promotional campaign:*** *A combination of advertising messages that share the same ideas*

***Promotional objectives:*** *Target set for the promotional campaign to achieve*

***Social media:*** *mobile technology based communication between businesses, communities and individuals*

**Discuss**

*In pairs discuss:*

1. *Why do businesses spend so much on promotional campaigns?*
2. *Is it worth it for the business?*

**Research**

*Research how much Coca-Cola spends on promotion of its brand each year.*

What is the business trying to gain from the brand? It may be focused on raising the awareness of the product or service. For example, a new product or service will need a larger promotional campaign than those that are already established.

It may want to remind customers of its product or service. Businesses must constantly promote in order to remind so that customers do not forget about their products. This should include continually informing customers of the product and changes to price or options.

Newer businesses will want to create market presence with their promotional campaign. This is common in the confectionery market. For example, the new Cadbury Bubbly. Any product that is different from others will still need to be promoted.

Larger businesses may also want to increase market share. This is more likely if the business is promoting itself on a regular basis. The more someone sees a product, the more likely they are to buy it.

A business should try and differentiate itself from others. This could be through humour or new ways of promoting a product. For example, Gillette used a viral advert of Roger Federer knocking a bottle off of someone's head with a serve, to do just that.

**Figure 3.9 When planning a promotional campaign for a brand, a business must consider these promotional objectives**

## Choosing the promotional activities

A business must also make sure it chooses the correct market segment. If a brand is targeted incorrectly, it will reduce potential sales and could even ruin the brand for good. Some brands alter the target segment over time. For example, Lucozade used to be aimed at older, retired people – and was often seen as a drink for ill people – but now targets the younger athletic person.

All businesses will need to improve their campaigns continually, learning from previous experience and adapting future promotion. This may involve slight changes such as increased PR, more exposure within catalogues or the start of personal selling. However, this will need to be backed up by evidence. This could come from projected sales figures against actual figures, previous years and competitors.

# Promotional choice

## 2B.M4 Developing the most appropriate promotional mix

For some promotional campaigns, older and more reliable methods are often used. However, many businesses are looking for new, more innovative techniques to help boost their brand. The emergence of **viral adverts** has been one example of this. Every brand requires a slightly different mix of promotional tools. Not all brands will require as much promotion as they may generate more exposure through PR. The more innovative and new a product is, the more PR it will receive as public interest is higher.

For companies like Adidas and Nike, their promotional mix focuses on TV advertising and celebrity endorsement. This is because of their higher budgets and type of product. The use of celebrities allows the customer to see the product in action, and then associate the product with high quality. Companies can justify this mix because of the global returns the product will make.

Local take-away chains will often use cheaper promotional mixes, focusing on PR, local radio media and word of mouth. This is because they target the local customer base, are cheap and easy to organise. Choosing the appropriate promotional mix will require the business to consider the following:

1. The size of the organisation: what sort of campaign can it afford?
2. How have previous campaigns been designed? Have they been a success?
3. How important is the brand?
4. The industry the brand operates within.

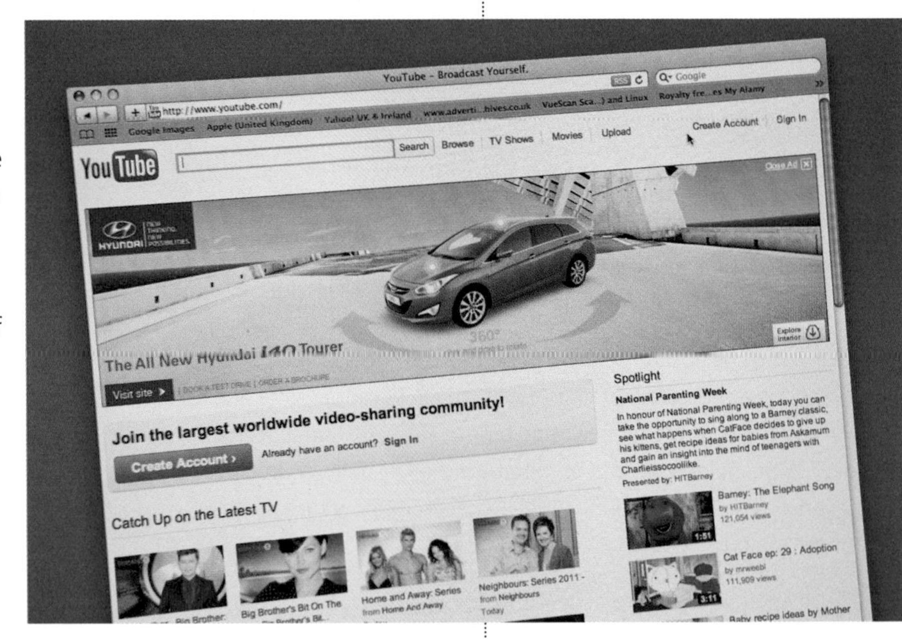

Online promotion for a leading brand

Your assessment criteria:

**2B.M4** Justify the choice of promotional mix for a brand

**2B.D2** Evaluate the effectiveness of a promotional campaign for a brand and recommend improvements

### Key term

**Viral advert:** *an advert that does not show or link directly with a brand*

Despite many famous brands spending large amounts of money on their promotional campaigns, they still underperform. It may be that sales figures are below that of the targets, market share doesn't grow as much as required or customer perception doesn't improve. Whatever it is, businesses must evaluate their promotional mix and improve it if necessary. By looking at the following, a business can evaluate its performance:

- sales figures
- market share
- customer feedback
- media reviews
- costings/sales returns.

For example, in 2007, Snickers had to redesign its promotional mix when it received lots of negative criticism. Using Mr T in its television adverts, it had many complaints from the public about its bullying, over-macho message. The adverts were redesigned for both magazines and newspapers, and a new PR campaign was started. It based this redesign on the fact that customers now perceived the brand as a bully, and sales figures had started to drop.

**Research**

*Using the internet, research into a new product that has just been released. This could be a computer game, new car or film. You should find out what the reviews say. Has this product been successful in its launch? If not, why is this?*

**Discuss**

*You have opened a local hair salon that specialises in expensive hair and beauty treatments for weddings. The local market is very wealthy and the potential clientele is high. You must now devise a branding and promotional strategy. In small groups, decide on the best strategy for this business. You should think about everything that has been covered in this chapter. The key to this is applying it to the business in question. Think about what is realistic.*

**Case study**

The rise of the 'Deans Doughnuts' range was a surprise to many industry experts. However, founder Andre Boss, was confident from the start. His brand is based around the product range, which offers personalised doughnuts for delivery up and down the UK. The products are designed online and then delivered within an hour to offices and homes everywhere.

The brand received plenty of PR in the early stages, with local media interested in the newest company to the industry. The promotional campaign, which involved online media pop-ups, social network pages and celebrity endorsements, also helped to gather interest. However, despite the advice of several experts, Andre Boss refused to use sales promotions.

A year later, the business is still going strong, but the brand lacks personality due to the huge range and variety of promotional tools used.

1. Do you agree with Andre Boss's decision not to use sales promotions? Explain your answer. (2A.P5)
2. Justify the use of celebrity endorsement in this promotional campaign. (2A.M4)
3. How would you improve the promotional campaign of 'Deans Doughnuts'? Why? (2A.D2)

# Assessment checklist

**To achieve level 1, my portfolio of evidence must show that I can:**

| Assessment criteria | Description | ✓ |
|---|---|---|
| 1A.1 | Describe the importance of branding for a business | ☐ |
| 1A.2 | Identify elements of the marketing mix for a selected branded product | ☐ |
| 1A.3 | Identify elements of the promotional mix used for a selected branded product | ☐ |
| 1B.4 | Outline an idea and select a target market for a brand | ☐ |
| 1B.5 | Outline elements of a promotional campaign for a brand | ☐ |

**To achieve a pass grade, my portfolio of evidence must show that I can:**

| Assessment criteria | Description | ✓ |
|---|---|---|
| 2A.P1 | Explain how branding is used in two businesses | ☐ |
| 2A.P2 | Assess the marketing mix for a selected branded product | ☐ |
| 2A.P3 | Describe the purpose of elements of the promotional mix used for a selected branded product | ☐ |
| 2B.P4 | Use branding methods and techniques to recommend a brand personality and a target market for a brand | ☐ |
| 2B.P5 | Plan a promotional campaign for a brand | ☐ |

**To achieve a merit grade, my portfolio of evidence must show that I can:**

| Assessment criteria | Description | ✓ |
|---|---|---|
| 2A.M1 | Compare the use of brand promotion in two businesses | ☐ |
| 2A.M2 | Explain the importance of selecting an appropriate promotional mix for a selected branded product | ☐ |
| 2B.M3 | Explain how branding methods and techniques are used to recommend a brand personality and a target market for a brand | ☐ |
| 2B.M4 | Justify the choice of promotional mix for a brand | ☐ |

**To achieve a distinction grade, my portfolio of evidence must show that I can:**

| Assessment criteria | Description | ✓ |
|---|---|---|
| 2A.D1 | Evaluate the effectiveness of the promotional mix for a selected branded product | ☐ |
| 2B.D2 | Evaluate the effectiveness of a promotional campaign for a brand and recommend improvements | ☐ |

# 4 Principles of customer service

## Learning aim A: Understand how businesses provide customer service

- Topic A.1 Definition of customer service. The ways in which businesses satisfy their customers
- Topic A.2 Different customer service roles in a business. How businesses deal with customers directly and indirectly.
- Topic A.3 The different types of customer service businesses have. Businesses deal with customers in different ways whether it is face-to-face, through call centres, online and working with other colleagues.
- Topic A.4 Customer satisfaction. This section explores why it is important to make sure customers are satisfied and the different ways this is achieved.
- Topic A.5 Different ways that businesses can provide consistent and reliable customer service. Customer service staff make the difference between good and bad customer service. The ways they offer consistent and reliable customer service are explored.
- Topic A.6 The effect of good customer service on the reputation of a business. Good reputations are built on good customer service and this will mean increased sales, more customers and job satisfaction!
- Topic A.7 Different ways of exceeding customer expectations. Customers' expectations are exceeded when they have value for money, are helped and assisted in their purchases and dealt with appropriately.
- Topic A.8 Providing effective customer service through organisational procedures. The ways that businesses deliver customer service are explored ensuring that all staff know what is expected of them and how this helps to contribute to good customer service.
- Topic A.9 Complying with legislative and regulatory customer service requirements. Organisations have to meet all legal and regulatory requirements in order to ensure effective customer service.

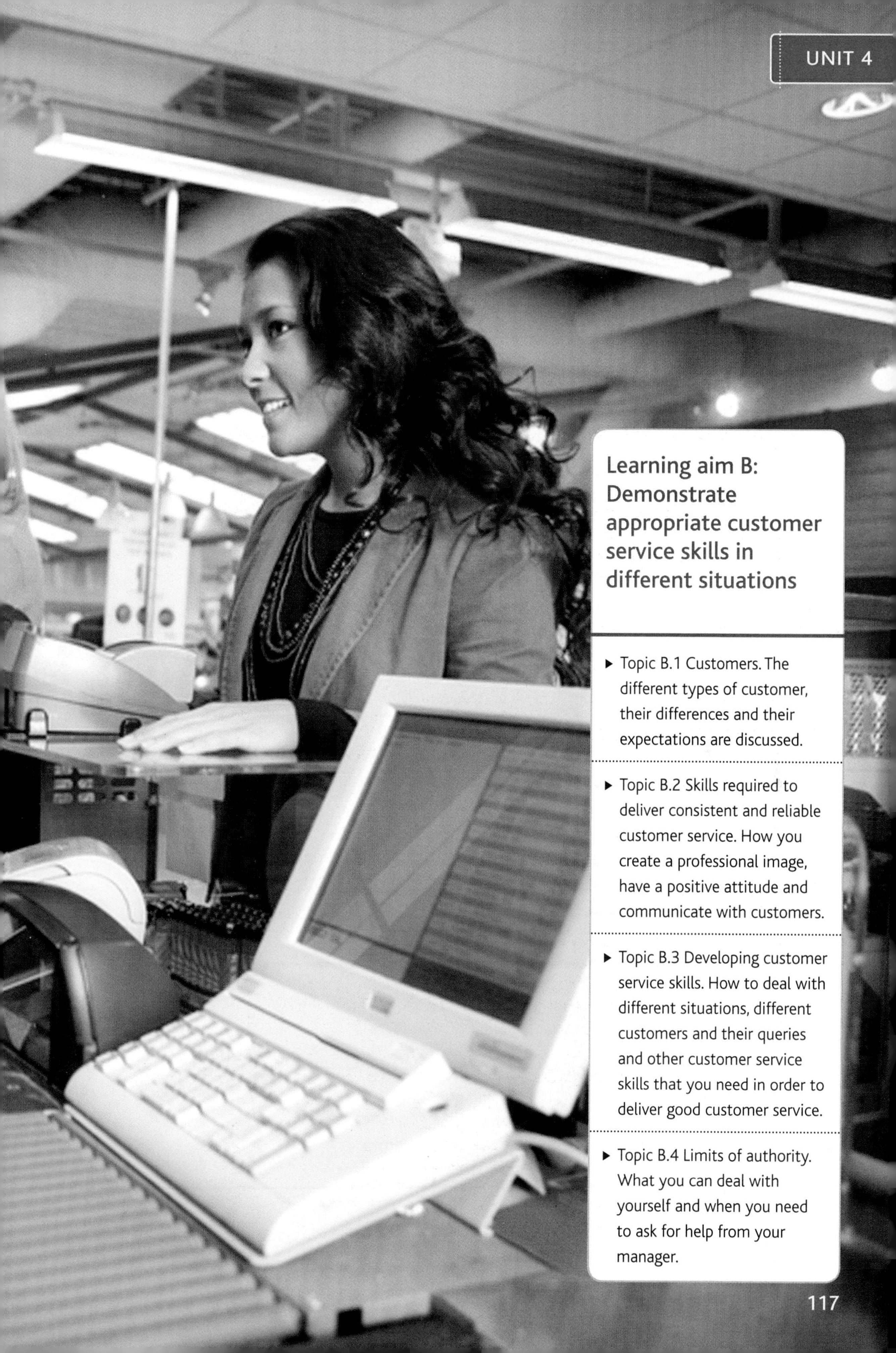

## Learning aim B: Demonstrate appropriate customer service skills in different situations

- Topic B.1 Customers. The different types of customer, their differences and their expectations are discussed.
- Topic B.2 Skills required to deliver consistent and reliable customer service. How you create a professional image, have a positive attitude and communicate with customers.
- Topic B.3 Developing customer service skills. How to deal with different situations, different customers and their queries and other customer service skills that you need in order to deliver good customer service.
- Topic B.4 Limits of authority. What you can deal with yourself and when you need to ask for help from your manager.

# Customer service

## 2A.P1 Customer service

Customer service describes the actions organisations take to make sure their customers are happy and satisfied. If customers are not happy and satisfied with the service they receive, they will go to another organisation. Therefore it is vital for an organisation's success that their customers' needs and expectations are met.

Your assessment criteria:

**2A.P1** Describe the different types of customer service provided by two selected businesses

**'There is only one boss. The customer. And he can fire everybody in the company from the chairman on down, simply by spending his money somewhere else.'— Sam Walton, founder of Wal-Mart**

In order to offer excellent customer service, organisations need to understand what their customers expect from them. For example, many people need to catch a train to get to work. However, they expect a seat on the train, a clean environment and the train to be on time. Successful train companies know their customers well, are aware of their expectations and meet them.

Customer service can be defined as the ways in which a business meets customers' expectations and satisfies their needs.

## Customer service roles

Customers' expectations are met through the staff who deal directly with them. These include receptionists, shop assistants and delivery drivers. For example, if the ticket inspector on the train is impolite to a customer, this will have a negative impact on the travelling environment for the customer and therefore not meet their expectations. Staff roles that do not involve direct customer service can also greatly impact customers' expectations. For example, if the train is dirty because the cleaners have not done their job properly, customers will not be happy and will use a different train company.

### Key terms

***Customer service:*** *the ways in which a business meets customer expectations and satisfies their needs*

***Customer service teamwork:*** *the network of staff in an organisation who deliver customer service, including individuals, departments and other businesses*

***Face-to-face customer service:*** *when the service deliverer and customer interact in person*

***Remote customer service:*** *when the service deliverer and the customer interact via telephone or the internet*

***Service deliverer:*** *the person seen by the customer as providing customer service and representing the business*

### Design

*Design your own definition of customer service, based on your own customer service experiences.*

## 2A.P1 Customer service businesses

Customer service can come in many different forms. In many organisations, customers' expectations are met by a **service deliverer**, the person seen by the customer as providing customer service and representing the business, for example a sales assistant. This is **face-to-face customer service**. Other examples of face-to-face customer service include:

- reception staff in hotels
- waiting staff in restaurants
- instructors in leisure centres
- nurses in hospitals.

Other businesses never come into face-to-face contact with their customers. This is **remote customer service**. For example, if you buy a product from an online retailer like Amazon (www.amazon.co.uk), you never come into contact with an employee. The customer service is delivered to you via e-mails and your online account. Remote customer service can also be delivered through call centres.

In order for an organisation to deliver effective customer service to meet customers' expectations, the individuals and departments within the company need to cooperate. This is known as **customer service teamwork**. For example, if a customer phones an organisation with a complaint about their mobile phone bill, the call centre staff need to communicate with the finance department and share information in order to solve the customer's problem. Some organisations need to work with other businesses in order to meet their customers' expectations. For example, a customer has a problem with a product bought on www.amazon.co.uk. However, the product was sold by a different company that sells through the Amazon website. When the customer makes a complaint, Amazon has to cooperate with the seller to rectify the problem.

**Research**

*Research the different ways that two different businesses handle customer complaints and problems.*

**Remote customer service**

**Case study**

Joseph ordered a birthday gift for his girlfriend online. The gift did not arrive in time for her birthday so Joseph contacted the company. The customer service representative apologised and explained and that his order had left the depot and was due to be delivered the next day. Joseph was angry. The company had originally said that the product would be delivered in five days. It was now the seventh day.

1. Define customer service.
2. What role does the customer service representative play?
3. Describe the customer service that Joseph received. (2A.P1)

**Discuss**

*In groups, discuss your experiences of face-to-face and remote customer service in your dealings with two different businesses.*

# Customer satisfaction

## 2A.M1 Customer satisfaction

Satisfying customers is vital to a business's success. **Satisfied customers** feel that the product or service received has met their needs and expectations and that they have received value for money. If customers are satisfied they become loyal repeat customers. They will continue to return to the same business and recommend it to their friends and family (word of mouth reputation). Turning people into satisfied customers means that the organisation's reputation is enhanced, which will help it become successful.

There are many ways in which organisations strive to satisfy customers and ensure they feel that they have value for money.

### Providing reliable products or services

Organisations strive to ensure that their products are the best that they can be. For example, John Lewis states on its website that customers who are not satisfied with its products can simply return them to one of their stores. Customers can also track their orders through John Lewis's website to ensure that they receive a reliable delivery service.

### Providing extra services

These include free delivery and follow-up services. For example, John Lewis offers free delivery on items over £30 and also a 'click and collect' service where customers can order their items online and collect them in store the next day. Apple, the technology company, also provides extra services such as Apple Care where customers receive '90 days of complimentary technical support and a one-year limited warranty'.

### Being accurate, reliable and efficient

Customers are satisfied if the business delivers what it says it will deliver and when. For example, Next promises next-day delivery on items ordered online by 9 pm. It also gives customers the option to request a call back for urgent enquiries.

### Providing value for money

Organisations must ensure that customers believe they are getting value for money for the products or services they purchase. This means they want maximum quality for the price they pay. Customers constantly

Your assessment criteria:

**2A.M1** Compare how two selected businesses satisfy customers

**Key term**

***Customer satisfaction:*** *customers are satisfied when they feel their needs and expectations have been met and that they have received value for money*

select items and services to buy, and aim for the right balance between quality and cost. They take into account the additional services available and the time it takes to receive the service or goods.

## Providing information and advice

Organisations satisfy customers by providing effective and comprehensive information and advice on their products. If customers have confidence in the advice and information given, they are more likely to be satisfied. Currys PC World ensures that the guidance it offers online is as comprehensive as possible. Staff are also trained continually on the products and services sold.

## Dealing with problems

In order to be satisfied, customers need their problems dealt with quickly and efficiently. For this reason most organisations have very detailed complaints procedures that staff must follow. JD Sports, for example, has a customer service section on its website, featuring frequently asked questions (FAQs), delivery information, order tracking and size charts. There are also options for contacting the organisation so that problems can be put right on a personal level.

**Research**

*In pairs, research how two businesses of your choice satisfy their customers. What are the differences and similarities between them?*

**Case study**

John Lewis is a large customer-focused retailer. There are many ways in which is ensures its customers are satisfied. You may not be aware of it, but your school or college is also committed to ensuring that you and your parents are satisfied customers.

1. Research and explain the ways in which John Lewis tries to satisfy its customers. (2A.M1)
2. Research and explain the ways in which your school or college tries to satisfy its customers. (2A.M1)
3. What are the similarities between the two? (2A.M1)
4. What are the differences between the two? (2A.M1)

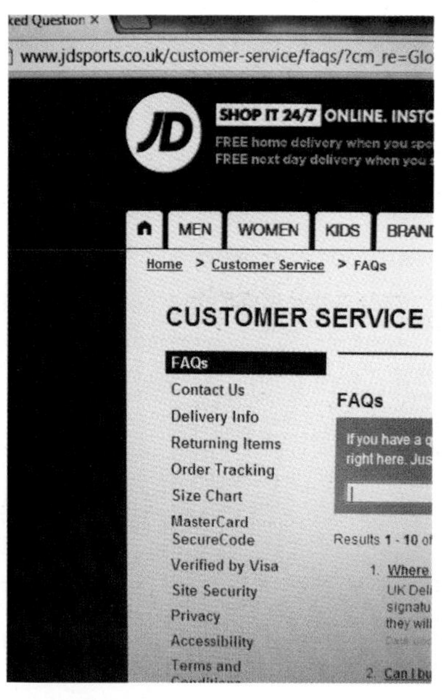


**Many businesses use FAQ sections on their website as a way of dealing with customers' problems**

# Different ways that businesses can provide consistent and reliable customer service

## 2A.P2 Consistent and reliable customer service

Customers expect to experience the same high levels of service no matter whom they come into contact with in an organisation. Achieving consistency requires an organisation to spend a lot on staff training to meet customer expectations.

### Staff knowledge of the scope of the job role and products or services

All employees need to be trained on what they can and cannot do as part of their job. They need to know the situations where customers should be passed on to their manager. They must also understand the different products and services on sale so that they can offer reliable assistance and advice. Employees should also know where they can find out information about the products, for example in manuals or catalogues, and understand the terms (jargon) used about them.

### Staff attitude and behaviour

Employees need to understand the importance of having a positive attitude and being polite and professional to customers. They also need to understand that customers do not like to waste their time, for example by having to wait in long queues. Similarly, being aware of how much time they have and when to approach them to offer help is also important. If employees keep customers waiting, they need to ensure that they apologise and deal with the problem as quickly and effectively as possible. Staff also need to know what products are available and the procedure for helping customers if the product they want is not in stock. This may include putting the customer's name on a waiting list and calling them when the product comes in store.

### Meeting specific customer needs

Staff need to know the correct questions to ask customers so that they can identify and fulfil their needs as quickly as possible. For example, service deliverers should ask customers how they can be of assistance.

### Working under pressure

Employees should be able to act appropriately towards customers even when they are busy and under pressure. Service deliverers should

Your assessment criteria:

**2A.P2** Describe the characteristics of consistent and reliable customer service

**Key term**

***Jargon:*** *technical or slang terms used widely within an industry*

always maintain high levels of customer service regardless of their own thoughts and feelings.

## Confirming service meets needs and expectations

Organisations that try to improve their customer service may check that their customers are satisfied. This may involve phoning them to check that they are happy with the service, or asking them to complete a customer service questionnaire, for example feedback forms in restaurants or on online sites such as Amazon.

## Dealing with problems

When customers are unhappy and have a problem, staff need to know how to deal with them. Is the customer always right? Staff need to know what they can offer an unhappy customer. Do they want their money back? Do they want some other form of compensation, for example discounts, vouchers or a free meal?

**A customer service questionnaire**

**Design**

*Design an induction booklet for new staff giving examples of consistent and reliable customer service. Explain how this ensures that customers are satisfied.*

**Case study**

Christine Bleakley and Adrian Chiles were sacked from presenting ITV1's *Daybreak* show in December 2011. Their dismissal was blamed on inadequate viewer ratings due to their consistently poor presenting performances.

1. Come up with your own definition of consistent.
2. Why is it important that customers receive consistent customer service? (2A.P2)

# The effect of good customer service on a business and its customers

## 2A.M2 Exceeding customer expectations

Meeting customer expectations ensures that customers are satisfied; however with increased competition, organisations now try not only to meet customer expectation, but to exceed them. There are several ways in which they can do this.

### Providing value for money

If customers believe they have received exceptional quality goods and excellent after-sales **customer service** for the price paid, they will perceive that they have had value for money.

### Providing information and advice quickly

Often companies exceed customers' expectations by responding to their information requests more rapidly than customers expect. Online companies often have a time frame within which they promise to respond to requests. If information and advice are offered before this time has elapsed, customers' expectations are exceeded.

### Providing exceptional help and assistance for customers with special requirements

Businesses that recognise that their customers have special requirements and do their best to go beyond them will ensure that customers' expectations are exceeded. For example, most supermarkets have baby-changing facilities for customers with young children.

### Providing additional help and assistance

Dealing with customers' problems is often to key to exceeding their expectations. For example, the Gro Company is an organisation that sells baby and children's products. It sells predominantly through www.amazon.co.uk and is very aware of the impact that customer reviews have on its business. The owner and inventor responds personally (and promptly) to any negative customer reviews and problems. As a result, most of the negative reviews are deleted by customers who explain that the response has exceeded their expectations. This has led to increased sales as potential customers describe how this has persuaded them to buy products from the company.

**Your assessment criteria:**

- **2A.M2** Explain how a selected business attempts to exceed customer expectations
- **2A.D1** Assess the effect of providing consistent and reliable customer service on the reputation of a selected business

**Key terms**

***Customer service:*** *providing a service that consistently meets or exceeds customer needs.*

***Good reputation:*** *when customers have a favourable opinion of a business*

***Value for money:*** *the belief that the goods or services provided by a business are worth the price paid*

***Word of mouth:*** *when customers tell other people about their experiences*

**Discuss**

*In groups, discuss what constitutes excellent customer service. Use examples from your own experiences and your research. How does this impact on the reputation of the businesses you are describing?*

**Research**

*Research how a company like Gro (or a company of your choice) attempts to exceed customer expectations.*

Companies are not always in a position to deal with customers in such a personal way. However, they may offer discounts or additional products and services. An effective and efficient returns policy more than compensates customers for their inconvenience and gives them the confidence to buy from the business again.

## 2A.D1 The reputation of a business

A **good reputation** is built by offering good quality products, **value for money**, consistent and high quality customer service and reliable and trustworthy service. Emirates, the Dubai owned airline, prides itself on its reputation as one of the world's best airlines. It has consistently won awards for the services it offers. Customers know that when they fly with Emirates they will receive high-quality catering, in-flight entertainment and, on certain routes, be offered the biggest and best aircraft.

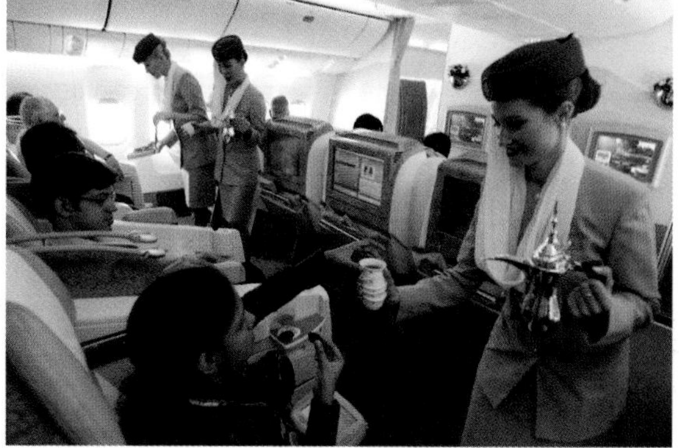

**Emirates has a reputation for excellence in the airline industry**

Emirates' excellent reputation has earned it:

- Increased sales year on year since the business started in 1985
- Increased profit since the third year of operation
- Retention of existing customers
- New customers who have heard about Emirates' reputation for excellent quality and service. New customers can also read reviews about the airline on the Emirates website
- **Word of mouth** publicity as customers tell their friends and family about its superior service
- Competitive advantage with high standards that other airlines struggle to compete with
- Staff job satisfaction and motivation – working for a company with such a high reputation motivates staff to continue to offer customers the highest levels of service

**Research**

*Assess the effect of providing consistent and reliable customer service on Emirates' reputation.*

**Case study**

Partyrama (www.parytrama.co.uk) is a successful online party product business. It has an easy to use website, excellent range and quality of products, reasonable prices and first-rate customer service. They pride themselves on offering their customers value for money and a comprehensive returns and exchange policy. This means that their customers can buy their products with confidence.

1. Explain how Partyrama attempts to exceed customer expectations. (2A.M2)

# Providing effective customer service through organisational procedures

## 2A.P3 Organisational procedures

There are many ways in which an organisation can provide effective customer service in its everyday activities.

### Monitoring customer service

Organisations invest money in finding out what their customers think, what they are doing right and what needs to be improved. They can do this by asking for informal feedback from their customers, asking customers to complete comments cards or questionnaires, asking for feedback from their employees, using mystery shoppers or evaluating the compliment and complaints letters they receive. For example, McDonalds uses **mystery shoppers** to monitor its customer service levels.

### Following codes of practice

**Codes of practice** are voluntary guidelines that identify the standards of service customers can expect. They may also give customers advice about what to do if they are not satisfied. Codes of practice operate at different levels. They include:

- Industry codes of practice: these set out the minimum standards expected throughout an industry, for example banking and finance.
- Organisational/business codes of practice: guidelines written by specific companies on their own standards and ways of dealing with customer complaints. For example, retailers with high standards, such as John Lewis, are likely to have 'no quibble' money back guarantees.
- Professional codes of practice: guidelines that all professional workers, for example doctors or solicitors, should abide by. They are drawn up by professional institutions such as the British Medical Association.

### Having ethical standards

**Ethical standards** set out how organisations should trade fairly and honestly with customers and suppliers and ensure that their employees are trained to be aware of the correct procedures. For example, staff need to know when to refer a customer to someone in authority (for example, a manager), how to deal with refunds, how to deal with questions they cannot answer and how to treat customers fairly.

Your assessment criteria:

**2A.P3** Explain how organisational procedures and legislation contribute to consistent and reliable customer service

**2A.P4** Explain how legislative and regulatory requirements affect customer service in a selected business

**Key terms**

***Codes of practice:*** *voluntary guidelines that identify the standards of service customers can expect*

***Competitive advantage:*** *the advantage a company gains by providing customers with better service than its competitors*

***Ethical standards:*** *standards that set out how organisations should trade fairly and honestly with customers and suppliers*

***Mystery shopper:*** *a person hired by a market research company to pretend to be a real customer and report on customer service*

Organisations have to comply with all these organisational procedures to be law abiding, provide consistent and reliable customer service and ensure that they can achieve their aims and objectives.

If businesses can develop organisational procedures that mean their customer service exceeds that of their competitors, they will gain a **competitive advantage**. John Lewis, for example, has not seen a fall in profits despite trading in difficult economic times. This is because the John Lewis shopping experience is focused on excellent customer service. A key factor in its success is its partnership structure, which means that all its staff own a stake in the business and are more inclined to offer good levels of service.

**Research**

*Research John Lewis's codes of practice. How does John Lewis ensure that its employees are always willing to offer excellent customer service?*

**Outstanding customer service gives John Lewis competitive advantage**

## 2A.P4 Legislative and regulatory requirements

Businesses have to comply with all legal and regulatory requirements in order to deliver consistent and reliable customer service. These are the requirements that organisations have to follow by law. They include:

- Sale of Goods Act – any goods sold must be of satisfactory quality and fit for purpose (free from defects, durable and safe).
- Health and Safety Act – organisations must ensure that any hazards and risks to their customers are minimised. This includes identifying where customers could be injured; informing people about hazards (for example, signs warning about wet floors); complying with fire regulations (making fire exits identifiable, displaying the locations of fire extinguishers, showing evacuation and fire practice procedures and meeting points); and knowing how to deal with security alerts (for example, taking messages, evacuation procedures and meeting points).
- Data Protection Act – any organisation that retains and processes customers' and employees' personal information must be registered under the Data Protection Act 1998. This means information retained about individuals must not be excessive or kept for too long, be kept secure, accurate and up to date.
- Equal Opportunities – every business has to make an Equal Opportunities statement available to all staff. A business must make sure it has effective anti-discrimination policies so that all staff are treated fairly and are valued equally whatever their race, gender, level of disability, health, religion, nationality or age.

If you go into a business such as Marks & Spencer, you will see how the business complies with these legislative and regulatory requirements in order to offer good customer service. All the goods it sells are of good quality and as described. If something has been spilt on the floor, yellow hazard signs are displayed and it is clear where the fire exits are around the store. Where it has taken customers' details, for example in online orders, it asks permission from customers

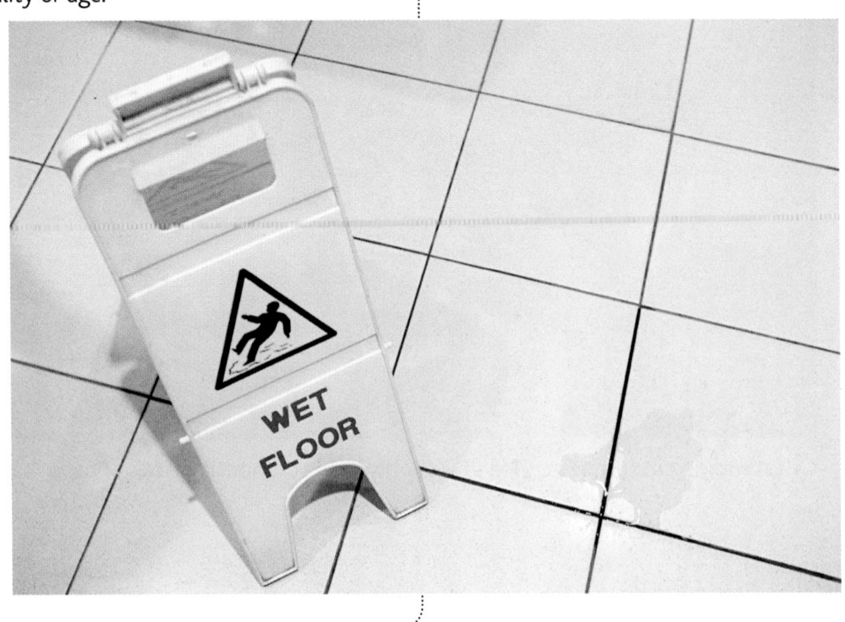

### Design

*Design a document that can be given to new staff at John Lewis (or a company of your choice) summarising the legislation it has to comply with to protect its customers and how this dictates its customer service delivery procedures.*

if these details can be passed on to third parties. Finally, it complies with equal opportunities legislation and this is outlined in the job vacancies section on its website.

## 2A.M3 The impact of legislative and regulatory requirements

In order to achieve 2A.M3, you will need to compare the impact of the legislative and regulatory requirements and how these affect customer service in a selected organisation. In order to do this, you will need to explain the similarities and differences in the organisation between the legislative and regulatory requirements. This then needs to be developed into how these impact the customer service offered to customers. This could include looking at customer complaints and compliments and reviews of customer service posted on websites.

**Research**

*Research any businesses that have been featured in the media for not meeting legislative or regulatory requirements.*

**Case study**

Insideout is a homeware and gift business in Devon. They also have an online shop, www.gottahaveit.co.uk. In order to comply with the Sales of Goods Act, they ensured that they got to know all about the Act, inspected their products and developed a customer service policy.

1. What other organisational, regulatory and legislative requirements would a company like Insideout have to comply with in order to ensure that it offers consistent and reliable customer service?
2. Explain how the legislative and regulatory requirements affect the customer service that Insideout offers to its customers. (2A.P3 and 2A.P4)
3. Compare the impact of legislative and regulatory requirements affecting the customer service at Insideout. (2A.M3)

# Customers

## 2B.P5 Customers

### Internal customers

Everybody within an organisation works with and for other people. Just as customers expect goods to be delivered on time, managers expect staff to deliver a report on time or arrive at a meeting on time. Staff should regard all colleagues as **internal customers**. They are called customers because they depend on the services they provide each other.

An organisation can only achieve excellent customer service if all employees work, regardless of whether or not they deal directly with external customers. In schools, the teachers, education welfare officers, catering staff and caretakers work together to ensure students have a good experience.

In most businesses the key internal customers are colleagues, managers and other departments.

### External customers

**External customers** are the people who buy or use a business's products or services. An organisation must tailor its services to meet the expectations of customers. Here are some factors a business might consider:

- Existing or new customers – offering promotions to new customers and rewards to loyal customers, for example loyalty cards offering discounts
- Individuals – offering promotions to individual customers
- Groups – offering group discount tickets
- Members of the public – offering new promotions to members of the public to encourage them to become customers, for example one-off 'giveaways' on the high street
- Business to business – most businesses trade with other businesses, for example their suppliers. Organisations sometimes offer special discounts for loyalty to the same supplier and these cost savings can be passed on to the end customer.

### Customers with special requirements

It is important for organisations to tailor their products and services to the specific needs of their customers (see Figure 4.1).

Your assessment criteria:

**2B.P5** Outline how the business environment can impact on a start-up business

**Key terms**

***External customers:*** *the people who buy or use the products and/or services of an organisation*

***Internal customers:*** *everybody who is directly connected to a business, for example employees, shareholders and other stakeholders*

**Businesses have to cater for customers' special requirements**

**Figure 4.1 Meeting customers' special requirements**

| Type of customer | Ways to meet their needs |
|---|---|
| Non-English speaking | Staff may need to speak slowly or write things down. |
| Customers of different ages | Organisations have to cater for both the young and the elderly. For example, they may have a play area for children. Some organisations play music in their stores that they think will attract their target customers. |
| Customers from different cultures | Customers from different cultures may have different needs. These may be met by having leaflets and signs in different languages. |
| Customers of different genders | Men and women have different needs, such as segregated toilets and changing rooms. |
| Families | Organisations may offer family parking bays or family discount tickets. |
| Customers with disabilities | Visually impaired customers may need assistance to find products and announcements to make them aware of obstacles. Many hearing impaired customers can lip read and staff should look at the customer and speak slowly when talking. Mobility impaired customers may need help to use the facilities provided. Many of these facilities are a legal requirement under the Disability Discrimination Act, for example disabled parking, ramps or lifts. Staff should always be ready to assist. |

Many factors can impact on customers' service expectations: older customers may expect a higher level of personal service than younger customers. Customers from different cultures may have different expectations from the British. For example, American customers are used to very friendly and talkative cashiers in supermarkets, while British cashiers are more reserved. If a business portrays itself as high quality or highly ethical, customers may expect higher levels of customer service. Customers with high incomes may have higher customer service expectations than customers on lower incomes because they are able to pay for better quality service.

**Case study**

Jerry works in Argos on the customer service desk. Today, a woman came in with children to return some unwanted gifts. She was then followed by an elderly gentleman who was partially sighted.

1. Identify the external and internal customers in Argos.
2. How could Argos meet the needs and expectations of the two different customers in this case study? (2B.P5)

**Design**

*Design a poster describing the needs and expectations of three different types of customer. Ensure you have at least one internal and one external customer. Explain how a company of your choice meets the needs and expectations of these three different customers.*

# Skills required to deliver consistent and reliable customer service

## 2B.P7 What skills are required?

Consistent and reliable customer service is crucial, particularly if the employee is face-to-face with customers. Good customer service skills are essential to maintaining satisfied customers in any type of business. A good salesperson can make an overpriced product feel like a bargain while a poor customer service worker can make the customer buying an inexpensive product feel they are being scammed! Most companies train new employees in the skills required to make customers feel that they are receiving the customer service they deserve.

Several skills are necessary in order for employees to deliver consistent and reliable customer service. They include:

- Being professional and creating a good impression. This means having good manners, dressing appropriately and professionally, using appropriate language (no slang), good posture (the way you stand and sit), positive body language (smiling and looking alert), and a tidy work area. Customers will perceive you as organised and efficient.
- Having a positive attitude, for example being on time, being conscientious and being motivated regardless of how you feel
- Communicating effectively with customers. This includes:
  - **Verbal communication** Most people make a judgment about staff in the first minute of meeting them, so making a good first impression is vital, for example shaking hands and introducing yourself. Speaking clearly is also very important. Customers need to understand what the member of staff is saying and the tone of an employee's voice should reflect that they are talking to a customer, whether it is formal, informal, concerned, apologetic, persuasive or grovelling. Staff should also be aware of the volume of their voice. A calm and placid voice is often best. If an employee has to speak to a customer whose first language is not English, speaking slowly and clearly will be essential.
  - **Non-verbal communication** What you don't say to customers can be just as important as what you do say. Smiling and making eye contact can make customers feel at ease and the staff look approachable and willing to help. Looking directly at customers and appearing interested in what they are saying can improve customers' perceptions of the service they receive. Staff body language should make customers feel comfortable. No aggressive movements or physical contact should be used and facial expressions should be

Your assessment criteria:

**2B.P7** Demonstrate effective communication skills to meet customer needs when dealing with three different customer types in customer service situations

**Key terms**

***Non-verbal communication:*** *messages given without words, for example body language or eye contact*

***Verbal communication:*** *spoken and written communication*

controlled so that staff do not display inappropriate feelings towards customers. It is important also to use hand gestures when explaining or demonstrating a product or service, as this can make the customer feel more relaxed.

- The skills used to end an interaction with a customer are as just as important as the greeting and interaction. Staff must thank the customer, use an appropriate tone of voice, positive body language, address the customer appropriately and professionally (for example, 'Mrs Jones') offer them further assistance and confirm what service they require. It is always important to be polite and well mannered and therefore saying goodbye or wishing them a good day also ensures a positive end to the conversation.

**Design**

*In groups, design a diary where you can record when you have to demonstrate appropriate communication skills to deliver consistent and reliable customer service. Over the next two weeks, use this diary to record all of the times you have to demonstrate these skills.*

**Non-verbal communication is important in creating the right first impression**

# Developing customer service skills

## 2B.P7 Customer service skills

Customer service skills are needed in the following situations:

- Face-to-face – where the member of staff deals directly with customers, for example a receptionist greeting a hotel guest.
- Telephone – where the customer calls the organisation for information or to buy a product or service,, for example a customer calling a shop to check when an item will be in stock.
- Writing – writing a letter or email to the company enquiring about a service, for example a customer e-mailing Amazon to check the delivery time for an order.

The skills needed to deal with these different situations vary depending on the nature of what the customer requires from the member of staff. In a face-to-face **customer query** about the returns policy, for example, the member of staff must politely inform the customer about what action will be taken.

**Face-to-face customer service**

### 2B.M4 Customer service skills

Staff need specific skills to handle customers' **problems or complaints**. They may offer the customer an alternative product or an exchange. However, they must always follow the business's policy. If they are unsure how to deal with the situation, they must refer the customer to a manager. Sticking to the company policy is often the best way to handle

Your assessment criteria:

**2B.P7** Demonstrate effective communication skills to meet customer needs when dealing with three different customer types in customer service situations

**2B.M4** Demonstrate effective communication skills when responding to customer problems and complaints in three customer service situations

**2B.D2** Evaluate the effectiveness of own customer service skills, justifying areas for improvement

**Key terms**

***Customer problem and complaint:*** *when a customer has a difficulty or is dissatisfied with the product or service*

***Customer query:*** *when a customer enquires about a product or service*

**Describe**

*Describe three different situations, in your personal life, at school or work experience, where you have had to demonstrate effective communication skills.*

a demanding customer. If a customer is abusive, it is best to pass the problem on to a manager.

Staff should know what facilities are available to customers with disabilities (for example lifts) and assist customers in using them. If customers need technical information, and the member of staff has not been trained to provide it, they should be referred to somebody who has been trained, or to information leaflets.

Ensuring that staff are trained to provide accurate information and advice about products and are able to promote additional products and services is vital in delivering efficient customer service.

### 2B.D2 Customer service skills

Developing reliable and consistent customer service depends on employees implementing the necessary customer service skills. Keeping accurate records of customers' orders; dealing with problems; handling complaints effectively; understanding what you are able to offer customers to remedy a situation (for example a discount); understanding any organisational disclaimers; and following the correct procedures in emergency situations are all customer service skills that have to be developed.

In order to achieve 2B.D2 you need to evaluate your own customer service skills. You will need to explain what you do well and what you do less well and suggest ways you can improve your customer service skills.

**Assisting a customer effectively**

**Describe**

*Describe three different situations, perhaps in your personal life, at school, or at your work experience placement, where you have had to deal with somebody making a complaint.*

**Staff need to be trained to understand exchange and refund policies**

**Case study**

In pairs, act out these three scenarios and follow the instructions.

1. You are a receptionist in a hotel. A guest arrives and you greet them and direct them to their room. They later return complaining that their air conditioning is not working.

2. You work on the customer services desk at Marks & Spencer. A customer has rung to find out when an item will be in stock. He was originally told by one your colleagues that it would be today. You have to inform him that the item is not due in until next week.

3. You work for Amazon.co.uk in the customer service centre. You have received an email from a customer who tells you that she will be out when the item she has ordered is due to be delivered. The item needs to be signed for.

1. Demonstrate appropriate and effective communication skills. (2B.P7)
2. Demonstrate effective communication skills when responding to the customer's problem. (2B.M4)

**Describe**

*Evaluate how you dealt with the three different situations you have described in 2B.M3 and explain how you would deal with them better if they happened again.*

# Limits of authority

## 2B.P6 Authority

Staff need to know what they can offer customers and when it is necessary to refer them to someone in a more senior position within the company, for example a supervisor or manager. Sometimes staff can offer only limited customer service to customers, either because they are not trained or experienced enough to offer them anything or because of company policy.

- Service deliverers – Service deliverers are the sales staff that you encounter when entering a business. They often inform customers of the organisation's refund or exchange policies when customers buy goods and services. There are, however, limits to the services that they can offer customers. If a customer returns an item and wants a refund, there may be a problem if it is not in a condition to be resold. Staff may not have the authority to offer a free or replacement product to customers when they relate to large purchases, for example offering a month's free servicing when someone buys a TV. In these situations, they will have to refer to their line manager who may have more authority to grant the customers' wishes. Service deliverers need to be trained to be familiar with the organisation's policies.
- Line manager/supervisor – Line managers or supervisors tend to have more power to authorise refunds. They can also authorise free products and services for customers. There is a clear line of **authority** in companies where the line manager supervises staff at lower levels and ensures that they carry out the correct refund policies and procedures. Line managers and supervisors are more experienced staff who are very familiar with the organisation's policies.
- Senior management – Senior managers are experienced members of staff who have a lot of power in an organisation (for example store managers). They are able to authorise refunds when line managers or service deliverers can't. This is usually to protect the reputation of the organisation or to make exceptions for valued customers. For example, a customer returns a coat to the store without the receipt. The customer explains that it has only been worn on a few occasions but the fabric has already worn thin. The manager may agree a refund to protect the reputation of the store, even if the store's policy is not to offer a refund when there is no receipt.

Your assessment criteria:

**2B.P6** Describe, using examples, the limits of authority that would apply when delivering customer service

**Key terms**

***Authority:*** *someone who is higher up in the decision making process than you*

**Discuss**

*Discuss with your friends and family members examples of when they have had to ask for assistance from somebody with authority at their place of work.*

**Managers have the authority to authorise exceptional changes to company procedures and policies**

**Case study**

Look again at the three role-plays you acted out from the case study for 1B.7, 2B.P7, 2B.M4 and 2B.D2.

1. When would it be necessary for you to refer the customer to someone in authority in role-plays 1, 2 and 3?
2. Describe, using the case study examples, the limits of authority that would apply when delivering the customer service. (2B.P6)
3. Why is it important to refer problems to someone with authority?

**? Reflect**

*In groups, reflect on situations, perhaps in school, college, at home, part-time work or work placement, when you asked someone with authority (for example a parent or a teacher) to rectify a problem.*

# Assessment checklist

**To achieve level 1, my portfolio of evidence must show that I can:**

| Assessment criteria | Description | ✓ |
|---|---|---|
| 1A.1 | Define customer service, giving an example of a customer service role in a selected business | ☐ |
| 1A.2 | Identify features of consistent and reliable customer service | ☐ |
| 1A.3 | Identify how organisational procedures contribute to consistent and reliable customer service | ☐ |
| 1A.4 | Outline how legislative and regulatory requirements affect customer service in a selected business | ☐ |

**To achieve a pass grade, my portfolio of evidence must show that I can:**

| Assessment criteria | Description | ✓ |
|---|---|---|
| 2A.P1 | Describe the different types of customer service provided by two selected businesses | ☐ |
| 2A.P2 | Describe the characteristics of consistent and reliable customer service | ☐ |
| 2A.P3 | Explain how organisational procedures and legislation contribute to consistent and reliable customer service | ☐ |
| 2A.P4 | Explain how legislative and regulatory requirements affect customer service in a selected business | ☐ |
| 2B.P5 | Describe how a selected business meets the needs and expectations of three different types of customer | ☐ |
| 2B.P6 | Describe, using examples, the limits of authority that would apply when delivering customer service | ☐ |
| 2B.P7 | Demonstrate effective communication skills to meet customer needs when dealing with three different customer types in customer service situations | ☐ |

**To achieve a merit grade, my portfolio of evidence must show that I can:**

| Assessment criteria | Description | ✓ |
|---|---|---|
| 2A.M1 | Compare how two selected businesses satisfy customers | ☐ |
| 2A.M2 | Explain how a selected business attempts to exceed customer expectations | ☐ |
| 2A.M3 | Compare the impact of legislative and regulatory requirements affecting customer service on a selected business | ☐ |
| 2B.M4 | Demonstrate effective communication skills when responding to customer problems and complaints in three customer service situations | ☐ |

**To achieve a distinction grade, my portfolio of evidence must show that I can:**

| Assessment criteria | Description | ✓ |
|---|---|---|
| 2A.D1 | Assess the effect of providing consistent and reliable customer service on the reputation of a selected business | ☐ |
| 2B.D2 | Evaluate the effectiveness of own customer service skills, justifying areas for improvement | ☐ |

# 5 | Sales and personal selling

## Learning aim A: Explore the role of sales staff

- Topic A.1 The functions of the role of sales staff: selling, providing information.
- Topic A.2 The skills that sales staff should have: understanding customers, sales techniques.
- Topic A.3 The knowledge that sales staff should have: products, legislation, motivation.
- Topic A.4 The process of personal selling and additional aspects of the role of sales staff: customer requirements and care, product promotion.

## Learning aim B: Demonstrate personal selling skills and processes

- Topic B.1 Demonstrate personal selling skills: appropriate attitude and appearance, communication, closing sales.
- Topic B.2 Demonstrate personal selling processes: initiating and closing sales, customer care, recording information, liaison with other departments.

# The functions of the role of sales staff

## 2A.P1 What do sales staff do?

Sales staff perform a variety of functions. The most obvious one is selling, but in a crowded and competitive retail market they actually do much, much more.

Sales staff do not only sell goods (TVs, mobile phones, sofas) and services (insurance, hair treatments, holidays); they also sell the product surround or augmented product. These are the benefits a customer gets when buying a particular product, such as free installation, free delivery or a guarantee. In many cases the product surround is the deciding factor for a customer in making their choice between products. Think about a time when you have had the choice of two similar products. What made you decide between them? If you are buying a take-away pizza, the take-away that gets your business could win that sale by offering free delivery or a promise that if you don't get your food within 15 minutes it is free. Your choice of take-away is based on a lot more than the taste of the pizza.

Sales staff provide information about the products or services they are selling. If a mobile phone package was being sold, the sales staff would provide information on the number of monthly texts and minutes, the length of the contract, the data allowance and the range of phones included in the offer. Sales staff need to know about their product/service and about that of their competitors to be able to make comparisons.

**Providing customer care is about more than selling**

Your assessment criteria:

**2A.P1** Describe, using examples, four functions of sales staff in a selected business

### Key terms

***Product surround:*** *the non-physical part of the product; it usually has added value (for example, the warranty on a car) – also known as augmented product*

***Selling:*** *exchanging goods/services for payment; also focused on fulfilling the needs of customers*

### Discuss

*In groups, share experiences you have had where sales staff gave you a good or bad impression of a company.*

*Are there more good experiences or bad ones?*

Many customers make routine enquiries to sales staff that will not always lead to a sale. A customer could be looking into different products or deals, or could just be interested in an item that they have no intention of buying. Enquiries can include if an item is in stock, if it can be delivered, if finance is available or if it is available in other colours. These initial enquiries are a customer's way of selecting not only what they buy but who they buy it from. If store staff don't have the knowledge, a customer will choose to go elsewhere, while very informed staff can turn an enquiry into a sale.

In all their communications with customers, sales staff are representing the organisation. This extends throughout the day – if you went into a store and staff were chewing gum and chatting on their mobiles you would not be impressed; equally, if you saw a member of staff in their uniform being rude to a bus driver it would not give you a good impression. Sales staff are on the front line and their actions leave an impression on customers – good or bad.

**Investigate**

*What is the product surround a customer receives for:*

1. *an Apple iPhone*
2. *satellite television with Sky*
3. *a cruise with Royal Caribbean?*

**Always project the right image**

**Case study**

In 2008, 13 members of Virgin Atlantic were sacked for inappropriate comments about the airline and its customers on the social networking site Facebook. The staff had called passengers 'chavs' and the airline sacked them for bringing 'the company into disrepute'. Virgin Atlantic believed that if staff had these views about passengers they would not be able to provide the high levels of customer service expected of them.

1. Name two items a member of the cabin crew may try and sell to customers.
2. What other function apart from selling would cabin crew be expected to carry out during a flight?
3. The cabin crew are representatives of the Virgin brand. Explain how, in the case study, they failed to meet this function. (2A.P1)

# The knowledge and skills that sales staff should have

## 2A.P2 Knowledge and skills in sales

What do customers want and, more importantly, do they realise they want it? Good sales staff will find out what customers want and then make suggestions to encourage them to buy add-ons – think about restaurant staff who ask you if you also want to order a side dish!

Some of the biggest complaints made by customers are that they are mis-sold products or that sales people do not know enough about the products they are selling. Would you buy a car from someone who could not drive? Many retailers insist on a level of product understanding before they allow sales staff near their customers.

One way of finding out why people buy certain things and to understand the sales **motivation** behind their purchases is to list the benefits they are seeking. These benefits can be real – I am thirsty and if I buy water the benefit will be that I am no longer thirsty – or they can be perceived – water is healthier than a fizzy drink so if I buy water I will be healthier.

By understanding potential customers and their needs, the sales staff can better match products and services to their needs and are more likely to make the sale. For example, a family booking a holiday will probably want entertainment for the children, such as a kids' club, while a couple booking a honeymoon will probably prefer a child-free hotel. By having this insight it helps make sure that customers get the right holiday and that next time they want to book one they will come back to you.

Customers go through a process when making a purchase:

- Recognise problem ('I have run out of chocolate!')
- Search for alternatives ('What have I got in the cupboard? Cornflakes? Biscuits?')
- Evaluation of alternatives ('Would I like a biscuit or a bowl of cornflakes instead?')
- Choice ('No, I want some chocolate!')
- BUY (go to shop and buy some) or DO NOT BUY (still want some chocolate!)
- Post-purchase consumption ('Mmm, that was yummy, I'll buy it again' or 'That was disappointing, I wish I'd bought something else.')

Good sales staff will be on hand to identify the problem, offer alternative products and encourage customers to make a choice and buy the most expensive product being offered.

Your assessment criteria:

**2A.P2** Describe the sales skills used by sales staff in three different selling situations

**Key terms**

***Interpersonal skills:*** *communication skills that include active listening, body language and tone of voice*

***Intrapersonal skills:*** *confidence and how we cope with disappointments and criticism; sales people need to be able to deal with rejection*

***Motivation:*** *this is what drives customers to make a purchase; it could be a genuine need (a new fridge because one has broken) or a desire (they have an iPhone but want the latest model)*

There are a number of techniques involved in personal selling. The techniques employed by sales staff will vary according to the product being sold.

- Cold calling – sales people make calls to potential customers in order to try and make a sale. For example, they will ring up people to ask them if they have thought of buying a new kitchen or if they have double glazing. This very often ends in the potential customer putting the phone down, so sales people need resilience!
- Face-to-face – sales people deal personally with the customer. An example of this could be at a beauty counter, where the sales assistant may try the product out on the customer to show them its benefits.
- Drop-in visits – a sales person visits customers in the workplace or their home to persuade them to make a purchase. One example is medical sales reps, who visit doctors' surgeries to demonstrate their equipment.
- Telemarketing – the use of the telephone, mobile phone or internet to make contact with customers to try and make a sale. Unlike cold calling, this is very often to customers who have previously bought from the company. An example could be from a car dealership who sold a new car to someone two years ago, calling to see if they would like to upgrade to a newer model.

Sales people need to have good **interpersonal skills** like listening to customers, making eye contact and speaking confidently, and good **intrapersonal skills** so they can deal with customer rejection.

**Telesales staff**

**Research**

*Many people complain about cold calling, saying it is an invasion of their privacy and a nuisance. In 2012 businessman Robert Herman made sure he didn't receive cold calls again. Carry out internet research into what he did.*

**Discuss**

*In groups, discuss what impact Robert Herman's actions could have on the sales industry.*

## Closing sales

Good sales people will identify the doubts the customer has and turn them into a positive. Some examples are shown in the figure below.

**Figure 5.1 Examples of turning customer doubts into positives**

| Example of a customer doubt | How a good sales staff would turn the doubt into a positive |
|---|---|
| Worried about the cost? | We can do you a 'buy now pay later' deal. |
| Worried about the maintenance? | We will throw in a reduced three-year warranty. |
| Worried about getting the item home? | We will deliver for free. |
| Worried your husband/wife/ mum/dad won't agree with your purchase? | We will exchange or refund if you change your mind in the next 30 days. |

**Key terms**

***Browsers:*** *people who are 'only looking'; they have no desire to make a purchase*

***Customer profile:*** *who a typical customer is – their age, where they live, how much they earn, what newspapers/magazines they read, hobbies, qualification level, marital status, number of children and so on*

| Interpersonal skills | Intrapersonal skills |
|---|---|
| Good listener | Confident |
| Tone of voice | Team player |
| Persuasion | Resilience |
| Good manners | Leadership |
| Product knowledge | Innovative |
| Customer awareness | Resourceful |

**Research**

*Complete the table on the left, giving examples of interpersonal and intrapersonal skills.*

## Sales preparation skills

Could you imagine walking into an exam hall without preparing first? You would probably not expect to be successful. The same is true in a sales situation. Before approaching a customer, whether by cold calling, on the telephone or face-to-face, a sales person has to be prepared.

- Step 1: Know the product. Sales people need to know everything about the product they are selling: its benefits, features, purpose and how it is different from competitors' products.
- Step 2: What will the objections be from the customer? There are many reasons that may prevent a customer from buying; the sales staff need to know what they are.

- Step 3: Customer profile – who buys the product? Understanding this will make it easier to identify customers.

Different situations will require different skills. Consider these situations:

*Situation 1*

Farid works for a voucher/deal company. He has to persuade customers to sign up with his company so they can buy vouchers for discounted deals. He approaches a local restaurateur, Frank, who is struggling to attract customers at lunchtimes. Farid has recognised Frank's problem and suggests he runs a discounted voucher for lunches. He does this face-to-face, meaning he has to dress appropriately, speak clearly and confidently and make eye contact. He has up-to-date sales figures on his laptop for a restaurant that ran a similar promotion with him a month ago; he shares these with Frank, and from them is able to make predictions about possible sales that Frank can expect. Frank is concerned, as he read about a cake maker who ran a deal on rival voucher site, Groupon; she could not cope with the demand and made huge losses. Farid is very empathetic about that situation and assures Frank that they can limit the number of vouchers sold to avoid this. Frank is still hesitant, so Farid shows him testimonials from satisfied restaurant owners and this gives Frank the confidence to go ahead.

In this situation it is Farid's interpersonal and intrapersonal skills and his product knowledge and data from similar campaigns that clinches the deal.

**Understand your customer profile**

**Discuss**

*In pairs, discuss the skills that would be needed for:*

1. *a travel agent to sell a holiday to Orlando for a family of four.*
2. *a telesales person cold calling someone to try and arrange a sales visit by their double glazing sales team.*

*Situation 2*

Jess has a Saturday job in a busy shoe shop in the Trafford Centre. Jess has to be able to target genuine customers who are likely to make a sale. This means she won't waste her time on **browsers** who are there to kill time and have no intention of making a purchase. This isn't easy.

The shoe shop has commissioned market research to understand better who its customers are, and from this it was able to create a **customer profile** showing typical age, gender, lifestyle and fashion preferences. This is shared with the sales staff to make their job easier, as Jess can use this information to help her to target. In this case understanding who the potential customers are ensures that Jess is effective at work; she doesn't ignore people who don't fit the profile but focuses most of her efforts on those who do.

## Reflective practice and Gibbs' Cycle of Reflection

One way that retailers encourage their sales people to improve is by training them to be **reflective** by using tools such as Gibbs' Cycle of Reflection.

### Key terms

***Reflective***: *where you look back on your experience and replay what happened, thinking about what you could do differently next time*

### Reflect

*How well are you working in this unit? Use Gibbs' Cycle of Reflection technique to look at how you could achieve a higher grade.*

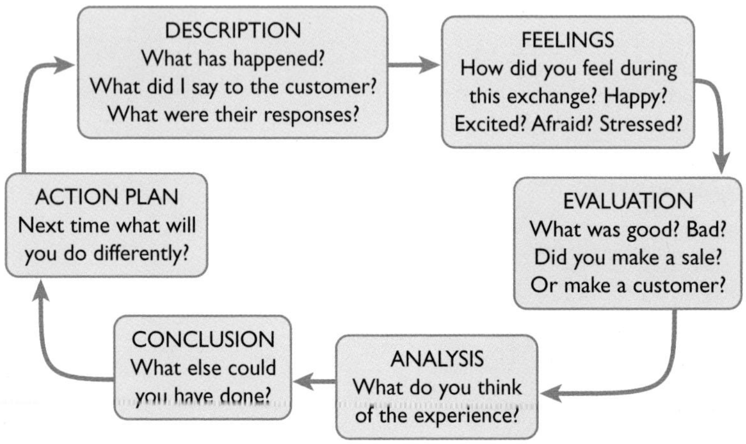

DESCRIPTION
What has happened?
What did I say to the customer?
What were their responses?

FEELINGS
How did you feel during this exchange? Happy? Excited? Afraid? Stressed?

EVALUATION
What was good? Bad?
Did you make a sale?
Or make a customer?

ANALYSIS
What do you think of the experience?

CONCLUSION
What else could you have done?

ACTION PLAN
Next time what will you do differently?

**Figure 5.2 Gibbs' Cycle of Reflection**

By using Gibbs' Cycle of Reflection the sales staff can look back on their experiences, make changes to the way they deal with customers and improve sales.

**Case study**

Dylan is a sales trainee at Polar Ford in Winwick. Yesterday he failed to make a sale with Mrs Stubbs, who wanted to upgrade her Citroen C3. Mrs Stubbs arrived in the showroom with her two-year-old daughter and her husband at 12.45 p.m., just as Dylan was about to go for lunch. No other members of staff were available, so Dylan had to miss lunch and deal with her. Her car is three years old and she wanted to replace it with something a bit sporty. She loves the Fiat 500 but needs a five-door car. Dylan went through the stock available and suggested a Suzuki Swift. Mr Stubbs thought it was a great car and the family test drove it. On their return, the couple's daughter was fed up and kept whining and running around, being a nuisance. There are crayons and colouring books available for children to use, but Dylan felt the sale was in the bag and didn't want to waste time because he was starving, so he ignored her. Mrs Stubbs liked the car but wanted it in red; there is an eight-week delay for a red one, but the black one she tested was available today. Mr Stubbs felt she should just buy it but Mrs Stubbs was unsure. Dylan could have offered a discount if she would take it in black and could have listed the benefits to her of buying it from him today (extended warranty, interest-free credit, free alloys and a free service), but he was too hungry. While she was dithering, her daughter was running about and fell over, cutting her head. The couple went off in a panic to hospital. They have not returned to buy the car.

1. Which sales technique did Dylan use?
2. What knowledge did Dylan demonstrate?
3. Use Gibbs' Reflective Cycle to reflect on the case study. What went wrong? (2A.P2)
4. How Dylan can make a sale in a similar situation next time? (2A.P2)

**Learn from your mistakes**

**Discuss**

*In groups, share experiences of poor service you have received while shopping. How could Gibbs' Cycle of Reflection have helped improve the situation?*

**Investigate**

*Create a fictitious situation like the one Dylan encountered in the case study. Swap situations with a partner and using Gibb's Cycle of Reflection analyse what went wrong and how the situation could be improved next time.*

# The process of personal selling and additional aspects of the role of sales staff

## 2A.P3 The importance of product knowledge

How important is product knowledge in making a sale? Product knowledge is a key skill to give customers the confidence to buy a product. If you are buying a laptop there are a number of requirements you will have, ranging from its size and weight, to its RAM, graphics, display and connectivity. Having this knowledge will also give the salesperson the confidence to be able to answer customers' queries and secure a sale.

## 2A.P3, 2A.M1 Additional aspects of the role

### Remaining competitive

Most people would consider that selling is the only role of sales staff. However, this is incorrect. Sales staff are key to a company remaining competitive. Retail is a very competitive business to be in and many retailers have failed in recent times. In 2010 and 2011 Faith Shoes, Adams Childrenswear, Habitat and Focus DIY all fell victim to the credit crunch. In 2012 the same fate befell SeaFrance and Portsmouth F.C. and yet many other retailers continued to thrive in the global recession.

Tesco managed to increase its profits from previous years and Sainsbury's saw its sales grow. How have they managed to do this in such hard times? The answer is that they have managed to encourage customers to buy, ensuring they remain competitive while others have failed.

Your assessment criteria:

- **2A.P3** Explain the knowledge and skills needed to sell a selected product
- **2A.M1** Compare the functions of the sales staff and the different sales skills used in two selected businesses
- **2A.D1** Assess the effectiveness of sales skills and knowledge used by sales staff in two selected businesses

### Key terms

***Competitive:*** *where a business is able to attract customers better than other companies in the same market*

***Customer care:*** *providing a service before, during and after customers have made a purchase*

***Feedback:*** *the information gathered from customers about a product/service – this can be positive or negative*

**Victims of the global recession**

## Customer requirements

Salespeople need to find out what customers require and then find a product that matches their requirements. Alun Davies is a sales supervisor for a car dealership. He believes that the key to good personal selling is finding out exactly what the customer needs (a family car, a run around) and their budget, and then finding the product that best suits both. This is known as establishing customer requirements and then matching them to the appropriate goods and services.

## Customer care and relationship building

Making that sale is only part of a sales staff role; they must also provide appropriate **customer care**. This involves providing after-sales service such as arranging repairs, replacements or refunds. They need to follow-up customers to ensure loyalty so that the customer comes back next time they want to make a purchase. One example of this is a travel agent sending a 'welcome home' card to a client, timed to arrive as they get back from their holiday. Good sales staff build relationships with their customers so they know their likes and dislikes and can make recommendations; many people are loyal because they like the salesperson. Customer care also involves handling queries and complaints from customers about products/services. Failure to deal with a complaint effectively will leave an angry customer who not only won't come back but, according to research, will also tell nine other people about his or her poor experience.

## Gathering feedback

Many stores now recognise that selling is a two-way process and that **feedback** from customers (positive and negative) is the key to improving sales. Negative feedback highlights problems with a product/service or identifies a training need among the sales force that firms can act upon. Positive feedback can be used to reward staff.

### Research

*Hamza wants to buy a laptop. He enjoys playing games, especially ones with 3D graphics, and wants to be able to access the internet. The laptop needs to be lightweight to carry round to his friend's house. He has saved up £400.*

*Research laptops – which one would you recommend to Hamza?*

## First point of contact

When you walk into a store the sales staff are usually the first point of contact. Customers complain if they are over-eager and pounce with a smile and a 'Can I help you', but complain if they are ignored – getting the balance right isn't easy. It is important to get this right so that customers feel comfortable in the environment and trust the salesperson – first impressions matter. Have you ever left a shop due to a poor first impression?

## Promoting the product

Very few products sell themselves and it is often the job of sales staff to promote the product. Next time you visit a department store, count how many people try to spray you with perfume. While some of us may find this annoying, the sales staff are performing an important role in helping to promote the product by allowing customers to smell a new fragrance. Promotion is about informing customers what the product is and what it does, and persuading them to make a purchase. It is also about reminding us of things we may have forgotten, like batteries or light bulbs for our new purchase.

The functions of sales staff are different in different selling situations, which may be dependent on the type of customer being served or the type of product being sold – consider selling a car or selling a sofa.

**Mystery shoppers will try to blend in**

### Key terms

***Mystery shopper:*** *someone employed by a retailer to act as a shopper; they visit stores to test different situations and the information they gather is used to improve customer care*

### Research

*What knowledge and skills would be needed to sell:*

1. *an iPad?*
2. *a pair of trainers?*

### Research

*Research two different selling situations: for example, face to face in a travel agent and in an electrical shop. How do the knowledge and skills differ between the staff? How are they similar? How do they help the business be competitive?*

## 2A.D1 How effective are sales staff?

One way of assessing how effective sales staff are at their jobs is to employ a **mystery shopper**. This allows the business to check on specific aspects of a sales role and to check how its staff behave in different situations. It can identify areas of training that are needed and the feedback is used to make improvements.

### Research

*In pairs, you are going to act as mystery shoppers.*

*You need to select two contrasting businesses (for example, a service business such as a café and a retailer such as a supermarket) and test aspects of the service provided there.*

*For example, you could ask about a specific product, ask for advice choosing between two products or ask about how to return an item.*

*Draw up a list of the different functions and skills that staff in these businesses need and compare how they differ.*

*You also need to assess how effective the staff are in the two businesses. What were they good at? What could they improve upon?*

*Which business has the best sales staff in your opinion? Why?*

### Case study

The increase in social networking has meant that Twitter and Facebook have now become an interface for customer feedback. In addition, retail guru Mary Portas has a section on her website dedicated to feedback about Britain's shops – most of this feedback is negative. American airline Delta uses customer service staff to manage its Twitter feed and complaints are resolved as quickly as possible. One passenger who tweeted that he had missed a flight got a response 40 minutes later that he was booked on the next available flight. Other passengers have had problems such as lost luggage and flight delays swiftly dealt with. Delta has recognised that to be effective and build customer loyalty it needs to listen to customers and act quickly on their complaints. However, surprisingly research has shown that 71 per cent of customer complaints posted on Twitter are ignored. Many companies, it would seem, are missing a trick.

1. Delta is an international airline based in America and it flies to countries all over the world. Why is it important that its sales staff know which countries Delta flies to?
2. A customer has called Delta and wants to make a round the world trip, starting from London and ending in Sydney, stopping over in a number of different countries on the way. What product knowledge will the salesperson need and what information do they need to know about the customer to help make the sale? (2A.P3)
3. What product knowledge and customer information does a retail assistant at Tesco need? How are they different from the skills of Delta staff? (2A.M1)
4. Explain why responding to negative feedback helps increase sales. (2A.D1)
5. Delta is identified in the case study as being outstanding in responding to customers on Twitter. Why do you think that other companies ignore Twitter comments? (2A.D1)

# Demonstrate personal selling skills

## 2A.P4 Personal selling and the law

Salespeople have to operate within the law and there are a number of laws that they must adhere to:

- Sale of Goods Act – this means that goods must be as described, be of satisfactory quality and fit for the purpose for which they are sold (this means free from defects, durable and safe): if I bought a pair of Wellingtons and they leaked I would be entitled to a refund; if a tent was described as waterproof and it wasn't I could have a refund or a replacement.
- Trade Descriptions Act – goods sold must be as described and companies have to support any statements they make about their products and show them to be 'demonstrably true'.
  - In the 80s Australian Peter Foster was prosecuted for selling black tea that he claimed would make people slim – it didn't; it was just tea.
  - In 2005 Marks & Spencer was fined £10 000 for making misleading claims about a collection of men's clothing. The high street retailer admitted five breaches of the Trade Descriptions Act by falsely suggesting items in its 'Italian' range were made in Italy. The goods were actually made in Egypt, India and Romania, the court heard. The store was fined £2000 for each offence and also ordered to pay the local authority's costs of £6500.

**Peter Foster, who made fraudulent claims about his 'slimming' tea, pursued by reporters**

Your assessment criteria:

**2A.P4** Explain the legislation that affects personal selling in a selected business

**2A.M2** Assess the importance of complying with the legal requirements for customer care and selling products in a selected business

**Key terms**

***APR (annual percentage rate):*** *the rate of interest you will be charged; for example, a store card with Oasis currently charges 28 per cent whereas a Barclaycard charges 17.9 per cent APR*

***Legislation:*** *laws made by parliament*

***Manufacturer's warranty:*** *the assurance given to a customer that when they buy something it will perform in a certain way; for example, a three-year warranty on a washing machine means that if it doesn't work properly in the first three years it will be repaired/replaced*

***Statutory rights:*** *these are legal rights determined by the law*

- Consumer Credit Act (1974) – companies offering credit must make the **APR (annual percentage rate)** clear to customers.
- The Weights and Measures Act (1985) – this law states that goods sold must be the weights and measurements they are labelled as – if I buy a kilo of apples then it should weigh 1kg!
- Food Hygiene Act (1990) – anyone selling food must adhere to food safety rules and members of staff need to be trained in food hygiene.

Door-to-door sales staff now have strict guidelines to follow after complaints by customers about aggressive and bullying sales techniques. Many of us have seen these aggressive practices on television, where door-to-door salespeople have lied about discounts, inflated the initial price to look as though they are offering a 'one day only' bargain and bullied people into signing up.

Organisations have to adhere to **legislation** so that they do not break the law. However, many companies have their own policies and procedures in addition to the laws that exist to protect their customers.

Many of us assume we have a legal right to a refund and in most cases we do. If you buy a faulty computer game it is not fit for purpose and you would be entitled to a refund. However if you decided you didn't want it after all and returned it unopened to the shop you would not legally be entitled to a refund. Many shops in this case offer an exchange or refund as an act of goodwill under their own policies – legally they don't have to.

Have you ever seen the phrase 'customers' **statutory rights** are not affected' on your receipt or in a store? This means that your rights to buy goods that are fit for purpose, not sold fraudulently or faulty still stand whatever the store's own policies are. These are still the shop's legal obligations so, if they tell you that because an item is in the sale it cannot be exchanged, your legal rights will override the store's policy if it should turn out to be faulty.

### Research

*Which retailers offer the best refund deal to consumers?*

*It is not a legal requirement to give a full refund if customers change their mind but many do. Which retailer allows the customer the most flexibility in terms of a refund and for the longest period?*

*Do retailers on the high street offer a better refund deal than e-tailers on the web? Explain your answer.*

Other policies that help secure sales include:

- Price matching: John Lewis claims it is 'Never knowingly undersold' and will match any other high street retailer. If Debenhams has a blue cross sale then John Lewis will also discount its products to price match Debenhams'.
- Discounting: car salespeople are often allowed to give discounts on the cars they sell to ensure the sale.
- Guarantees: many stores will extend the **manufacturer's warranty** to ensure that consumers make a purchase. John Lewis offers a free five-year warranty on all its electrical items.
- Aftersales service: providing customers with a Help desk like the one in the Apple store means that customers feel reassured if things go wrong. If a customer finds they can't work their Apple product they can see one of the store's experts for help and guidance.
- Customer care: a successful organisation will look after customers at all levels of the organisation. John Lewis has someone at the entrance of the store available to offer help and advice as shoppers enter. It provides staff in each department to advise. It has facilities such as baby changing rooms complete with free nappies. If an item is out of stock John Lewis will order it and then deliver it for free.
- Dealing with problems and complaints: Marks & Spencer has a dedicated customer service desk in its stores. Customers can return goods within 35 days of purchase, and if they have the receipt will get a full refund. Customers can also order items not in stock, arrange delivery and make complaints.

**Investigate**

*The case study opposite shows how these laws are as important for the business as they are for the customer.*

*Carry out research into other cases where it was the business that was protected rather than the consumer. What do your findings tell you?*

**Case study**

Marks & Spencer has a dedicated division at its offices in Chester that deals with complaints. You would be very surprised at how some customers complain. For example, if you bought a ready-cooked chicken and it didn't taste nice, would you return it to the store and complain or would you package it up and post it to Chester? Believe it or not, many customers do the latter. The complaints department at Chester receives so many food items in the post that each member of staff has their own plug-in air freshener by their desk! But every single complaint is followed up with suppliers and all customers receive a written response. All incoming telephone calls have to be answered within three rings and all e-mails have to be responded to within three days. By having these policies and practices, Marks & Spencer aims to keep customers loyal and sales high.

1. Marks & Spencer has to adhere to legislation regarding selling goods and services. Name three laws it has to follow.
2. Why does Marks & Spencer have its own policies regarding customer returns that are over and above the requirements of the law? (2A.P4)

**Research**

*Carry out web research into what happens when retailers break these laws. Why is complying with the law key to being a successful business?*

## 2A.M2 The importance of legal requirements

The law exists to protect consumers and businesses. In 2010 an 82-year-old woman died from salmonella poisoning at a wedding; 20 guests who were also taken ill took legal action against the caterer. An investigation suggested that the source of the poisoning was beansprouts, meaning that the caterer's supplier was the source. In this case the law protected the business owners as much as the consumers.

**Traders are prosecuted for breaking the law**

## 2B.P5 Make that sale!

'He who fails to plan, plans to fail' is a saying that is very true for sales staff, who need to plan carefully for when they sell.

- Step 1: Preparing for the sales process. Salespeople need to ensure they have appropriate product knowledge of every aspect of the product they are trying to sell. They need to be able to identify the features and benefits of a product and know its **unique selling point**, or **USP**. This information needs to be presented effectively to customers and they must also be able to answer any questions customers may have. This is key to making that sale and retailers provide product training about new ranges to ensure that staff are prepared and fully understand the functions of a product/service.
- Step 2: Maintaining an appropriate appearance. Salespeople need to ensure that they are dressed correctly, have clean and tidy hair and good personal hygiene. They need to ask themselves whether they present the correct **image**. Employees of Club Holidays selling trips to holidaymakers will have a different image from a Business Travel consultant selling business trips. This is why many retailers provide their staff with a uniform, to ensure that staff convey the correct image.

**Your assessment criteria:**

| | |
|---|---|
| **2B.P5** | Prepare for the sales process for making personal sales to two different types of customer |

### Key terms

***Closing technique:*** *a way of making the customer make the purchase and 'close the deal'*

***Image:*** *a salesperson's image is a representation of the business; how they dress, behave and communicate with customers must represent the business they work for*

***Unique selling point (USP):*** *the unique features of a product that make it different from its competitors*

**This would not create a good impression**

- Step 3: Preparing the sales area. Sales staff need to make sure the selling area, whether it's the shop floor, a display stand or a desk, is well presented and that any displays comply with health and safety laws and are not dangerous. Trying to book a family holiday would be off-putting if the travel agent's desk had dirty coffee cups and biscuit crumbs on it. Sales staff also need to be aware of personal space and not stand too close to customers, as this will make them feel uncomfortable.
- Step 4: Maintaining an appropriate attitude. Sales staff have to behave in the way that the business and, more importantly, their customers expect them to. Some considerations will include what language they will use (Club Holiday reps might use words like 'awesome' or 'cool', but SAGA Holiday reps would not) and their manners; they should act positively and be courteous and considerate to their customers.
- Step 5: Communicating with customers. Sales staff have to plan for spoken communication, which could be face-to-face or over the telephone. They will need to listen to what customers are saying and to answer questions and queries. Good sales staff also recognise the limits of their authority; no-one expects them to be able to solve everything and there will be times they will need their manager's help.
- Step 6: What types of communication will be used with customers? How will they be greeted? How will a salesperson introduce themselves to customers'? How will they gain the customer's attention and interest? ('Can I help you?') How will they identify what the customer needs? How can they meet the customer's needs? How will the information about the product be presented? – Is it a demonstration of the product showing how it works? Is it a discussion with the customer? Or is it a presentation?
- Step 7: Closing techniques. A **closing technique** is a way of getting the customer to agree to the sale. There are a number of closing techniques staff can employ, which are shown in the figure on page 162. The sales staff have to employ the correct technique for the customer; getting it wrong at this final stage can mean all their planning and hard work has been wasted. Role-play exercises as part of staff training are used to train staff in the correct closing technique, but as any experienced sales person will tell you, they can still get it wrong.

Getting this wrong can lose a sale.

Imagine that a customer is shopping with her daughter and is undecided about an 18th birthday gift and is concerned that the price is too high and they cannot afford it. The salesperson making a presumptive close puts the customer in an awkward position and they may feel forced to make a purchase rather than disappoint or embarrass their child.

### Research

*Research what these steps are for a member of staff working for a mobile phone store selling a mobile contract to a teenager.*

*What would they be if they were selling a PC to an elderly customer?*

**Figure 5.3 Possible closing techniques**

| Technique | Explanation |
|---|---|
| Presumptive close | This presumes the customer will buy: 'When shall we deliver to you?' The idea is to make it embarrassing for the customer to then say they don't want it! |
| Alternative close | This is like the presumptive close; the salesperson presumes the customer will buy the product and offers them alternatives: 'Would you like it delivered or are you taking it with you today?' |
| Concession close | This is used when a customer is hesitant and the salesperson will offer them something in return for buying today, for example a discount or a free gift. |
| Distraction close | This is where the salesperson waits for them to be interrupted, for example by their phone ringing; as they go to answer it, 'So you would like this now?' |
| Direct close | This is where the salesperson asks for the sale. |
| Silent close | This is like the game of who speaks first loses. The salesperson does not speak after they have finished their pitch; they just wait for the customer to buy. |

**Key terms**

***Presumptive:*** *this is making a presumption, accepting that something (i.e. a sale) is going to happen*

The salesperson will make the sale but will lose a customer. It left the customer feeling as if she had no choice and she will probably never go back! However, using the concession close in this case could not only have secured the sale but also made a customer. Offering a free gift or a warranty on the expensive gift would have left the mother feeling it was worth the additional expense and left the daughter feeling she had got a lot more than she expected. The customer would have felt that she had got a good deal and that she had negotiated the sale and not been forced into it.

Distraction sales work well but again don't often make a customer. Maria was recently in a jewellers looking for a gift for her sister. She was undecided and wanted to visit other stores, but her phone rang and because it was the babysitter Maria turned away to answer the call. By the time she had finished, the necklace was giftwrapped and the salesperson was waiting to be paid. Did it work? Yes it did, but Maria felt she had been 'had' and won't be going back!

**Case study**

In 2009 the Dalton family (comprising mum and dad Vicky and Ryan, their two-year-old daughter and Vicky's 70-year-old parents Carmel and Tommy) enjoyed a family holiday with Thomson Holidays to Menorca. They stayed full board in a 'family friendly' hotel that had a crèche, kids' club, children's disco and family entertainment each night. They had a fabulous time, enjoying the holiday so much that they returned to the same travel agent to rebook the following year. The travel agent in this case had a good understanding of the family's needs and wants from a holiday and had found a suitable trip for them. In doing so she had encouraged loyalty and repeat business.

In 2010 the family returned to the same hotel in Menorca only to find that the hotel had changed its package; it was no longer promoting itself as 'family friendly' and was now marketing itself as a 'couples' hotel. There was no longer a crèche, kids' club or children's disco. The family found themselves the only guests with a child who most other guests felt might spoil their tranquillity. The family complained to their rep and requested a move. No move happened and on their return they went to see their travel agent to complain. Had the agent been lazy and sold them a holiday without first checking if it still met their needs? No, she hadn't. It transpired that Thomson had failed to update its brochure and the travel agent with the changes. The agent acted on the Daltons' behalf, securing the family a £1 000 refund. The Daltons were delighted and have continued to book their holidays with her ever since.

1. What customer knowledge was needed to find the right holiday for the family?
2. Why did the travel agent persuade the Dalton family to rebook with her after their first holiday? (2B.P5)
3. How did the travel agent make sure the family remained loyal in the future? (2B.P5)

**Research**

*Select a product and a type of customer for a sale in a class role-play. It could be: a mobile phone to a teenager, a holiday for a family with young children, a 3D TV for a young couple. Research the product thoroughly. What is the purpose of the product? What are the benefits and features of the product? What is the product's USP? What questions are customers likely to ask you (and what are the answers)? Show how you have completed the seven steps in preparing for a sale.*

*For your assessment you will need to deal with two different types of customer, for example, a family with young children or someone with a disability.*

**Families have different holiday needs from couples**

# Demonstrate personal selling processes

## 2B.P6 Customer enquiries

When working in sales you will have to deal with different customer enquiries throughout your working day:

- Have you got any in stock?
- How much are they?
- Where are... ?

Good salespeople not only sell to customers but manage to **upsell**, generating more income for the business (and if they are on **sales commission**, for themselves) while retaining customer loyalty, and encourage repeat business by developing a relationship with customers that makes them keep coming back.

### Customer delivery note

Your assessment will require you to make sales and record the sales you make. This may involve arranging delivery by collecting customer information such as address, contact number and delivery time slot, accepting payments and inviting customers to join a loyalty scheme. This will have to be recorded in an organised way so that the other departments you may need to liaise with (such as accounts, delivery, customer collection) know how to find the information they need. You will have to overcome barriers to closing a sale by reinforcing the benefits, offering an **incentive** while demonstrating **empathy** with the customer and showing them respect.

In some cases customers will have a complaint; this will have to be dealt with according to the policy of the organisation you are working for and operating within the law.

Your assessment criteria:

| | |
|---|---|
| **2B.P6** | Demonstrate handling two different types of customer enquiry |
| **2B.M3** | Demonstrate handling a customer problem or complaint |
| **2B.D2** | Demonstrate the confident use of personal selling skills when making sales in at least three different personal sales situations |
| **2B.P7** | Demonstrate effective customer care skills in two personal sales situations |

### Key terms

***Empathy:*** *being able to share someone's feelings*

***Incentive:*** *a reward or a motivator to persuade people to buy, such as interest-free credit, discounts, free delivery, free warranty or a free gift*

***Sales commission:*** *a percentage of the sale paid to the salesperson – the more they sell the more they earn*

***Upsell:*** *where the salesperson persuades the customer to upgrade their purchase, this may be through selling add-ons (side orders in a restaurant) or a better product than they initially planned to buy*

## 2B.M3 Handling complaints

Complaints are a part of a salesperson's job; sometimes they are the salesperson's fault for failing to match the customer's needs to an appropriate product. This inevitably leads to disappointment as the product is not what was expected. In your assessment you need to demonstrate how you can handle a customer problem or complaint.

## 2B.D2 Being confident

To achieve a distinction you have to be confident in your demonstrations of at least three different selling skills. It is having this confidence in your ability to make sales, answer questions and overcome problems that makes the difference between a customer leaving the store satisfied or disappointed. Preparation is key to this.

## 2B.P7 Demonstrating your skills

For your assessment you will need to demonstrate your customer care skills in two personal sales situations. For example, you may have to demonstrate the use of a mobile telephone to an elderly person (like your Business teacher) who has limited technological understanding, and explain the types of contract to them.

You may be a member of the customer care team at a large supermarket who assists a parent in locating a lost child.

**Finding lost parents is all part of the job**

### Discuss

*In the previous topic you researched a product. With a partner acting as your customer, practise your skills. Your partner should raise objections and you will need to overcome these. You should eventually close the sale and then arrange delivery/collection/credit and complete the paperwork for another department.*

*After completing the exercise, discuss what went well, what didn't and what could be done differently next time. Consider all the aspects we have looked at in this unit.*

### Discuss

*In pairs, discuss an experience you have had where you were disappointed with a product or service. This could have been a meal in a restaurant, a holiday, a haircut or a mobile phone. How was the problem dealt with? How did you feel? How would you deal with this problem?*

### Research

*What preparation do you need to complete to ensure that you have this confidence?*

**Case study**

How many stories of amazing customer service have you heard? Probably not that many – when we have experienced excellent customer service most of us thank the member of staff then carry on with our lives. However, if we experience poor customer service we will tell friends, family, colleagues and now, with the internet, almost everyone!

GASP is a clothing store in Australia. When a bride-to-be was shopping there with her friends and asked if the dress she was trying on was available in a different size, she was told unhelpfully 'Just get it' and 'Is it the price you are worried about?' She didn't make a purchase and on leaving, the sales assistant shouted after her that she should go to Supre (a budget shop) and that he knew the group were a joke when they walked in. The bride contacted the store in an e-mail to complain and the reply was again rude, suggesting that not all customers were GASP customers. The e-mails went viral, with other customers joining in the debate and a Facebook campaign to boycott the store.

Google 'GASP Retail' and items on this story are at the top of the list.

1. The customer had asked a question: 'Is this available in another size?' How should the salesperson have responded?
2. You are a trainer for GASP. List the selling skills the staff should use.
3. GASP failed to treat the customer with respect in this case study. How? (2B.P6)
4. If you worked for GASP, how would you remedy this situation? (2B.P7)
5. The customer e-mailed the store to complain. In response to her complaint, compose an e-mail that you believe is how GASP should have responded. (2B.M2)
6. In pairs, act out this scenario, ensuring that this time the customer leaves the store having made a purchase. (2B.D2)
7. How effective were you in question 6? What went well? What didn't? How does your effectiveness compare to the case study? (2B.M3)
8. Write a report to GASP recommending how its sales staff can improve their personal selling skills and customer care. (2A.D3)
9. In light of the Facebook campaign, write a letter to all GASP customers to try and rescue the situation. (2A.D3)

## 2B.M4 How effective are you?

When looking at the effectiveness of your selling skills you need first to look at how successful you were. Did you make that sale?

What were your strengths? What aspects of the sales process did you do well in (for example, your preparation)? What aspects were you weak in? Did your product knowledge let you down? How effective was the close?

Your assessment criteria:

**2B.M4** Assess the effectiveness of the selling skills and processes used in two different situations

**2B.D3** Evaluate the preparation, skills and processes used in two personal sales situations and recommend improvements

## 2B.D3 Improvements

In order to assess your skills and decide upon improvements, it is necessary for you to revisit Gibbs' Cycle of Reflection:

- Step 1: Describe what you did.
- Step 2: How did you feel? (Confident? Uncomfortable? Why? Had you done enough preparation?)
- Step 3: What was good? What was bad?
- Step 4: What did you think of the experience?
- Step 5: What else could you have done?
- Step 6: What will you do differently next time? What are your actions? (Do you need to do more preparation?)

By working through this reflective cycle you should be able to assess your performance and formulate recommendations for the future.

**Discuss**

*In groups, discuss how well you performed in the two situations. What went well? What didn't? Write a report about your effectiveness.*

**Research**

*Use Gibbs' Cycle of Reflection to analyse your own performance. How effective were you? How would you improve in the future?*

**Success!**

# Assessment checklist

**To achieve level 1, my portfolio of evidence must show that I can:**

| Assessment criteria | Description | ✓ |
|---|---|---|
| 1A.1 | Identify two functions of sales staff in a selected business | ☐ |
| 1A.2 | Identify the sales skills used by sales staff in a selected business | ☐ |
| 1A.3 | Outline the importance of product knowledge when making sales | ☐ |
| 1A.4 | Outline legislation that affects personal selling in a selected business | ☐ |
| 1B.5 | Identify product knowledge required to make personal sales | ☐ |
| 1B.6 | Answer two routine customer enquiries in a personal sales situation | ☐ |
| 1B.7 | Use selling skills in two personal sales situations | ☐ |

**To achieve a pass grade, my portfolio of evidence must show that I can:**

| Assessment criteria | Description | ✓ |
|---|---|---|
| 2A.P1 | Describe, using examples, four functions of sales staff in a selected business | ☐ |
| 2A.P2 | Describe the sales skills used by sales staff in three different selling situations | ☐ |
| 2A.P3 | Explain the knowledge and skills needed to sell two selected products | ☐ |
| 2A.P4 | Explain the legislation that affects personal selling in a selected business | ☐ |
| 2B.P5 | Prepare for the sales process for making personal sales to two different types of customer | ☐ |
| 2B.P6 | Demonstrate handling two different types of customer enquiry | ☐ |
| 2B.P7 | Demonstrate effective customer care skills in two personal sales situations | ☐ |

**To achieve a merit grade, my portfolio of evidence must show that I can:**

| Assessment criteria | Description | ✓ |
|---|---|---|
| 2A.M1 | Compare the functions of the sales staff and the different sales skills used in two selected businesses | ☐ |
| 2A.M2 | Assess the importance of complying with the legal requirements for customer care and selling products in a selected business | ☐ |
| 2B.M3 | Demonstrate handling a customer problem or complaint | ☐ |
| 2B.M4 | Assess the effectiveness of the selling skills and processes used in two different situations | ☐ |

**To achieve a distinction grade, my portfolio of evidence must show that I can:**

| Assessment criteria | Description | ✓ |
|---|---|---|
| 2A.D1 | Assess the effectiveness of sales skills and knowledge used by sales staff in two selected businesses | ☐ |
| 2B.D2 | Demonstrate the confident use of personal selling skills when making sales in at least three different personal sales situations | ☐ |
| 2B.D3 | Evaluate the preparation, skills and processes used in two different personal sales situations and recommend improvements | ☐ |

# 6 | Introducing retail business

## Learning aim A: Explain the structure and organisation of retail business

- Topic A.1 The nature of retailing: what retailing is and how products get to us
- Topic A.2 Retail sub-sectors: the different areas of retailing
- Topic A.3 Retail business ownership: explores different ownership types
- Topic A.4 Retail outlets: describes different types of retail outlets including micro, SMEs and large outlets
- Topic A.5 Non-outlet retailing: where else we purchase goods from if we do not go into shops
- Topic A.6 Location: where retailers are based
- Topic A.7 Jobs in retail business: job options in the retail industry
- Topic A.8 Supporting retail businesses: many organisations and industries support the retail industry to ensure that goods find their way to the end customers
- Topic A.9 Aims and objectives: the aims and objectives of retail businesses
- Topic A.10 Measuring performance: how retailers measure their success using KPIs

## Learning aim B: Investigate the relationship between retail business and the external environment

- Topic B.1 Retail business in the UK: the issues that UK retailers face
- Topic B.2 Doing business with the rest of the world: the issues that UK retailers face when they want to go global

English
Apples and Pears
£1-50 Kg
40p
AGRIMUR, S.A.
TOMATES DE MAZARRON
PERFEKT
SARSONS

# The nature of retailing

## 2A.P1 The nature of retailing

Retailing consists of all the activities required to sell products to end customers. It is one of the UK's biggest industries and is the largest private sector employer, employing around one in 10 of the working population. Within retail, there are an estimated 295 000 businesses, selling a wide range of products, employing anything from one person to thousands of people.

Retailers provide a way for manufacturers to get their products to end customers. They do this by providing facilities (shops, supermarkets, websites) where customers can look at and buy the products. Retailers will often specialise in a particular type of product and will attract customers by offering a choice of products, expert advice on what product to buy and after-sales services, such as the opportunity for the customer to return a product if they are not satisfied.

Retailers operate by buying products in bulk from suppliers, such as manufacturers and wholesalers, and then selling the individual products to customers. The term retail originates from the French word 'to cut' (to cut down in size).

Retailers are the final stage in the **supply chain**, which is the term used to describe the process of getting products to the final customer. The supply chain starts as the goods are produced (turned from raw materials into products) by the **manufacturer**; these are then sold in bulk either directly to the retailer or, in some circumstances, to a **wholesaler** who will then sell to a retailer.

A wholesaler is a middle man who buys in large quantities from the manufacturer and then sells in smaller quantities to the retailer. Wholesalers are often useful to retailers, especially if they sell lots of different products, because using them cuts down on the number of manufacturers the retailers have to deal with directly and the amount of stock they have to hold for each product.

Your assessment criteria:

**2A.P1** Describe the sub-sector, channels, format size, ownership and location of two retail businesses operating in different sub-sectors

**Key terms**

***Manufacturer:*** *the organisation that makes the product from raw materials sold by the retailer*

***Retail channels:*** *the routes that retailers use to get products and services to market (the end customer)*

***Supply chain:*** *the chain of processes and activities involved in transforming raw materials to final products and selling the final product to the end customer – typically, this can involve several different organisations working together*

***Wholesaler:*** *the organisation that buys and sells products in bulk, and often acts as a middle man between manufacturers and retailers*

**Many high street retailers rely on wholesalers to supply them**

## Research

*Choose a retail company of your choice and research what retail channels it uses in order to get its products and services to market.*

## A typical retail supply chain

There are many different ways that retailers can get their products or services to us, the end customers. These are known as **retail channels**. In order to be successful, a retailer has to ensure that it is using the best channel to get its product to its customers. For example, the retail channel for music and films is increasingly moving from selling CDs and DVDs in shops to selling downloads from websites and mobile phone applications.

**Figure 6.1 The different retail channels that exist**

| Retail channel | What is it? |
|---|---|
| Shops/Stores | A building where products and services are sold. |
| Showrooms | A room used to display goods that can be bought, for example BMW cars. |
| E-tailing | Otherwise known as e-retailing, this is where products and services are sold via the internet. |
| Mobile technology | The collective term used for all cellular technology (such as smart phones like iPhones and PDAs) that can be used to purchase goods and services online. |
| Catalogues | Books that list all the products and services that an organisation sells, for example the Argos catalogue. |
| Home shopping | The selling of goods and services through a TV channel such as QVC. |
| Market stalls | A temporary store that is erected to show and sell goods to the public, usually in a street or other outside location, for example Camden Market. |

# Retail sub-sectors

## 2A.P1 Classifying retail sub-sectors

Retail businesses can be classified into **sub-sectors** depending on what products they sell. For example, BMW, Mercedes and Ford are all in the automotive sub-sector. Topshop, Marks & Spencer and Armani are in the clothing sub-sector.

**Figure 6.2 The different sub-sectors that exist within the retail industry and examples of businesses that operate within them**

| Retail sub-sector | Example of a retail business within the sub-sector |
|---|---|
| Automotive | BMW |
| Clothing | Topshop |
| Electrical goods | Currys/PCWorld |
| Food and grocery | Tesco |
| Footwear | Footlocker |
| DIY | B&Q |
| Homewares | IKEA |
| Music and video | HMV |
| Specialised stores | Jessops |
| Personal care | Boots |
| Second-hand goods | Oxfam |

The size of the retail sub-sectors vary. For example, the clothing retail sub-sector is estimated to be worth £29–31 billion whereas the DIY sector is estimated to be worth £8 billion. Each retail sub-sector has its own characteristics; however, they are all prone to change over time and none more so than in recent years.

The food and grocery retail sub-sector has changed over recent years as customers are becoming more health aware, and this has meant a growth in organic and farm-assured. However, the major players in this market (Asda, Tesco, Sainsburys, etc.) have ensured that they have met these new trends by offering their customers a wide range of organic and farm-assured products. There has also been a huge increase in the popularity of farmers' markets across the UK as customers demand more locally sourced produce.

Your assessment criteria:

**2A.P1** Describe the sub-sector, channels, format, size, ownership and location of two retail businesses operating in different sub-sectors

**Key term**

***Retail sub-sector:*** *a group of retail businesses that sell the same type of product*

The homewares sub-sector has seen rapid change in a relatively short space of time. Within seven years of opening stores in the UK, IKEA went from being a new player in the market to being the market leader. This suggests that this particular sub-sector is susceptible to new developments.

The music and video sub-sector has found it very hard to keep a presence in the high street. However, this has been uplifted by the new ways of purchasing music, with music downloads becoming increasingly popular.

The automotive sub-sector has seen a slow decline in the UK in recent years due to the increase and investment in automotive technology and design from countries such as India and China. This has meant that UK-based firms have been struggling to sell cars and components as they cannot compete with the ever improving technologies and cheap workforce of the East.

Retail analysts look at each retail sub-sector in order to comment on the changes that are occurring. For example, the personal care sub-sector has seen changes in the products that it offers to customers due to the fact that we are living longer. This has had implications for certain products such as hair colouring and health products.

**Retail businesses operate in different sub-sectors. HMV operates in the music and video sub-sector.**

**Discuss**

*In pairs, pick two different retail businesses that operate in different sub-sectors. Discuss what the differences are between the sub-sectors and explain why you have chosen these particular businesses.*

# Retail business ownership

## 2A.M1 Different ownership structures

Retail businesses differ greatly in their size and their ownership structure. Small retail businesses, such as the local florist, are run and operated by their owners. The manager of your local Pizza Hut may also own the business, but run this as a **franchise**. Other people own larger businesses. In some cases they may actually work there and control the way that it is run; others may never work there but instead own shares in the business. Some people, such as solicitors and accountants, jointly own and run a business and this is known as a **partnership**.

Your assessment criteria:

**2A.M1** Assess two different types of ownership of selected retail businesses

**Research**

*Choose five different retail businesses. Research their ownership and describe this type of ownership.*

**Figure 6.3 Six main ownership structures for retail businesses**

| Business ownership | Usual size of the business | Details of the type of ownership | Examples of this type of retail business |
|---|---|---|---|
| Sole trader | Small, owned by one person | The owner is responsible for all aspects of the business including the finances, selling, hiring and firing of staff. The owner keeps all of the profit after paying tax.<br>No limited liability. | Local florists, hairdressers, independent clothes shops |
| Partnership | Usually small<br>Owned by two or more people<br>Also used by some larger retailers | The partners are jointly responsible for the running of the business.<br>No limited liability. | John Lewis, the Cooperative |
| Limited companies | Small–large | Company name ends in 'ltd' so it is easy to identify.<br>The owners own a share of the business and are therefore the shareholders. If the company is successful, the shareholders will receive a financial reward, known as a dividend. If the company fails the owners' liability is limited to their original investment in the shares. | New Look |
| Public limited companies | Large | Company name ends in 'plc' so easy to identify.<br>A type of limited company where the shares are traded on the Stock Exchange and can be owned by members of the public. The directors are paid a salary to run the company and may or may not own shares. Selling shares to the public means that the business can raise large amounts of money to expand, although they are subject to more public scrutiny. | Next, Marks & Spencer |

| Franchises | Small–medium | A business is started using the name of a well-known organisation. The owner of the small business (the franchisee) pays the larger company (the franchisor) a share of the profit and a fee to use the name. In return, the franchisor lets the franchisee use its trade name, sell its products and helps the franchisee to run the business. | Body Shop, Benetton |
|---|---|---|---|
| Dealerships | Small–medium | This is a type of franchise where the business has the authority to sell or distribute a company's goods in a particular area. | Car dealerships such as Stratstone Jaguar |

**All retail businesses can be classified by their type of ownership. Next is a public limited company.**

### Key terms

***Dealership:*** *retail businesses that have the rights in certain locations to sell and market a particular product*

***Franchise:*** *an agreement with a larger established business where a smaller business pays to use the trade name, sell the products and receive guidance from the larger business*

***Limited company:*** *a form of business ownership where, if the business fails, the liability of the owners (the shareholders) is limited to their original investment*

***Partnership:*** *a form of business ownership where two or more people set up a business together and share the profits, with no limited liability if the business fails*

***Public limited company:*** *a type of limited company where the shares (and hence ownership) in the company are traded on the Stock Exchange and can be bought and sold by members of the public*

***Sole trader:*** *a form of business ownership where one person owns and is responsible for the running of the business, with no limited liability if the business fails*

## Assessing retail business ownership

In order to assess the different types of ownership of two retail businesses, it is necessary to look at their similarities and differences and then to comment on why they operate as that type of ownership. What advantages and disadvantages does it give to the companies?

### Discuss

*In groups, assess the different ownerships of two different retail businesses.*

# Retail outlets

## 2A.P1 Types of retail outlets

Across the UK, many different types and sizes of outlets are used by retailers to sell products to customers, from independent traders through to large department stores. These outlets are described in the figure below.

Your assessment criteria:

**2A.P1** Describe the sub-sector, channels, format, size, ownership and location of two retail businesses operating in different sub-sectors

**Figure 6.4 Summary of different outlets for retail businesses**

| Type of retail business | Size of retail business | What is it? | Example |
|---|---|---|---|
| Independent trader | Micro | A shop owned by an individual, which is not part of a larger retail business. | Local hairdresser/florist |
| Convenience store | Micro | A shop that usually has extended opening hours and is in a convenient location, stocking a range of household goods and foodstuffs. | Local 'corner shop' |
| Symbol group | SME | A type of franchise in the retail industry. Symbol groups do not own or run shops but supply small grocers and supermarkets, which then trade under a common name. | Spar, Londis, Costcutter |
| Specialist outlet | Micro/SME | Stores that sell a specialist range of products and normally offer a high level of service to their customers. | Mothercare, Evans Cycles |
| Market stall | Micro | A stand used by someone who is selling goods, usually in an outdoor setting. | Camden Market |
| Kiosk | Micro | Small open-fronted store selling drinks, magazines and newspapers. | WHSmith retail kiosk at train stations |
| Multiple/chain store | Large outlet | Where one company owns a series of shops all selling the same products – usually a fairly narrow range. They usually have more than 10 branches. | Matalan |
| Discount store | SME/Large outlet | Shops that offer a wide variety of products at low prices, usually goods that tend to be out of fashion or season. They concentrate on selling large quantities at discount prices. | Currys/PC World |
| Cooperative | SME/Large outlet | A partnership business that is owned and run by its members, who all have a share of the profits. | The Co-operative |

| Franchising/ concessions | SME/Large outlet | A type of franchise in the retail industry where smaller companies occupy space in the retail outlets of larger companies. Known as 'shops within shops'. Commonly found in department stores and service stations. | Selfridges, Debenhams and House of Fraser offer concessions/franchises to smaller retail businesses |
|---|---|---|---|
| Superstore | Large outlet | A shop that is larger than average (around 2500 square metres), which stocks a larger than average number of products and has its own car parking. | IKEA, Sainsbury's |
| Hypermarket | Large outlet | Large superstores (around 5500 square metres) that provide huge numbers of varied products, often exclusive to them, at a low price. | Tesco Extra |
| Department store | Large outlet | Very large stores offering a huge variety of goods. They sell lots of different categories of goods and lots of different brands at different prices. They also usually offer very good customer service. | Debenhams |

**Debenhams is an example of a UK department store**

### Key terms

***Micro businesses:*** *businesses that employ up to 10 people*

***SME:*** *Small and Medium Enterprises are companies that employ 10–250 employees*

### Design

*In pairs, design a handbook explaining the different types of retail outlets in the UK. Try to think of different examples of companies from those in the table.*

# Non-outlet retailing

## 2A.P4 What is non-outlet retailing?

Although we may think of retail businesses as having actual shops, this is not always the case: many retail businesses are now emerging that are classified as non-outlet retailing. This is often an attractive option to anyone starting their own retail business. This is because the costs are lower as they do not have to pay rent and bills relating to a physical shop.

## E-tailing

E-tailing has seen the largest growth in recent years due to the convenience that it offers to customers. Customers do not have to travel, queue or pay for parking and can buy at their leisure in their own homes. In addition, e-tailing offers customers a lot more choice than the high street/shopping centres, and goods are generally cheaper online as e-tailers do not have the same high costs as retailers with physical shops.

### Mail order

Mail order is when a catalogue is sent to customers advertising their products (for example Next Directory and La Redoute). The customer then browses the catalogue, chooses which products they would like to buy, and orders them through a website or by telephone. The goods are then delivered to the customer's house. Some retail businesses, such as Argos, have their whole catalogues available online and therefore customers can reserve products for store collection or pay for the goods to be delivered.

### Telephone selling

Telephone selling, otherwise known as telesales or tele-marketing, is when staff are trained to phone customers to try to sell their products or services. Nowadays, firms sometimes use recorded messages that are played to potential customers. However, telesales have come under scrutiny in recent years and can be seen as an annoyance by some customers.

### Vending machines

Vending machines are also a type of non-outlet retailing, as although the customer has to go to a physical machine to purchase goods, they do not involve any interaction with selling staff. They are useful as they

Your assessment criteria:

**2A.P4** Describe how two retail businesses operating in different sub-sectors make use of non-outlet retailing

**Key term**

***E-tailing:*** *The selling of goods and services via the internet*

provide customers with service 24 hours a day, seven days a week. For many years, vending machines have been selling cigarettes, drinks and confectionery; however, recently there has been a rise in other products sold, such as hot drinks, disposable toothbrushes and toothpaste, and even iPods!

## Shopping channels

Channels such as QVC enable customers to buy products that are advertised on their channel. This usually involves the customer having to ring the company to purchase the goods. However, in more recent years, shopping via the television has become more interactive. Digital television allows customers to order goods and services through their remote control, for example films via Sky Movies Box Office.

**Vending machines have come a long way from simply selling drinks and confectionery!**

### Research

*In pairs, research two different businesses that use non-outlet retailing. Describe how they use it and what advantages it offers to the businesses.*

### Case study

There has been a recent trend in the USA for Apple products, including iPods and iPads, to be sold in vending machines. Most commonly found in American airports, the iPod vending machine offers customers a quick solution to purchasing their Apple products.

Since first opening IKEA has enjoyed an explosive global success, most notably by way of its website. It enables global expansion but still keeps its Swedish identity. By localising the website (selecting which country you are in on the homepage), it offers customers multilingual websites, which has seen its global expansion increase.

1. Identify the types of non-outlet retailing used by IKEA and Apple. (2A.P4)
2. Identify the retail sub-sectors in which IKEA and Apple operate. (2A.P4)
3. Describe how IKEA and Apple make use of non-outlet retailing. (2A.P4)

# Location

## 2A.P1 Location

Retail outlets can be found in a variety of different locations, from city and town centres, out-of-town retail parks/shopping centres to local village centres. The performance of retail outlets in different locations can vary dramatically, so choosing the best location is often critical to a retailer's success.

In recent years, the increase in the number of **out-of-town shopping centres** and retail parks has seen customers attracted away from the traditional high street and towards these new shopping complexes. This, combined with the rise of online and other non-outlet retailing, has led to many retail outlets in our city and town centres closing down due to a declining number of customers.

Out-of-town shopping centres and retail parks are huge regional shopping complexes built in out-of-town sites around the UK. They are attractive to customers as they offer free parking, a range of facilities (such as baby changing, crèches, weatherproof buildings and toilets), a diverse range of shops and leisure activities (including cinemas, restaurants and bowling alleys) and good transport links, as they are generally close to main road networks.

In contrast, many city and town centre locations cannot offer the breadth of choice of most shopping centres due to space restrictions, and they can be difficult to get to, with high parking charges and traffic congestion as particular problems. As a result, a growing trend is for fewer and fewer people to visit town and city centres primarily to shop.

**Shops situated in the Manchester Arndale shopping centre are classified as having a primary location**

Your assessment criteria:

**2A.P1** Describe the sub-sector, channels, format, size, ownership and location of two retail businesses operating in different sub-sectors

**Key term**

***Out-of-town shopping centres:*** *shopping complexes located outside of city or town centres*

**Figure 6.5 The largest out-of-town shopping centres in the UK by size**

| Rank | Shopping centre | Region | Size (metres squared) |
|---|---|---|---|
| 1 | Metro Centre | North East | 194 000 |
| 2 | Trafford Centre | North East | 177 000 |
| 3 | Westfield Stratford City | Greater London | 175 000 |
| 4 | Bluewater | South East | 155 700 |
| 5 | Westfield Merry Hill | West Midlands | 154 002 |
| 6 | Westfield Shepherd's Bush | Greater London | 149 461 |
| 7 | Manchester Arndale | North West | 148 600 |
| 8 | Meadowhall | Yorkshire and the Humber | 139 355 |
| 10 | Eldon Square | North East | 132 879 |

(Source: http://www.enotes.com/topic/List_of_the_largest_shopping_centres_in_the_United_Kingdom_by_size)

Retail outlets can be classified as being in a primary or a secondary location. A shop in the high street could be described as having a primary location, whereas a shop within walking distance of the high street and which is not easy to find would have a secondary location. A shop in an out-of-town shopping location, providing that it was alive and prosperous, would be categorised as being in a primary location.

**Design**

*Design a map of your local area describing the primary and secondary retail locations. Explain why they are primary and secondary. You can also include any out-of-town sites on your map.*

**Case study**

Grace and Glory is a clothes retailer in a small village in the outskirts of Wolverhampton (www.grace-and-glory.co.uk). Grace started the shop on her own a few years ago and sells fashionable and contemporary women's clothing. Grace works on her own; she does not employ anybody else.

Cineworld is a chain of successful cinemas operating in the UK and Ireland. It started life as a private company in 2006 and quickly grew and registered as a PLC in 2007. It operates 79 cinemas of which 76 are multiplex and have five or more screens.

1. Identify the sub-sector, channels, format, size and location of Grace and Glory.
2. Describe the sub-sectors, channels, formats, size, ownership and locations of Grace and Glory and Cineworld. (2A.P1)
3. Assess the two different types of ownership of Cineworld and Grace and Glory. (2A.M1)

# Jobs in retail business

## 2A.P2 Different jobs in retail

There are many different retail jobs available with well-defined career progression routes to ensure that you are constantly being challenged.

### Retail assistant, sales floor assistant and shop assistant

Generally, the first job people have in retail is as a **retail, sales floor or shop assistant**. These jobs have different names, but they carry out the same tasks and lead to similar career progression routes. These assistants look after customers when they are shopping. They answer customers' questions and give advice and information on products. They keep the shop looking well presented and restock the shelves as necessary. They generally earn the minimum wage for their age.

### Cashier

A **cashier** operates the tills correctly, has a good knowledge of the products and understands the refund/returns policies of the business. Cashiers generally earn the minimum wage for their age.

### Sales floor supervisor

The next step on the career ladder may be a **sales floor supervisor**.

A sales floor supervisor helps the shop assistants/cashiers whenever they have any questions or problems and ensures that they carry out their duties. Sales floor supervisors have to understand the objectives and policies of the business, so experience is essential.

### Customer service assistant

A **customer service assistant** is often the first point of contact for the customer when they have a question. This can be face-to-face or via a telephone in a call centre. They have to advise customers on products, services and policies. They handle complaints, provide information for customers and process exchanges and refunds.

There are usually plenty of opportunities for progression as a customer service assistant once you have gained enough experience, to team leader and on to accounts manager or customer services manager.

Your assessment criteria:

**2A.P2** Describe the functions of two job roles in store operations and their progression routes

**Key terms**

***Cashier:*** *an individual responsible for recording sales in the cash register/till*

***Customer service assistant:*** *an individual responsible for dealing with customer enquiries*

***Receptionist:*** *an individual responsible for answering phone calls, putting customers through to the right person, organising meetings, and greeting customers when they enter the company's offices*

***Retail/sales floor/shop assistant:*** *an individual responsible for dealing with customers on the shop floor and ensuring the shop floor remains presentable*

***Sales floor supervisor:*** *supervises the retail/sales floor/shop assistants and cashiers*

***Stock room assistant:*** *an individual responsible for processing deliveries from suppliers*

***Stock room supervisor:*** *supervises the stock room assistants*

Working in customer service provides you with transferable skills, such as communication skills and experience of working with people. Therefore, the job offers a whole range of opportunities for career progression, not directly linked to the customer service sector.

## Receptionist

A **receptionist** offers administrative support for employees, for example by answering telephone calls, taking messages and arranging meetings, and is often the first person customers speak to when they contact a business. A professional manner is very important. In some retail businesses, the receptionist can also perform the customer services assistant role.

With experience, receptionists often progress to the role of administrator or secretary, supervisor or customer services manager.

## Stock room assistant and supervisor

**Stock room assistants** work behind the scenes in the retail industry and are vital in the smooth running of any shop. They process deliveries quickly and ensure stock is labelled, sized and stored correctly.

There is usually the chance of promotion to **stock room supervisor**. Supervisors coordinate the activities of the stock room assistants, organise and supervise the movement of stock in and out of the stockroom, ensure that all deliveries are processed and ensure productivity targets are met.

**Retail assistants offer help and guidance to customers**

**Case study**

Jodie works as a sales assistant. She enjoys looking after and advising the customers, answering their questions and giving them information on the products. When she leaves school she hopes to go full time as she enjoys the work. She is, however, very ambitious and hopes to progress quickly and become a sales floor supervisor.

Gary is a stock room assistant. He works full time but has only been in the job a couple of weeks. He has been working closely with his line manager, the stock room supervisor, to process the deliveries and label all the stock.

1. Outline the functions of the sales assistant and the stock room assistant.
2. Describe the functions of the sales assistant and stock room assistant and their progression routes. (2A.P2)

**Describe**

*Choose two retail in-store job roles that appeal to you. Find relevant job vacancies that are available and describe what the jobs entail and what career progression they offer.*

# Supporting retail businesses

## 2A.P3 Support networks in retail

Retail businesses rely on the support of different kinds of businesses. The most common supporting businesses are discussed below.

### Manufacturers

Manufacturers supply retailers with the products that they sell. A retailer needs to have a good relationship with its network of suppliers so that it can:

- obtain products at the best price
- ensure the products are tailored to customers' needs
- ensure its brand quality requirements are met.

Each manufacturer will also have its own network of suppliers that provide the raw materials used to make the products. For example, a clothes manufacturer would need to buy cotton, fabric and buttons from different suppliers in order to make trousers. Some retailers, such as the Cooperative, like to have control of their supplier network and hence manufacture a lot of their own products; others are content to use a few well-established suppliers.

### Distribution

Retail businesses use distribution companies to deliver products from their suppliers to the retail outlets and then to the end customer. Sometimes they also use them to store their products in warehouses.

In some cases, retail companies need to have distribution networks that can differentiate them from their competitors by providing excellent customer service. For example, they might offer delivery and installation of large items such as dishwashers. In other cases, they need a distribution network that can provide a competitive advantage in terms of cost and timing. For example, John Lewis offers free delivery on orders over £30.

### Technology

Computers are used to record transactions in the tills and cash registers, to track and manage the levels of stock in retail outlets, and maybe even to help track employee and customer information, or control security systems such as CCTV cameras.

Retail businesses use computer companies to design, implement and maintain their computer systems. This is important as a poor stock

Your assessment criteria:

**2A.P3** Explain, using examples, the role of two businesses that support retail businesses

**Key term**

***Shop fitter:*** *individual who plans shop layouts and installs any fittings*

management system may result in retailers running out of stock or having the wrong kind of products in stock.

## Finance

The finance function provides a retail business with the information it needs to survive – what products are selling most, how much profit is made for each product, how much cash is in the bank to buy stock, and so on.

Often, smaller retail businesses employ specialist financial services firms to help them analyse their information and to prepare their financial accounts. Bigger businesses often have their own finance department.

## Shop fitting

If retail businesses want to attract their target customers, their retail outlets must look good. The design of a store can vary depending on the products being sold. Retailers employ designers and **shop fitters** to design, plan and install the shop layout.

Shop fitters typically employ tradespeople such as electricians and carpenters to ensure that the shop is fitted out according to the designs, and also that equipment is in good working order.

## Marketing

An effective marketing campaign informs customers why they should buy from the retailer, and can help a retail business to attract more customers and therefore increase its sales and profits.

Retail businesses often use specialist advertising and marketing agencies to create TV adverts, billboard campaigns and special promotions. For example, T-Mobile's very successful 'T-Mobile Dance' advert, created by Saatchi and Saatchi, resulted in a 16 per cent increase in customers entering T-Mobile shops and a 20 per cent increase in online sales. (http://www.koozai.com/blog/video-marketing/why-t-mobile-are-succeeding-in-viral-video/)

### Research

*In groups, take two retail businesses of your choice; research businesses that have supported these two companies. Share your findings with your class.*

### Case study

In order to open her new clothing shop, Grace and Glory, Grace needed other businesses to help her. She had never opened or run a shop in the past. She rented a small outlet and then hired a shop fitter to fit out the shop to her design. In order to get her shop known in the local area, she then hired a local marketing firm to create posters, a local radio advert and her website.

1. Identify two types of businesses that have supported Grace and Glory.
2. Explain the role of these two support businesses. (2A.P3)

**Advertising agency Saatchi and Saatchi supported the retail business T-Mobile**

# Aims and objectives

## 2A.P5 Aims and objectives in business

Aims and objectives are used by businesses to help them achieve their long-term ambitions. Aims are the long-term targets that need to be met for a business to achieve its ambition, and objectives are the specific steps needed in order to achieve each aim. Having clearly stated aims and objectives is critical to the success of the business as it ensures that employees are all working together towards the same goal.

In retail businesses, the aims and objectives of each business can be very different. A new retail business may have the aim to simply survive, yet a more established business may aim to be a market leader.

Your assessment criteria:

**2A.P5** Describe the aims and objectives of two retail businesses operating in different sub-sectors

**Figure 6.6 The most common aims and objectives for retail businesses**

| Aims | Description |
|---|---|
| Provision of service | Some businesses focus on providing the best service possible. This could be because they want to increase sales by charging customers more, or want existing customers to keep coming back. Retail businesses whose aim is to provide excellent service have to consider how they will provide customer satisfaction, how they will monitor the quality of the services they provide and how much this will cost the business. |
| Breaking even | In order for a business to survive, it first of all needs to break even. This is the point where a business becomes self-sufficient, so the money it makes from sales is equal to the money it spends. This may be an aim when a business is just starting out. |
| Profit maximisation | Profit maximisation means that the business is focused on making as much money as possible. This is done through increasing sales or prices and/or by cutting costs (for example, using cheaper suppliers). |
| Growth | Growth means increasing sales. This can be done by increasing market share, expanding into new areas/locations, attracting new customers or developing new products and services. |
| Business ethics | Customers are now more aware of where the products they buy come from, and the impact this can have on human rights and the environment. Therefore, it is important that retail businesses consider the ethical impact of their aims and objectives to avoid any reputational damage, especially in relation to their suppliers. (Do they use Fair Trade suppliers?) For example, Primark has received negative publicity in the past as some of their overseas suppliers have been accused of exploiting their workforce. |

A key reason why retail businesses set aims and objectives is to motivate their staff. However, for this to really work, an objective must be SMART: Specific, Measurable, Achievable, Realistic and Time-related.

- Specific – specific objectives are clearly understood. For example, if a business wants to increase sales, the employees will need to know which products they will be focusing on to sell more of, which types of customers they want to sell to and where these customers are likely to be.

- Measurable – objectives need to be measurable so that the business knows when they have achieved them. Usually this means having a number or a percentage in the objective, for example, to increase sales by 15 per cent in the next year.
- Achievable – the staff must believe that they can achieve the objectives. If they are too hard to achieve the staff may become demotivated.
- Realistic – although objectives are there in order to motivate the staff to work harder, if they are too ambitious, they will have the opposite effect!
- Time-related – objectives also need to be achieved in a certain amount of time. There is little point having an objective that the business may achieve in 50 years' time! Therefore the objective needs to outline when it is to be achieved, for example by next year or in 2015.

### Key terms

***Aim:*** *where a business wants to be in the future*

***Market share:*** *one firm's sales as a percentage of total sales in the whole market*

***Objective:*** *a specific target that must be achieved in order to reach the long-term aims*

### Describe

*In groups, choose two different retail businesses that operate in different sub-sectors. Research their aims and objectives and describe how they are SMART.*

**Tesco's aim is stated as 'Continually increasing value for customers to earn their lifetime loyalty'**

## 2A.M2 How and why retail businesses use aims and objectives

Aims and objectives are used by retail businesses to help them achieve their long-term ambitions. Aims are the long-term achievements and objectives are the specific steps needed to achieve each aim. Essentially, they provide the targets to help staff know that they are heading in the right direction.

Retail businesses use aims and objectives for many reasons. These include:

- to help them develop plans to achieve their ambitions
- to provide targets to check their progress against their aims
- to provide a focus and motivation for employees and to give them instructions on what to do.
- to help with team building and communication so that everybody is working together towards specific goals.

Often, retail businesses cannot achieve their aims and objectives on their own. They therefore form partnerships with other businesses to get where they want to be. For example, Tesco and Sainsbury's run voucher schemes in partnership with local schools so that they can fulfil their aim of being seen to make a positive difference in the local community.

To explain how and why two different retail businesses use aims and objectives, do the following:

- Choose two different retailers from different sub-sectors, such as Marks & Spencer (clothing sub-sector) and BMW (automotive sub-sector).
- Research their aims and objectives by looking at the company's corporate site (often called investor relations). Links to these sites can often be found at the bottom of the retail websites. Marks & Spencer's can be found by going onto www.marksandspencer.com, scrolling to the bottom of the page and clicking on 'The company'. BMW's can be found by going onto www.bmw.com and clicking on 'the BMW group'.
- You will need to investigate the history of the retailers, their markets, and the products and services they sell, as well as the changes in fashions and tastes that have affected the businesses.
- You will then need to explain how the businesses have used their aims and objectives in order to be successful.

Your assessment criteria:

**2A.M2** Explain how and why two retail businesses operating in different sub-sectors use aims and objectives

**Discuss**

*In pairs, discuss how different retail businesses use aims and objectives in order to be successful.*

**Marks & Spencer and BMW are retailers operating in different sub-sectors and they will therefore have different aims and objectives**

**Case study**

Cineworld PLC is a chain of cinemas operating in the UK and Ireland. Its aim is to create welcoming, contemporary cinemas that movie-goers will want to come back to time and time again. It boasts that it offers customers a consistent, first-class experience across all of its cinemas. Its primary objective is to advance its position as one of the leading cinema groups in the UK – in terms of sites, screens and admissions. In order to achieve this, Cineworld will develop and improve its offer to customers, expand by opening new cinemas and look to expand into complementary markets and use technology to improve its customers' experiences.

Grace and Glory, on the other hand, is a small retailer selling women's contemporary clothing. Its primary aim is to survive in the first few years of trading and break even in year three. This should be achieved through offering its customers good quality, designer clothes and operating a loyalty scheme where customers have a card to be stamped every time they spend over £75. Once the card has been stamped six times, the customer receives 10 per cent off all future purchases.

1. Outline one aim and one objective of Cineworld.
2. Identify the sub-sectors in which Cineworld and Grace and Glory operate. (2A.P5)
3. Describe the aims and objectives of Cineworld and Grace and Glory. (2A.P5)
4. Explain how and why Cineworld and Grace and Glory use aims and objectives. (2A.M2)

**Research**

*Research the aims and objective of three retail businesses in your local area.*

# Measuring performance

## 2A.D1 KPIs

Key Performance Indicators (**KPIs**) help retail businesses to monitor their progress against their aims and objectives. KPIs can vary for each type of business, but they must always be measurable, specific and related to the key drivers of success. For example, the Business Department at your school/college may use the number of merits and distinction certificates achieved by their students as their KPI. The different types of KPIs used by retail businesses are set out below.

### Like-for-like sales

Like-for-like (LFL) sales is when a retail business compares the sales in one period from a group of stores to sales in a different time period (the same month in the previous year, or to a previous month or quarter). It is useful because it strips out the impact of stores that have been opened or closed during the year, which often distorts movements in sales between different periods.

For example, HMV reported in January 2012 that like-for-like sales fell 8.1 per cent in the five weeks to the end of December and that total sales were down 16.6 per cent compared with the previous year. This was particularly concerning as HMV had closed several stores during the period (as evidenced by the decline in total sales being higher than the like-for-like sales) but sales in the stores that remained open (the like-for-like sales) had still declined. You would have expected like-for-like sales to have at least remained the same given there were fewer stores for customers to visit (http://www.bbc.co.uk/news/business-16465170).

### Sales per square metre

Sales per square metre is calculated by dividing the sales for a given period (perhaps one month or one year) by the total floor area of a shop. It is used by retail businesses to compare the performance of different sized stores, to measure how different layouts and products affect sales and to benchmark the performance of new stores.

Waitrose, for example, achieved a sales per square feet increase of 2.5 per cent in 2011 compared with 2010. It puts this increase down to 'investing in value, innovative top-tier product ranges, new space and new store formats'. (http://www.johnlewispartnership.co.uk/content/dam/cws/pdfs/financials/annual%20reports/John_Lewis_Partnership_annual_report_and_accounts_2011.pdf)

Your assessment criteria:

**2A.D1** Evaluate how two retail businesses operating in different sub-sectors measure their performance, with reference to Key Performance Indicators (KPIs)

**Key term**

***KPI:*** *Key Performance Indicator – measurable statistics that businesses use to track their progress towards meeting their aims and objectives*

## Sales per employee

Sales per employee is calculated by dividing the sales for a given period (perhaps one month or one year) by the number of employees. It is used to compare the performance of employees between different stores, and helps a retail business calculate the number of employees it will need if it wants to increase sales or open up new stores.

## Average revenue per customer

Average revenue per customer is calculated by dividing the revenue of a particular product by the number of customers. It helps a retail business to determine which products or services produce the most revenue per customer and therefore need to be invested in, and which can be discontinued. Deutsche Telekom (owners of T-Mobile), reported in November 2011 that their average revenue per customer was $14, a 13 per cent increase from 2010. It put this down to increasing the call rates paid by customers (http://www.pcmag.com/article2/0,2817,2396230,00.asp).

## Profit

Profit is the most important KPI for retail businesses as it shows how much money they are making from their sales after deducting all their costs. It is used by retail businesses to monitor the movement in selling prices and the cost of raw materials and overheads. For example, in November 2011, Primark reported that its operating profit had fallen 8 per cent to £309m compared with the previous year (http://www.bbc.co.uk/news/business-15632934) and blamed this on the rising cost of cotton, which they did not pass on to customers in the form of higher prices. This year, however, Primark expects annual sales in its 242 stores to rise 15 per cent, while like-for-like sales are expected to rise 3 per cent for the full year, ahead of the first half's 2 per cent rise.

### Research

*Research two very different retail businesses that use sales and profit Key Performance Indicators. Evaluate how and why they are used.*

**T-Mobile's average revenue per customer is $14**

# Key Performance Indicators (KPIs)

## 2A.D1 Stock, returns and being green

### Customer service levels

Customer service level KPIs measure how well a customer has been treated by a retail business. This could include monitoring how long it takes for customer orders to be processed or how long it takes to respond to customer queries. These KPIs can then be compared to earlier periods to see if customer service levels are improving or getting worse.

### Customer satisfaction

Retail businesses measure customer satisfaction by using customer surveys (asking them what they think!) and **mystery shoppers**. A mystery shopper is an individual who pretends to be a real customer and reports on the customer service they have received in a particular shop. The retail business can then compare the results from mystery shoppers' reports with the previous year to see if customer satisfaction has improved. Customer surveys consist of questionnaires, feedback forms and rating websites. Retail businesses can use the information gathered from these surveys to improve their services levels. For example, Amazon.com was one of the first online retailers to use customer surveys in 1995 and now 44 per cent of online retailers use them too!

### Stock turnover

**Stock turnover** measures the time taken for a retail business to sell the products it keeps in stock. It is calculated by dividing the number of products in stock by the average number of products sold each day.

Retail businesses normally compare the number of days' stock they have left for each product to an earlier time period. This helps retail businesses to understand how much of a particular product they need to keep in stock to satisfy customer demand, to identify products for which stock levels are too high and to identify slow-moving stock items that need to be discontinued.

Amazon.com uses the stock turnover KPI to ensure it only stores high turnover goods (their most popular goods) in its warehouses so that it can fulfil orders very quickly at a low cost. As a result, an item only spends an average of 33 days on Amazon's shelves compared with 70 days on Best Buy's shelves.

Your assessment criteria:

**2A.D1** Evaluate how two retail businesses operating in different sub-sectors measure their performance, with reference to Key Performance Indicators (KPIs)

**Key terms**

***Mystery shoppers:*** *individuals who pretend to be real customers and report on the customer service they have received in a particular shop*

***Stock turnover:*** *how long it takes a business to sell the products it keeps in stock*

## Returns and complaints

Retail businesses measure the number of products returned by customers so that they can identify potential problems with the products that they sell. This is especially important if a product has recently been released, as correcting a problem quickly may be the difference between success and failure.

They also track the number and type of complaints so that they can identify areas where their customer service can be improved. The number of complaints can be compared to different time periods to see if customer service levels are improving or getting worse.

## Environmental performance targets

Retail businesses use environmental performance targets to show how environmentally friendly they are compared to their competitors. The most common KPI used is the level of $CO_2$ emissions (carbon footprint). Sainsbury's aim is 'by 2020 we'll have reduced our... carbon emissions by 30 per cent... compared with 2005' (http://www.j-sainsbury.co.uk/responsibility/20x20/operational-carbon/).

**Sainsbury's uses environmental performance indicators to measure how green it is**

**Case study**

In order to monitor its performance, McDonalds makes use of mystery shoppers. It employs a company to send undercover customers into its restaurants and drive-thrus to comment on the performance of the staff and quality of the food and service. This is then used to monitor customer satisfaction and inform McDonalds about how it can improve its product and service offering. Following feedback from the mystery shoppers, it is commonplace for staff training opportunities to be identified.

John Lewis use sales per square metre in order to monitor performance across its stores. It has seen an increase in market share despite the recession and has performed better than all of its competitors in recent years. Using this KPI has meant that it has identified which stores are most successful and profitable and has invested in more luxury products, new spaces and new formats in these stores.

Evaluate how McDonalds and John Lewis measure their performance using KPIs. (2A.D1)

 **Research**

*Research and evaluate two different retail businesses that use returns and complaints and environmental performance indicators to measure their performance.*

## 2B.P6 UK retail developments

When a retail business decides to develop it is not an easy procedure. Lots of planning and preparation is involved. The management of the business has to look at all the advantages and disadvantages. First, the issues of choosing the site have to be examined:

### Environmental issues

When a retail business opens in a new location, there are significant issues that have to be addressed that affect the environment. These can include increased traffic in the area, due to more customers visiting in cars and more lorries making deliveries. If a food retailer is opening new premises, there are also issues surrounding food miles. If the new retailer is located far from where the food it is selling is produced, the food miles are greater and this has an environmental impact on global warming. Also, the carbon footprint of the area will increase due to this increased traffic and the increase in electricity being used to run the new premises. Retail businesses have been affected by issues surrounding increased waste due to the increased amount of packaging they are using for their products. In 2010, Sainsbury's was taken to court over its use of excessive packaging in its beef roasting joint.

When new retail site developments are being considered, the business has to consider the environmental impact of the new location. Green site developments are favoured in order to minimise building on new land. Retail sites that are built by renovating existing buildings are better for the environment than those that are built on brand-new sites, for example the Corn Exchange in Leeds. Demolishing old buildings uses energy and therefore costs a lot of money. Developing a retail site on infill land is also a green option. This is because it is not using agricultural land and does not destroy the landscape. In addition, building in urban areas means that usually all the electricity, sewage and gas services are already in place and therefore land does not need to be dug up to insert them.

### Ethical issues

These are issues concerning businesses 'doing the right thing'. For example, many retailers are now stocking more Fair Trade goods in an attempt to ensure that producers get a fair price for their goods.

Your assessment criteria:

**2B.P6** Explain, using examples, two issues of concern and two benefits that can arise from retail developments in the UK

**Key terms**

***Carbon footprint:*** *the amount of carbon dioxide a person or organisation uses*

***Corporate responsibility:*** *the programmes that businesses develop in order to be ethically, socially and environmentally aware*

***Food miles:*** *the distance that food has to travel to get from the producer to the consumer*

***Genetically modified foods:*** *foods that have had their DNA artificially enhanced to produce more favourable properties*

***Infill land:*** *vacant land that is in an urban area (near a town)*

Retailers such as Sainsbury's made a pledge that their own-brand coffee, bananas, sugar, tea and hot chocolate would be Fair Trade. Ethical issues relating to child labour should also be considered. Retailers such as Primark have come under criticism in the past for using child labour to produce their goods. The majority of retailers have now established **corporate responsibility** programmes as part of their business strategy. This impacts the local, national and even global communities. Argos, for example, has started a colleague volunteering programme where staff volunteer in their local communities. Attracting retailers with good corporate responsibility programmes to a location is vital to the development of an area.

Food retailers get their products from a variety of sources and these can present ethical issues in themselves. The use of **genetically modified foods**, processed foods and products that are tested on animals all raise concerns. With the growing importance of healthy living, retailers are more focused on providing customers with organic and healthy foods and this can have an impact on local and national communities. As the demand for more organic foods grows, so more specialist food retailers are entering the retail industry. For example, As Nature Intended is an organic food specialist with stores around London.

**The use of child labour is an ethical issue**

**The Corn Exchange in Leeds is now a shopping centre in the old refurbished Corn Exchange building**

**Research**

*In groups, research some retail developments that have had to consider ethical or environmental issues. Explain what the issues are and how they overcame them.*

## 2B.P6 Community concerns and politics

Since the 1980s, the majority of retail developments in the UK have been out-of-town developments, as the land is cheaper outside towns and there is more of it! This has also meant that there are lots of workers who live nearby and they are usually close to good transport networks. However, the growth of these kinds of developments has led to many problems:

- The nearby town centres have been affected as the larger shops move away from the high street and into out-of-town developments. This leaves many shops empty in the high street, which then attracts vandalism. This in turn means that fewer people visit the town centres, bringing further economic decline.
- Large out-of-town developments usually attract large retailers as small retailers cannot afford rents. This has a negative impact on the smaller retailers, who can only afford to have shops in secondary locations.
- Traffic congestion is increased as the out-of-town development attracts more customers who have to drive to the site due to its location. This can have a negative impact on the local **infrastructure** and transport systems.
- Often when new out-of-town retail developments are constructed, new road developments also take place to facilitate the increased traffic. This means a lot of disruption for local road users and can be environmentally unfriendly and very costly.

Developments in the retail industry have also brought about some political issues. Nowadays, competition among the large supermarkets is huge and each is trying to outdo the others by selling goods at lower prices. In the run-up to Christmas 2011, Asda were offering customers a £5 voucher when they spent over £40 in store, coupled with their price guarantee scheme (www.asda.com/priceguarantee). While this is good news for consumers, it is bad news for employees and producers. The lower the prices, the less profit the supermarkets make, which means they pay their producers less and could mean that staff are made redundant as the supermarkets struggle to pay their wages.

**Many high streets are in decline because of out-of-town developments**

### Key terms

***Advertising Standards Authority:*** *independent regulator of advertising in the UK that ensures that the adverts we see are legal, decent, honest and truthful*

***Competition Commission:*** *independent regulator that investigates mergers and takeovers to ensure that all markets stay competitive and are not dominated by a few large companies*

***Infrastructure:*** *the assets that a place has in order for people to work and live there, such as roads, water supply, sewage, electrical grids, gas pipes and telecommunications*

***Mergers and takeovers:*** *when two firms join together to make one firm*

Where out-of-town developments were once favoured by politicians, the current government is becoming more concerned with the state of our high streets, which are declining quickly. The government is developing new laws for the regeneration of town centres, which include making it more difficult for out-of-town developments to get planning permission, more assistance for small businesses to set up and relaxing the laws on parking in town centres. In addition, politicians are also concerned with how powerful supermarkets are becoming given that there are only five major supermarkets in the UK (Tesco, Asda, Sainsbury's, Morrisons and Waitrose) and they have the power to dictate the prices that consumers have to pay and the prices that they pay their suppliers, because they are such a big customer. The **Competition Commission** investigates any abuses of power by retailers and has blocked many **mergers and takeovers** taking place between the supermarkets.

Retailers are also affected by developments in political issues relating to their advertising campaigns. The **Advertising Standards Authority** (ASA) is an independent regulator that ensures that adverts are legal, decent, honest and truthful. It receives complaints from the public or from other businesses about certain adverts and then investigates the claims. For example, in December 2011 the ASA received complaints about one of Argos's promotions online and in its catalogue, stating that a toy was half its original price. However, it had underestimated the demand for the toy and had run out of stock, so customers had not been able to purchase the toy in the time period. The ASA judged that Argos had not conducted its promotion efficiently.

**The Competition Commission regulates mergers and takeovers (www.competition-commission.org.uk)**

## 2B.P6 Economic and social benefits

When new retail businesses develop in an area, there can be enormous benefits.

One of the major economic benefits of a retail development is providing employment. New retailers need new staff and this usually means they will employ people from the local area. It can also attract other businesses to the same area and therefore more employment. New customers are then attracted to the new shops and the area becomes prosperous. When a town becomes prosperous it usually means that people want to live there, new people move into the area and property prices increase. This is how areas regenerate.

**Research**

*Research any mergers or takeovers that are taking place at the moment in the retail sector. You can do this by looking on the Competition Commission website (www.competition-commission.org.uk).*

**Research**

*Research why certain supermarket takeovers were blocked by the Competition Commission.*

Retailers play a large role in supporting local charities and other voluntary bodies (such as **Rotary** and **Soroptimist International**), so when new shops open up in an area, charities and voluntary bodies benefit from increased donations and sponsorship.

There are also social benefits to a retail development opening in an area, including new meeting places for customers, cafés and restaurants in larger stores, and better facilities for the public. It also means that new community spaces are created, such as parks and libraries. When the Merry Hill Centre opened in Dudley, West Midlands on an old steelworks site, cafés, restaurants and a food court opened, along with open meeting spaces and conference facilities, play areas, parking facilities, a cinema and flats.

## Benefits to the local community

In order to achieve 2B.M3, you will need to choose a retail development in the UK that has been completed, proposed or is in development and then assess the benefits to different people in the local community, including local private businesses, charities, members of the public, staff and children. You will need to assess how the retail development has regenerated the area or could do so in the future.

## Evaluation

To achieve 2B.D2, you will need to evaluate the impact of the retail development that you have chosen in 2B.P6 and 2B.M3. In order to do this you will need to explain the relative merits and downsides of the environmental issues, ethical issues and political issues on the local community. This needs to be specific to the retail development that you have chosen.

**Retail developments such as Merry Hill can provide social and economic benefits for the area**

### Key terms

***Rotary:*** *a voluntary body made up of professionals and business leaders who raise money for local charities and promote goodwill*

***Soroptimist International:*** *a volunteer service organisation for business and professional women who work to improve the lives of women and girls in local communities and throughout the world*

### Discuss

*In groups, discuss the economic, social and customer benefits of a retail development in your local area.*

### Research

*Research some retail developments that are either being constructed at the moment or are proposed to be built in your local area. What benefits to you think they will bring to the local community?*

**Retail developments can have a positive and negative impact on the environment**

*Select a retail development in the UK. Discuss how this retail development will affect the environment (both positively and negatively) and then what affect this will have on the local community.*

**Case study**

The Merry Hill Centre in Dudley is a large out-of-town shopping centre. It offers customers a large number of shops, cafés, children's play equipment, free parking and facilities for people with disabilities. It employs thousands of people and has meant that the local road network has improved due to the large numbers of visitors. On the other hand, the town centre of Dudley has seen a sharp decline in visitor numbers, causing many shops to close or relocate to the Merry Hill Centre. There have also been traffic congestion problems around the town centre as customers queue to use the free parking facilities at Merry Hill.

The Leeds Corn Exchange is a Grade 1 listed building in Leeds city centre. After the closure of the Corn Exchange, its condition deteriorated and the building and its surroundings became one of Leeds' most run-down areas. The site has been regenerated and is now a modern shopping centre, home to a number of independent retail enterprises and designers, and has hosted exhibitions and events. However, as it has been refurbished several times, many retailers have been forced out due to its popularity and accompanying rent increases.

Not everybody was in favour of the regeneration at the time as the Corn Exchange has a lot of local history attached to it and the conversion into a shopping centre was not welcomed by some.

1. Outline and explain two issues of concern and two benefits that have arisen from the retail developments in Leeds and Merry Hill. (2B.P6)
2. Assess the benefits for the local community of the Merry Hill Centre. (2B.M3)
3. Evaluate the impact of the Merry Hill Centre on the local community. (2B.D2)

# Doing business with the rest of the world

## 2B.P7 Doing business in other countries

When a retailer decides to start exporting its goods, there are several factors that need to be considered.

### Choice of country

There are different economic pressures in different countries. The growth opportunities that exist in the UK may not exist in the new country. Retailers also need to know the types of customers that their products will attract, which may be different from their UK customers; they are also faced with different laws in new countries. All countries have different health and safety, employment and tax laws, and without looking into these a new retailer could break the law. When retailers set up to sell in other countries, they must satisfy all the legal requirements that exist in that country, which can add extra costs to the business.

### Product configuration

The products that retailers sell may have to be adapted so that they can be used. For example, electrical goods that have a UK plug attachment will not work in other countries as they have different sockets. There are also problems due to different customs, style preferences, lifestyles and tastes in other countries. For example, it is illegal to sell food products that contain animal fats in some Islamic countries. There are also some problems in translation between languages. In Italy, Schweppes tonic water was translated incorrectly as Schweppes toilet water!

### Entry route

Retailers also have to overcome other issues when deciding to sell their goods in other countries. They may decide to enter the foreign market on their own (self-entry) and this means using their own UK brand in the other country; for example, Tesco used its own name when it entered the French market. Although this means a brand becomes known on an international level, it also means that retailers have to do a lot of marketing when they first enter a country in order to get their name known and trusted, and this costs the company a lot of money. The other option that retailers have, when setting up abroad, is through acquisition – by buying a brand that is already well known in the country. This is the way that Wal-mart entered the UK market – they bought the already established brand, Asda. Another option is through franchising. In this way, the retailer can sell franchises in the new country and people from

**Your assessment criteria:**

**2B.P7** Explain, using examples, three issues facing UK retail businesses when they decide to operate in another country

**Key term**

***Exporting:*** *selling goods from the UK in other countries*

that country can buy the franchises and run them. This is less risky for the retailer as the franchisees take on the risk of the business failing. Joint ventures also offer retailers a less risky option for breaking into a new market. This is where they go into partnership (perhaps 50–50) with an already established retailer in the new country. In this way, they use the expertise of the foreign retailer and split the profits with them.

When doing business with the rest of the world, a lot of research has to take place in order to get the correct locations and property for the retail outlets, and this can be difficult without knowledge of the country.

**Research**

*Choose three of the different issues that would affect a retailer that chooses to do business abroad. Research three separate examples where these have happened to a real retailer.*

**Case study**

Harry Bunn owns and runs a chain of fish and chip shops in the north west of England. He wants to expand his business into France as he believes that the French could eventually learn to love this English delicacy! However, after doing lots of research he has found several issues with his plan:

- Big cultural differences between the English and the French, which need to be considered. The French like large restaurants as they like to sit down for long periods at mealtimes.
- Harry was hoping to buy all of his equipment from the UK as he knows the best suppliers and then use these in his French restaurant. However, there are problems as the plug sockets are different and health and safety laws governing the testing of electrical goods are also different.
- Harry's hopes of self-entry into France are going to be very costly. Not only has he got to overcome the differences in French food tastes, but he will also have to invest in some very heavy marketing to get himself known.

1. Identify and explain three issues that Harry must consider when deciding to operate in France. (2B.P7)
2. List the advantages and disadvantages for Harry operating in France.
3. Do you think Harry is wise choosing to operate in France? Justify your answer.

**In Italy, Schweppes tonic water was translated incorrectly as Schweppes toilet water!**

# Assessment checklist

**To achieve level 1, my portfolio of evidence must show that I can:**

| Assessment criteria | Description | ✓ |
|---|---|---|
| 1A.1 | Identify the sub-sector, channels, format, size and location of a retail business | ☐ |
| 1A.2 | Outline the functions of two job roles in store operations | ☐ |
| 1A.3 | Identify two types of business that support retail businesses | ☐ |
| 1A.4 | Identify types of non-outlet retailing used by two retail businesses | ☐ |
| 1A.5 | Outline one aim and one objective of a retail business | ☐ |
| 1B.6 | Outline two issues of concern and two benefits that can arise from two retail developments in the UK | ☐ |
| 1B.7 | Identify three issues UK businesses must consider when they decide to operate in another country | ☐ |

**To achieve a pass grade, my portfolio of evidence must show that I can:**

| Assessment criteria | Description | ✓ |
|---|---|---|
| 2A.P1 | Describe the sub-sector, channels, format, size, ownership and location of two retail businesses operating in different sub-sectors | ☐ |
| 2A.P2 | Describe the functions of two job roles in store operations and their progression routes | ☐ |
| 2A.P3 | Explain, using examples, the role of two businesses that support retail businesses | ☐ |
| 2A.P4 | Describe how two retail businesses operating in different sub-sectors make use of non-outlet retailing | ☐ |
| 2A.P5 | Describe the aims and objectives of two retail businesses operating in different sub-sectors | ☐ |
| 2B.P6 | Explain, using examples, two issues of concern and two benefits that can arise from retail developments in the UK | ☐ |
| 2B.P7 | Explain, using examples, three issues facing UK retail businesses when they decide to operate in another country | ☐ |

**To achieve a merit grade, my portfolio of evidence must show that I can:**

| Assessment criteria | Description | ✓ |
|---|---|---|
| 2A.M1 | Assess two different types of retail ownership of selected retail businesses | ☐ |
| 2A.M2 | Explain how and why two retail businesses operating in different sub-sectors use aims and objectives | ☐ |
| 2B.M3 | Assess the benefits for the local community of a retail development in the UK | ☐ |

**To achieve a distinction grade, my portfolio of evidence must show that I can:**

| Assessment criteria | Description | ✓ |
|---|---|---|
| 2A.D1 | Evaluate how two retail businesses operating in different sub-sectors measure their performance, with reference to Key Performance Indicators (KPIs) | ☐ |
| 2B.D2 | Evaluate the impact of a retail development in the UK on the local community | ☐ |

# 7 Providing business support

## Learning aim A: Understand the purpose of providing business support

- Topic A.1 Types of support: including visitors, travel and diaries among others
- Topic A.2 The purpose of providing business support: why business support is so important

## Learning aim B: Use office equipment safely for different purposes

- Topic B.1 Office equipment: what office equipment is necessary for business support?
- Topic B.2 Working safely: how do organisations ensure that you are safe at work?

## Learning aim C: Organise and provide support for meetings

- Topic C.1 Types of meeting: what different kinds of meeting are there?
- Topic C.2 Organising meetings: how do you prepare and organise a meeting?
- Topic C.3 Supporting meetings: how do you ensure a meeting runs smoothly?
- Topic C.4 Follow-up activities: what do you need to do after a meeting?

# Types of support

## 2A.P1 Types of business support

All businesses, large or small, have to ensure that their administrative tasks are carried out effectively. The tasks are usually undertaken by specific administrative staff to free up the time of specialist employees. Here are some common support tasks.

Your assessment criteria:

2A.P1 Explain the purpose of different types of business support in two contrasting businesses

**Figure 7.1 Common support tasks**

| Types of support | What does it mean? |
|---|---|
| Dealing with visitors | Greeting visitors, signing them in and out, contacting the necessary people within the organisation and directing visitors to the right place. |
| Organising travel and accommodation | Helping with the organising of events, for example conferences; making reservations for hotels and booking flights and train tickets. |
| Managing diaries | Arranging appointments and meetings and entering them into diaries. |
| Using telephone systems to make, receive and transfer calls | Making telephone calls to other businesses (external), answering the telephone, using the internal telephone system and transferring calls internally to the appropriate person |
| Organising and supporting meetings | Preparing meeting documents, for example agendas, minutes; booking rooms and catering. |
| Producing documents | Writing letters, emails, presentations and reports; using spreadsheets. |
| Processing and storing information, manually and electronically | Researching, finding, recording and storing information, for example expenses, in manual and electronic systems. |

### Purpose of business support

Administrative staff are very highly regarded in organisations and this is reflected in their pay – in London they can earn up to £30 000 per year. There are many reasons why they are so important:

- They ensure consistency – all office procedures have to be carried out in the same way, whoever does the job. If this does not happen, mistakes may be made and the quality of customer service affected.
- They enable time to be used effectively – managing your time in any job is extremely important. Tasks have to be prioritised, otherwise important jobs that need to be done urgently may be done too late. Administrative staff help their team plan their time effectively so that they do not miss deadlines or fail to meet their objectives.

**Administrative staff are usually the first point of contact for external customers**

- They provide support to managers – managers rely on their secretarial staff to carry out administrative tasks on time and in the agreed way. This frees up the managers' time to concentrate on their own responsibilities.
- They provide support to staff teams, other administrative staff and whole departments – this enables all team members and departments to concentrate on doing their own job. The administrative staff ensure that all the admin jobs, including organising meetings and ensuring effective communication between staff, are carried out consistently. This job can be very demanding. Time management skills are essential and secretaries need each other's support to deal with the pressure.
- They provide effective service to internal and external customers – internal customers rely on support staff to help them carry out their job more efficiently. If admin staff do not do their jobs properly – for example, answering the phone in a rude and abrupt manner – external customers will feel dissatisfied. Admin staff are often the first point of contact for external customers, and as we all know, first impressions count.

### Key terms

***External customers:*** *the people who buy or use the products and/or services of an organisation*

***Internal customers:*** *everybody who is directly connected to a business, for example employees, shareholders and other stakeholders*

**Case study**

Jo and Nick are both admin assistants working in very different businesses. Jo works in a beauty salon answering the phone, booking appointments, dealing with customers who visit the shop and organising her colleagues' schedules. She has to manage the diary for the beauticians' appointments and stores the details of their treatments on the database.

Nick, on the other hand, works for a large transport company. His role is to ensure that all the staff, including the managers, drivers and health and safety officers, are in constant and effective communication with each other. He deals with suppliers who visit the depot and organises the travel arrangements for the managers when they visit different sites and warehouses. He operates the firm's switchboard and organises all of the meetings between the different departments.

1. Identify the types of business support that Jo provides in the beauty salon. (2A.P1)
2. Identify the types of business support that Nick provides for the transport company.
3. Explain the purpose of the different types of support they both offer to their organisations. Consider consistency, time efficiency, supporting managers and staff and providing a service. (2A.P1)

### Discuss

*You have all been in contact with admin staff, either at a place of work, an organisation you have visited or at school or college. Discuss the different activities they have undertaken for you. For each activity, explain how this has helped you as a customer and the organisation. Explain what would happen if they did not perform any of these activities.*

# Office equipment

## 2B.P2 Office equipment

Administrative staff cannot work effectively without the correct equipment. Different office equipment is used to meet different business requirements:

- Computers are used for a variety of business requirements including producing word-processed documents and spreadsheets, using the internet to make bookings for travel and accommodation, using electronic diary systems and sending emails.
- Printers are used to make hard (paper) copies of documents that are produced on computers. Some documents may need to be signed and therefore need to be printed out, for example letters and contracts.
- Photocopiers are used to make copies of documents. They can make the documents smaller or larger and can make documents double-sided. They also have stapling functions so that documents can be bound together automatically.

**Many businesses have multifunctional machines that photocopy, scan, fax and print**

Your assessment criteria:

**2B.P2** Describe the use of office equipment to meet different business requirements

**2B.M1** Explain the appropriate uses of office equipment types, features and functions to suit different business purposes

**2B.D1** Analyse the contribution that office equipment makes to the provision of business support

- Telephone systems are used to communicate quickly with people inside and outside the organisation. They are used when a record of the conversation does not need to be kept. In larger organisations, a member of the administrative team will operate a **switchboard** where all calls into the organisation are directed. The switchboard operator then transfers the calls to the right people.
- Office chairs – it is important for everyone to have a comfortable chair that gives the right support to avoid back and neck injuries.

### Key term

***Switchboard:*** *a type of office equipment that allows telephone calls to be transferred from one person to another*

### Discuss

*Discuss the office equipment that you have used at school or college or at a workplace. Explain what you used it for and how it helped you to do your job.*

**The switchboard operator is often the first point of contact when a customer contacts an organisation**

## 2B.M1 The appropriate use of office equipment

In order for office equipment to be used appropriately, staff must be trained to use it. This will avoid injuries to members of staff and equipment malfunctions. Experienced members of staff demonstrate the equipment and instruction manuals are provided. Instructions may also be displayed next to the equipment as a reminder to users. The features, functions and purpose of different types of office equipment are summarised in Figure 7.2.

### Research

*Research other business uses for the office equipment described in Figure 7.2. Explain how these different uses could help to support the business.*

**Figure 7.2 The features, functions and purpose of different types of office equipment**

| Type of office equipment | Features and functions | Purpose |
|---|---|---|
| Computers | Keyboard, Excel, Word, storage capacity, Explorer and Outlook | Typing and word-processing documents such as letters and contracts; producing spreadsheets showing expenses; storing files such as copies of contracts; browsing the internet for research purposes (for example to make bookings for travel and accommodation requirements for staff); sending and receiving emails. Printing also enables electronic copies of documents to be made into hard copies, for example a letter for posting. |
| Printers | Scan, copy and print | Apart from printing, printers can scan and copy documents. Scanning means making electronic copies of paper (hard) documents. It can be useful in order to keep electronic copies of documents, for example signed contracts. Copying hard documents enables lots of people to have a copy of a document, for example the agendas for a meeting. |
| Photocopier | Makes copies of hard documents; staples documents together and resizes documents | Hard (paper) copies of documents are made so that more than one person can view the document. Automatic stapling enables large documents of several pages long to be bound together efficiently (for example contracts). Resizing enables a hard copy of a document to be enlarged or reduced in size; for example, health and safety notices may have to be enlarged to be displayed in the office. |
| Telephone systems | Answer, make and transfer calls | Answering the telephone, for example a supplier confirming an order; making calls, for example calling customers to tell them their order is in stock; transferring calls, for example transferring a customer with a complaint to the customer services department. |
| Office chairs | Adjusting the height; manoeuvring the chair to a different location; supporting the lower back and neck | Staff need to be able to be comfortable, especially if they are sitting down for long periods of time. The chair may need to be adjusted to suit the height of the person; it may need to be closer to the desk; and it may have lumbar and neck support to prevent back and neck injuries. |

## 2B.D1 The contribution of office equipment

In order to achieve a distinction, you will need to analyse the contribution that the office equipment listed in Figure 7.2 makes to supporting the activities of a business. You will need to provide two examples, one from your own experience of supporting a meeting and one from your research into the way an office works. You will need to examine what difference the office equipment made to the job that had to be carried out, what could have been done more efficiently, and analyse what other office equipment could have been used.

**Computers are used to create documents and spreadsheets, browse the internet and write and receive emails**

### Research

*Research the use of office equipment at your school or college. Analyse the contribution that it makes to the way the school or college is run. Consider the staff, teachers and students.*

**Case study**

You work as an administrative assistant for Right Move. Your boss is away and has left the following 'to do' list on your desk.

- Research travel arrangements for my trip to Rome
- Print off contracts for the sale of the flat on Wellham Road
- Organise meeting with buyers of 52 New Road
- Enlarge health and safety leaflet to a poster size to be put around office

1. Identify and describe the different office equipment that is needed to carry out your 'to do' list. (2B.P2)
2. Explain the appropriate use of the office equipment that you have identified and describe and explain their features and functions in order to carry out the 'to do' list effectively. (2B.M1)
3. Analyse the contribution that the office equipment that you have explained makes to carrying out the 'to do' list effectively. (2B.D1)

### Discuss

*Talk to your family members and friends about the contribution that office equipment makes in their places of work.*

# Working safely

## 2B.P3 Safety at work

Staff need to know how to use office equipment safely so that they do not injure themselves and comply with health and safety regulations. Health and safety legislation ensures businesses provide equipment and facilities that protect employees. In an office the key risk to employees is injuries connected with working at computers for long periods of time. Measures taken to protect against this include:

- Correct seating and posture – chairs with adjustable height and backrest are recommended. Thighs and lower arms should be in a roughly horizontal position when working at a keyboard. The seating should enable the employee to maintain a good posture when working at a computer.
- Positioning and distance of monitor – all new monitors should be fitted with tilt and swivel stands. Sufficient room is needed for the monitor to be moved backwards and forwards. Ideally, the top of the screen should be at eye level.
- Mouse and keyboard: the distance between user, keyboard and mouse must be sufficient to allow the user's lower arm to be placed horizontally on the desk in a comfortable position.

Health and safety at work is an important duty of care for managers. In reality, many expect staff to take care of this area themselves, as it has no direct bearing on the success of the business. However, poor health and safety standards can cause low morale among staff and bad publicity for the business.

Most businesses take the health and safety of staff very seriously. These businesses ensure that employees have access to the correct equipment, are trained to use it and are knowledgeable about health and safety standards. They ensure that their staff receive regular training on health and safety issues.

### Safe lifting

When lifting equipment, such as a heavy box of documents, it is important to take steps to avoid injuring your back. The heavier the item to be lifted, the more important it is to ensure that you use the correct technique. The best technique is to bend the knees and use your legs to do the lifting, rather than your back.

Your assessment criteria:

**2B.P3** Demonstrate using office equipment safely, in accordance with health and safety legislation

**2B.M2** Demonstrate understanding of the application of safe lifting techniques when using office equipment

**Key term**

***Posture:*** *the position of a person's body when sitting or standing*

**It is important to maintain good posture when working at a computer**

Lifting equipment correctly can avoid injuries to your back

## Design

*Design a manual for the office staff in your school or college, showing them on how to sit correctly at a computer desk. Research and explain the hazards of not sitting properly.*

**Case study**

You work as an administrative assistant for Right Move. Your boss is away and has left the following 'to do' list on your desk:

Research travel arrangements for my trip to Rome.

Organise meeting with some potential buyers.

Enlarge health and safety leaflet to a poster size to be put around office.

Use the correct office equipment to:

1. Research flights to Rome from London travelling next Monday and returning the following Wednesday.
2. Organise a meeting with some potential buyers, creating an agenda, carrying out the meeting and completing minutes.
3. Create a health and safety leaflet entitled 'Safe Lifting' and then enlarge the leaflet to poster size. (2B.P3)

You will also need to move a box of documents or books using the safe lifting techniques that you have described in the leaflet. (2B.M2)

## Discuss

*Discuss and then demonstrate how you lift equipment safely. Place a textbook on the floor, stand close to it with your feet shoulder-width apart. Tighten your stomach muscles, keep your back straight, bend your knees and squat to the floor. Grasp the textbook with both hands, keep it close to your body and use your leg muscles to stand up, lifting the textbook off the floor. Keep your back straight throughout.*

# Types of meeting

## 2C.P4 Different types of meeting

Meetings are a regular and integral part of any organisation. They improve communication, generate ideas and solve problems. Meetings must be organised and communicated to the necessary people in order to be effective.

Some meetings can be large and involve a lot of people, for example whole departments. Others may involve only a couple of people. Meetings are either internal or external. Internal meetings will involve only attendees who work for the company. External meetings will have guests, for example customers and suppliers.

Meetings are held for different reasons and can have different formats. Some are very formal, with specific rules and procedures, while others are informal and may not even feel like a meeting. They include:

- Confidential meetings – whatever is discussed in a confidential meeting is private and should not be discussed outside the meeting. This may involve human resource issues for example disciplinary procedures if somebody has breached company policy, or company strategy. If it is a strategy meeting, managers will discuss what the company intends to do in the future. The information must remain private as they do not want their competitors to find out what they are planning.
- Team meetings are meetings between people who usually work together within a particular department in a firm, or who have been put into a team to do a specific task or job. They may hold a meeting to discuss the plans for the task, delegate jobs and report back to the other group members.

### Organising meetings

Administrative staff have to do a lot of preparation and organisation before a meeting can take place. They need to draw up and use a checklist to ensure that the meeting will be a success. A checklist for organising meetings should include:

- Meeting brief and agenda – sending notice of the meeting to attendees, distributing the agenda, preparing and photocopying documents for circulation.
- Checking dates – confirming the date of the meeting with the chairperson and attendees.

Your assessment criteria:

**2C.P4** Organise a meeting according to specified requirements using a checklist

**Key terms**

***Agenda:*** *list of items to be discussed at a meeting*

***Attendees:*** *people who attend the meeting*

***Chairperson:*** *the person in charge of the meeting. All agenda items and questions go through the chairperson first. The chairperson also mediates when there are problems*

***Minutes:*** *a summary of the points made at a meeting*

- Confirming budget – confirm how much is to be spent on preparing the meeting, for example catering, photocopying costs, etc.
- Choosing and booking venues – reserving appropriate meeting rooms and checking the furniture and layout. This will need to be done again shortly before the meeting.
- Sending meeting invitations – this includes sending an email to the attendees confirming the date and time of the meeting, the agenda and any other relevant documentation, for example **minutes** of the previous meeting.
- Arranging catering, equipment and resources – ordering and checking the refreshments required and confirming the exact number required on the day before the meeting; checking what equipment and resources are required (for example flipcharts, projectors, paper, pens); ensuring there are extra copies of documentation, in case people have forgotten or lost them, and extra paper and pens.
- Sending delegates the venue address, transport details and local accommodation details via e-mail.
- Keeping a record of attendees – a record of the attendees is usually kept in a spreadsheet so that the correct amount of refreshments can be ordered and the room size is appropriate for the number of people attending the meeting. A list of apologies (notification from people who cannot attend the meeting) also needs to be drawn up.
- Special requirements – it is important to find out if any of the attendees have any special requirements, for example if they are vegetarian or are mobility impaired. If so, the admin assistant will have to ensure their requirements are met and checked prior to the meeting.

**For meetings to be a success they must be organised efficiently using a checklist**

### Design

*Design a checklist for organising an internal or an external meeting.*

# Supporting meetings

## 2C.P4 Supporting meetings

A well-organised meeting should go so smoothly that the administrative staff who organise it are hardly noticed. A badly run meeting, for example the refreshments arriving during a presentation, can affect its success. Providing effective support for meetings requires good training, and making and referring to a checklist:

- Documentation for attendees – it is important to ensure that all necessary documentation is in the room ready for attendees. This includes copies of the agenda and other documents for the meeting, for example minutes from previous meetings.
- Attendance list – it is important to know who is going to attend the meeting so that all documents and refreshments can be ordered in the right quantities and any special requirements can be met.
- Checking the room is set out correctly – for example, the correct number of chairs in the correct positions, around a table or facing a screen.
- Checking equipment is working – for example laptops and projectors.
- Serving refreshments – any special dietary requirements must be catered for. Refreshments must be served to the attendees on time, and there must be enough for the number of attendees present.
- Accurate list of those present – the chairperson needs a list of those attending the meeting.
- Apologies for absence – knowing who is not attending the meeting is also important so that relevant documents can be sent to them once the meeting has finished.
- Agreeing minutes of last meeting – the minutes taken at the previous meeting (if there has been one) must be checked by all attendees to ensure they are accurate and the outcomes of the meeting are agreed.
- Accurate minutes of the meeting – administrative staff are responsible for taking the minutes at a meeting. This is a very important task as minutes can be legally binding. Minutes must be accurate and include any actions agreed by the attendees.

**Taking minutes and agreed actions at a meeting is extremely important**

Your assessment criteria:

**2C.P4** Organise a meeting according to specified requirements using a checklist

**2C.M3** Explain the organisation and support required for different types of meeting

### Key terms

***Agenda:*** *list of items to be discussed at a meeting*

***Minutes:*** *summary of points made at a meeting*

### Discuss

*Find out when your teachers have their regular staff meetings. Discuss in groups what you would include in a checklist for organising and supporting these meetings.*

## 2C.M3 Organisation and support for different types of meetings

In order to achieve 2C.M3, you will need to explain the organisation and support that are required for the following types of meeting:

- Large meetings involving lots of attendees – consider what is required to send out the meeting briefs and agenda; how the times and dates will be communicated; the budget required for the meeting; how the number of attendees will affect venue choice, catering, equipment and resources; how the room needs to be set out to ensure everyone is involved in the meeting; the organisation of all of the relevant documentation; and how the minutes will be documented, given the large number of attendees.
- Small meetings involving only a couple of attendees – consider all the administrative tasks above but on a smaller scale.
- Internal meetings – how would these administrative tasks be affected if all the attendees were employees of the same organisation?
- External meetings – how would these administrative tasks be affected if some of the attendees were from outside the organisation and coming from different locations? What other items would have to be given priority in your checklist?
- Formal meetings – how important are these administrative tasks if the meeting is formal?
- Informal meetings – an informal meeting is usually not very well planned and may be in an informal setting, such as a restaurant or a café. How would these administrative tasks change for an informal meeting?
- Confidential meetings – what would you need to include in your checklist of administrative tasks for the organisation and support of a confidential meeting?
- Team meetings – how would your checklist of administrative tasks change for a team meeting?

**Discuss**

*In pairs, explain the organisation and support that are needed for internal as opposed to external meetings.*

**Large meetings require specialist organisation and support**

# Organising and supporting meetings

## 2C.P5 Meeting brief, agenda and making notes

Several documents are needed for a meeting to run effectively. Administrative staff need to prepare and circulate this documentation before and during the meeting.

The meeting brief and agenda are used to inform all attendees of the purpose of the meeting and when and where the meeting is to be held. It is distributed before the meeting and is used to structure the meeting while it is in progress. It includes the topics proposed for discussion. It is also used to establish who can attend the meeting and will usually include a contact number for people to call if they are unable to attend.

The meeting brief will include the agenda of the meeting. The agenda is usually a bullet point list of all of the items that are going to be discussed. The last item on the agenda is usually AOB, which stands for any other business. At this point in the meeting attendees can raise any issues they want to discuss that have not already been addressed. See Figure 7.3 below.

**Figure 7.3 Example of a meeting brief and agenda**

City of College PERFORMING ARTS

**Meeting brief**

23 September 2012

The next meeting of the College's Performing Arts Council will be held in the conference room in the Drama building at 3.30pm on 15 October 2012. Light refreshments will be provided.

**Agenda**

1. Apologies for absence (*the names of those who have said they cannot attend*)
2. Minutes of the previous meeting (*this gives attendees the chance to correct mistakes in the minutes*)
3. Matters arising (*enables people to give updates or report on action taken following the previous meeting*)
4. Report on the Performing Arts Society of their recent successes (*main business of the meeting*)
5. Proposed fundraising opportunities for the Performing Arts Council (*main business of the meeting*)
6. AOB (*any other business – minor issues that attendees want to raise*)
7. Date and time of next meeting

*Aurelia Grace*

**Performing Arts Council Chairperson**

Your assessment criteria:

**2C.P5** Produce accurate documents required prior to a meeting and take notes during the meeting.

**2C.M4** Produce accurate and detailed post-meeting documentation (including minutes) prepared from notes taken during meeting discussions

**2C.D2** Evaluate own contribution to providing support before, during and after the meeting and suggest improvements

**Key terms**

***Action points:*** *actions agreed in the meeting and who is responsible for getting them done*

***AOB:*** *any other business – minor issues that people want to raise in a meeting*

***Minutes:*** *notes made during a meeting, along with agreed action points*

It is essential that accurate notes are taken during the meeting, so that minutes can then be written up after the meeting and circulated to all the attendees. Having an agenda often makes it easier to take notes as you can note the points and actions agreed underneath each agenda item. Taking notes in the meeting ensures that the important items that are discussed are recorded and agreed actions are completed.

**Design**

*In groups, design a meeting brief and agenda for an internal or external meeting. Act out the meeting and take notes during the meeting.*

## 2C.M4 Post-meeting documentation

After making notes during a meeting, it is important that accurate and detailed post-meeting documentation (including **minutes**) is produced so that there is a record of what was said and agreed in the meeting. Minutes are noted during the meeting, written up after the meeting and circulated to all attendees. Writing minutes ensures that all of the important points that were discussed are recorded so that people know what they have to do following the meeting (**action points**).

### Other forms of post-meeting documentation

Other forms of post-meeting documentation may be produced, depending on the type of meeting. For example, if a presentation is delivered during the meeting, the presenter may want hard copies distributed to the attendees after the meeting. Or, if the attendees have had to travel to the meeting and will be repaid, expense claim forms may be needed. It is the job of the administrative staff to ensure that this is done within an acceptable time frame.

**Discuss**

*In groups, discuss the importance of taking notes and writing up minutes at a meeting. What would be the consequences if no minutes were taken? Give examples.*

## Evaluation

In order to achieve 2C.D2, you will need to evaluate your contribution to providing support for the meeting that you have organised. You will need to assess what you did well and what you did not do so well and suggest how you could improve your support for a similar meeting in the future.

**Discuss**

*In pairs, discuss what you think you did well in supporting the meeting you organised and what you could improve. What is your partner's opinion of how well you supported the meeting?*

# Follow-up activities

## 2C.P6 Following up

A successful meeting is usually followed by actions of some sort. The minutes of the meeting are therefore very important as they serve as a written record of what actions are to be taken. Once the minutes have been written up, the attendees must agree that they are a fair record of what happened at the meeting. This means that the person taking the minutes has to be alert in the meeting and accurate when documenting what was discussed. It is best to write up minutes as soon as possible after the event.

Minutes are not the only activity to be completed following a meeting. There are a whole host of other jobs. Use this checklist for following up after a meeting:

- Clearing the **venue** – the venue must be left as it was found so that it can be used for the next appointment without causing unnecessary work. This includes clearing the venue and tidying up and leaving it in a presentable state, clearing cups and papers away, stacking tables and chairs or returning them to their original position, and so on.
- Writing up minutes after the meeting – minutes are a written record of what was discussed, including any actions and deadlines that were decided at the meeting. They are an important legal document that needs to be produced following any meeting. Some minutes, for example those relating to financial information, should be signed off by attendees to confirm what was discussed and actioned in the meeting.
- Circulating documents to attendees within agreed timescales – minutes and other documentation requested at the meeting should be distributed within the agreed timescale. This is so that everybody has written evidence of what was discussed and what, if any, tasks have to be completed before the next meeting.
- Monitoring completion of agreed actions – there is little point in having action points if they are not followed through. An important job is ensuring that the action points that attendees are given at the meeting are actually completed. Action points that should be completed before the next meeting must be agreed on and noted in the minutes. This is an effective way of monitoring progress from one meeting to the next.

Your assessment criteria:

**2C.P6** Provide all required support for a meeting, including follow-up activities

**Key term**

***Venue:*** *the room or location where a meeting is held*

**Discuss**

*Talk to your family and friends about what they have had to do, or what has been done, following a meeting that they have attended.*

**It is important to clear up after the meeting to ensure the room is ready for the next user**

**Case study**

The principal is planning to hold a meeting of some Year 11 students to discuss teaching and learning. The date and time of the meeting is 2.30 p.m. on Friday 8 February in the boardroom. She wants refreshments to be available. She also has another meeting at 4 pm in the same room so needs to be sure that the room will ready for use again at that time.

1. Draw up a checklist for organising and supporting the meeting.
2. Organise the meeting using your checklist. (2C.P4)
3. Produce an accurate meeting brief and agenda and take notes during the meeting. (2C.P5)
4. Provide all the required support during the meeting and help to clear up after the meeting. (2C.P6)
5. Produce accurate and detailed minutes using the notes you made during the meeting. (2C.M4)
6. Explain the organisation and support you had to undertake for this internal meeting. How would this change if it was an external meeting with parents and governors? (2C.M3)
7. Evaluate your contribution to providing support before, during and after the meeting and make suggestions on how you could improve. (2C.D2)

**Reflect**

*Reflect on the jobs that need to be carried out following a meeting. What will you need to be responsible for in order to ensure that you provide all of the required support for the meeting?*

# Assessment checklist

**To achieve level 1, my portfolio of evidence must show that I can:**

| Assessment criteria | Description | ✓ |
|---|---|---|
| 1A.1 | Identify types of business support in two contrasting businesses | ☐ |
| 1B.2 | Identify office equipment to meet different business requirements | ☐ |
| 1B.3 | Demonstrate using different types of office equipment safely, with guidance and in accordance with health and safety legislation | ☐ |
| 1C.4 | Draw up a checklist for organising and supporting either an internal or an external meeting | ☐ |
| 1C.5 | Produce a meeting brief and agenda for either an internal or an external meeting | ☐ |
| 1C.6 | Provide some support at either an internal or an external meeting and assist in clearing the venue after the meeting has finished | ☐ |

**To achieve a pass grade, my portfolio of evidence must show that I can:**

| Assessment criteria | Description | ✓ |
|---|---|---|
| 2A.P1 | Explain the purpose of different types of business support in two contrasting businesses | ☐ |
| 2B.P2 | Describe the use of office equipment to meet different business requirements | ☐ |
| 2B.P3 | Demonstrate using office equipment safely, in accordance with health and safety legislation | ☐ |
| 2C.P4 | Organise a meeting according to specified requirements using a checklist | ☐ |
| 2C.P5 | Produce accurate documents required prior to a meeting and take notes during the meeting | ☐ |
| 2C.P6 | Provide all required support for a meeting including follow-up activities | ☐ |

**To achieve a merit grade, my portfolio of evidence must show that I can:**

| Assessment criteria | Description | ✓ |
|---|---|---|
| 2B.M1 | Explain the appropriate uses of office equipment types, features and functions to suit different business purposes | ☐ |
| 2B.M2 | Demonstrate understanding of the application of safe lifting techniques when using office equipment | ☐ |
| 2C.M3 | Explain the organisation and support required for different types of meeting | ☐ |
| 2C.M4 | Produce accurate and detailed post-meeting documentation (including minutes) prepared from notes taken during meeting discussions | ☐ |

**To achieve a distinction grade, my portfolio of evidence must show that I can:**

| Assessment criteria | Description | ✓ |
|---|---|---|
| 2B.D1 | Analyse the contribution that office equipment makes to the provision of business support | ☐ |
| 2C.D2 | Evaluate own contribution to providing support before, during and after the meeting and suggest improvements | ☐ |

# 8 Recruitment, selection and employment

## Learning aim A: Know about job roles and functional areas in business

- Topic A.1 Organisational structures and functional areas: the different organisational structures that exist and how they are split into functional areas
- Topic A.2 Job roles and responsibilities: the different job roles and responsibilities that exist within organisations

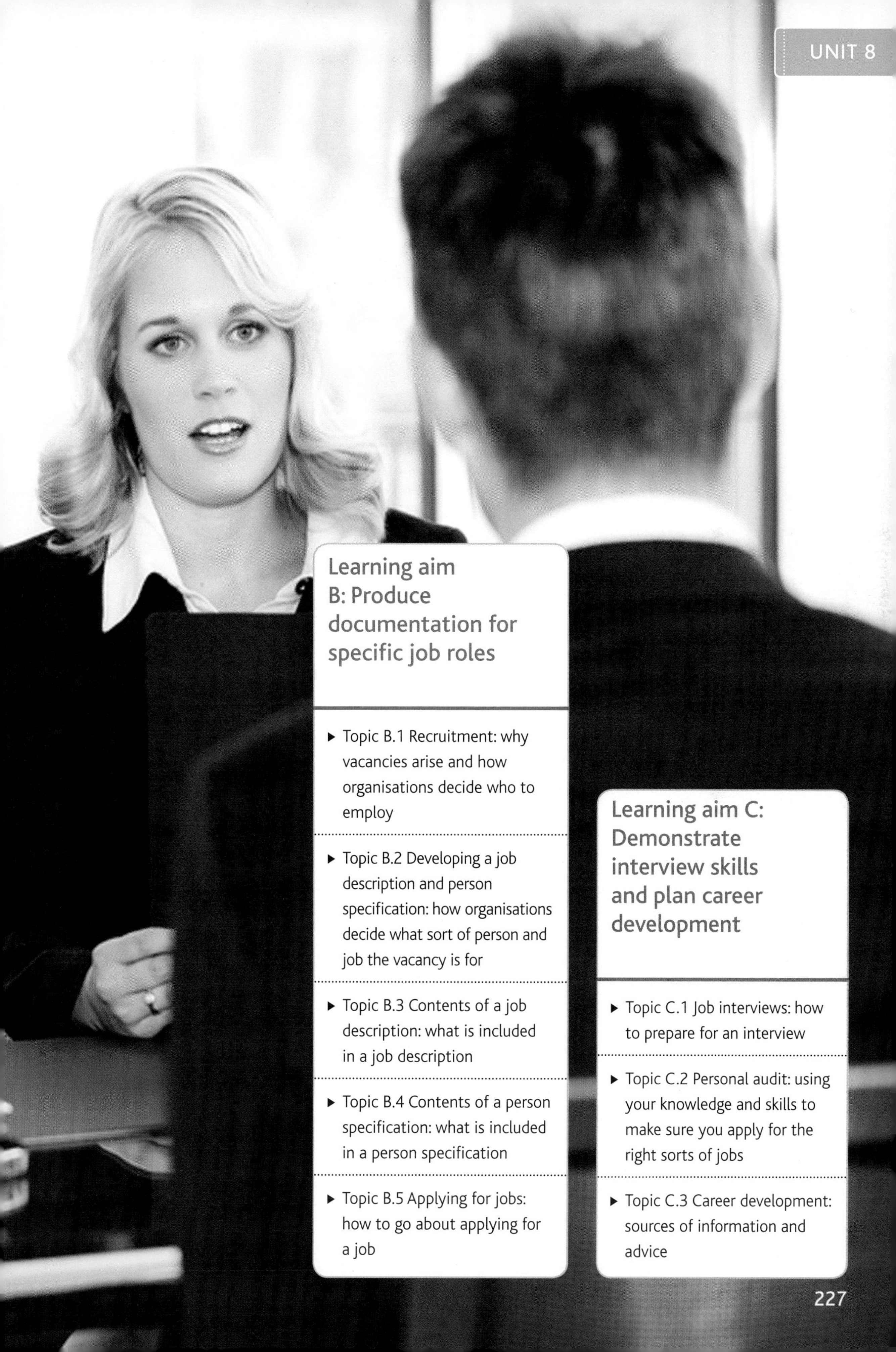

## Learning aim B: Produce documentation for specific job roles

- Topic B.1 Recruitment: why vacancies arise and how organisations decide who to employ
- Topic B.2 Developing a job description and person specification: how organisations decide what sort of person and job the vacancy is for
- Topic B.3 Contents of a job description: what is included in a job description
- Topic B.4 Contents of a person specification: what is included in a person specification
- Topic B.5 Applying for jobs: how to go about applying for a job

## Learning aim C: Demonstrate interview skills and plan career development

- Topic C.1 Job interviews: how to prepare for an interview
- Topic C.2 Personal audit: using your knowledge and skills to make sure you apply for the right sorts of jobs
- Topic C.3 Career development: sources of information and advice

# Organisational structures and functional areas

## 2A.P1 Organisational structures

The NHS employs round 1 300 000 people and is the UK's largest employer. Imagine how difficult it is in an organisation of this size to know who is to blame if something goes wrong or who to praise if there's a success. Businesses overcome this problem by organising themselves into departments, sections and sub-sections, which each have specific responsibilities, for example the sales department is responsible for increasing sales.

An organisation chart shows you how a business is split up into its different departments and teams.

- It shows all the departments, including the way each one is broken into different teams. The number of people employed in the various teams may also be shown.
- It shows the level of responsibility. All the people of roughly the same level of responsibility are shown on the same level in the chart. It shows how departments interact with one another.
- It shows the lines of communication in an organisation. Information is passed down from managers to the next level below. In the same way, it shows how matters are passed upwards from the employees to senior management.

Several different types of organisational structure can be used by businesses to allocate responsibilities.

### Hierarchical structures

This is an organisational structure where people are ranked one above the other. In a hierarchical structure, the higher up the structure you are, the more important you are and the more responsibility you have.

### Flat structures

This kind of organisational structure includes a hierarchy but does not have many layers. Flat structures are more common in smaller businesses. When businesses grow in size, the layers of responsibility increase as more managers are needed to manage the expanding workforce.

Your assessment criteria:

**2A.P1** Explain the purpose of different functional areas in two contrasting businesses

 Key term

***Organisation chart:*** *diagram that shows the structure of an organisation*

**Figure 8.1 An example of a hierarchical structure**

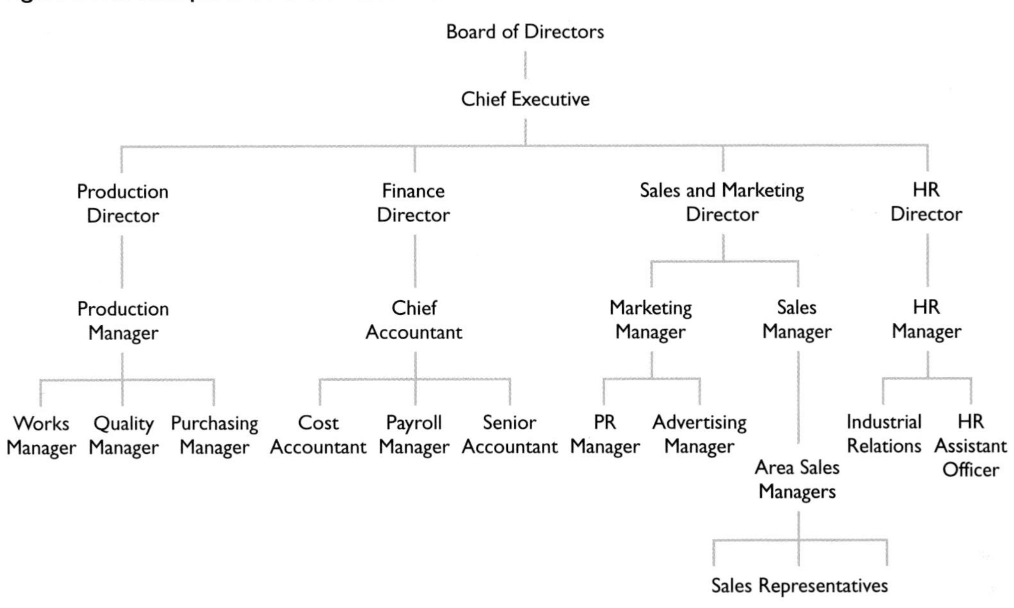


## Matrix structures

A matrix structure is used in organisations where a lot of project work is done. Project teams are normally put together to complete a specific task for a customer. These project teams are made up of people from all different specialisms within the organisation. In order for a matrix structure to work, they all need the support of the other members of staff, who are all specialists in different areas, such as finance, human resources and marketing. When the project is completed, that particular team is broken up and reassigned to a new project. A matrix structure is illustrated below:

**Figure 8.2 A matrix structure**

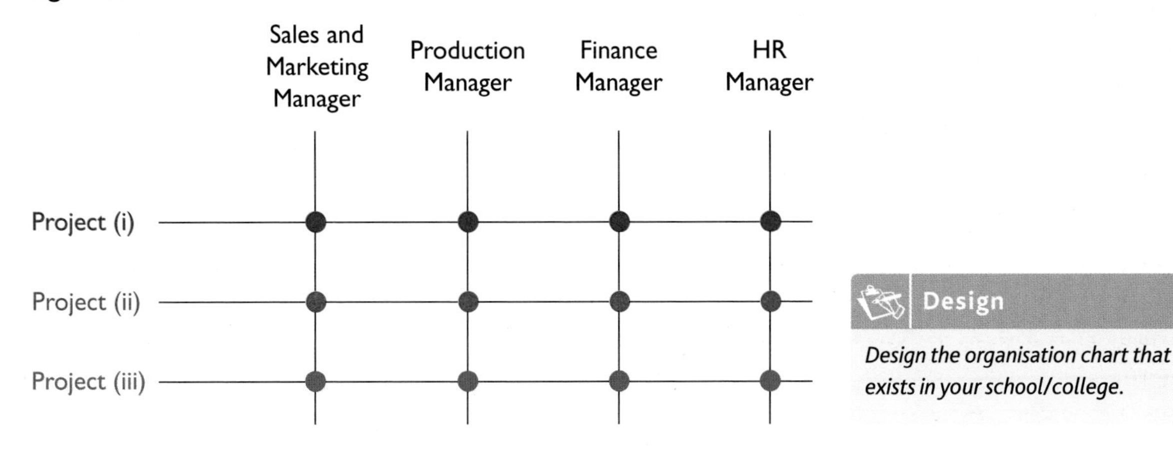


**Design**

*Design the organisation chart that exists in your school/college.*

## 2A.P1 Sales, production, purchasing, administration and customer service

Many organisations are organised into **functional areas**. These are the main departments of a business where people specialise in the jobs they are doing, for example sales and marketing, finance, production, human resources and so on. However, there may be variations on these; for example the NHS has the maternity department, oncology department, respiratory department, physiotherapy department, pathology department and many more.

Each functional area carries out specific tasks that are required for a business to achieve its aims and objectives. The main functional areas used by businesses are:

- Sales: this function is responsible for ensuring that sales targets are met. Sales staff need to be knowledgeable, able to demonstrate the benefits of a product and link these benefits to customers' needs and expectations. Usually, sales employees' pay is linked to the objectives of the business in the form of bonuses or **commission**. Customers expect more help and advice from sales staff if the products are more complex, expensive and technical, for example selling shoes in a shop is very different from selling a luxury car.
- Production: this function is responsible for making the products that are sold by the business. They assemble raw materials to create the final products to be sold to customers. For example, the production department at Sony takes all of the TV parts from its suppliers and assembles them to make the finished TVs. It must ensure the goods are made on time, the correct amounts are made, they are the right quality and are made as efficiently as possible. It must also ensure that the objectives set for the department are met; for example, if the business wants to increase sales by 20 per cent, it will need to increase production by 20 per cent.
- Purchasing: this function is responsible for buying all the products and services used by the business, such as the products sold by the sales department or the raw materials used by the production department to make the products. Purchasing staff are responsible for building good relationships with their suppliers, ensuring the prices they pay are competitive, the quality is up to standard and the goods are delivered on time and in the correct quantities. By doing this they help a business to maximise its profit as this can only be achieved if the lowest price is paid for the products, raw materials and parts.

**Your assessment criteria:**

**2A.P1** Explain the purpose of different functional areas in two contrasting businesses

**Key terms**

***Commission:*** *a type of payment for sales staff who sell products. This is often a reward, for example a percentage, for the number of products sold*

***Functional area:*** *the department responsible for completing a key operation, for example finance*

- Administration: this is a function needed by all businesses to support all of the other functional areas. Administrative tasks include opening mail, preparing and filing documents, sending e-mails and faxes, arranging travel, meetings and events. Efficient administration means that everything in the organisation runs smoothly and the managers can concentrate on running the business and achieving its aims and objectives.
- Customer service: this is the function that deals directly with customers and handles their enquiries, concerns and complaints. Unless customers receive a high level of service they are likely to take their business elsewhere. Customer service staff are highly trained to handle customers promptly and politely, especially if the organisation sells very specialist products where the staff need to know a lot of technical details about the products sold.

**Discuss**

*Discuss in groups who performs the customer services, administrative, purchasing and sales jobs in your school/college.*

**Customer services deal directly with customers**

## 2A.P1 Distribution, finance, human resources, ICT, marketing and research & development

- Distribution: this function ensures that goods are delivered to the right place at the right time. This may involve delivering directly to customers' houses or to stores and warehouses. It is important for businesses to keep their distribution costs as low as possible and therefore they plan vehicle routes to save fuel so that no unnecessary journeys are made. A good distribution function is important for businesses wanting to build a reputation for great customer service by always delivering on time.

- Finance: the finance function keeps track of all of the money earned and spent by a business so that the managers know how much profit or loss has been made and how much money a business has in the bank. This enables managers to make decisions accurately and can mean the difference between the business being a success or a failure. Without the information provided by the finance functions a business will not be able to track how it is performing against its aims and objectives.

- Human resources (HR): the HR function deals with employee-related matters. They are responsible for recruiting new staff and looking after existing employees. They ensure that new staff follow an **induction programme** and arrange training, and set up appropriate **continuing professional development** for existing staff. They also try to ensure that staff are paid appropriately, work in safe conditions, have opportunities for promotion and feel supported if they are ill or have personal problems. Well run businesses look after their employees so that they retain their best people. If employees are well trained, motivated and committed to the aims and objectives, the business is more likely to be successful.

- ICT: this function is responsible for looking after the computer equipment used in the business. Computers are essential for the smooth running of most businesses. For example, they are required to record customer orders, send e-mails, write reports and so on. ICT staff ensure that the computer systems in a business enable employees to do their jobs properly. They do this by improving communication between departments and developing improved systems so that tasks are carried out more efficiently.

Your assessment criteria:

**2A.P1** Explain the purpose of different functional areas in two contrasting businesses

**Key terms**

***Continuing professional development:*** *a commitment by a business to ensure that its employees continue to enhance their skills and training.*

***Induction programme:*** *A programme for new employees that tells them about the organisation, their rights and responsibilities, company rules and the requirements of the new job*

- Marketing: this function works closely with the sales department to ensure that sales objectives are achieved. The function is responsible for managing how a business and its products are perceived by customers. It uses market research to set prices, organise the promotion of products to identify the best place to sell products and to help the production and design department to develop products that its customers want to purchase.
- Research & development (R&D): this function is responsible for developing new products or improving existing products that are already on the market. It does this by researching products and services that are already available to customers and then creating their own new products or improving what they already offer. For example, car companies are constantly researching more fuel-efficient cars to address concerns over $CO_2$ emissions. The R&D staff help the business to achieve its aims and objectives by developing products that meet or exceed the needs and expectations of customers and are better than the competitors' products. For example, the new iPad has ensured that Apple is the market leader in tablet computers. The first iPad appeared in 2010 and less than three years later, the fourth generation iPad and iPad Mini were launched.

**R&D staff are responsible for the design of new products and improvements to existing products**

**Research**

*Research the people responsible for human resources in your school/college. Why do you think they are responsible for this?*

**Case study**

You may not realise it, but your school or college has all the different functional areas that would exist in any other business – although they may not necessarily be called the same names! You may be aware that there is an ICT technician who fixes any computers or interactive whiteboards when they are not working. However, you may be less aware of the staff who organise job interviews for prospective teachers or ensure that your teacher's contract has been issued and signed. This is equivalent to a Human Resources department.

Your own teachers are part of the distribution function! They work hard to ensure that you are taught the correct specifications and that all work is completed by the necessary deadlines. There will be a finance function where staff calculate budgets for the different departments, and there are even staff working in your school who are effectively doing R&D – the teachers! They will be constantly looking at developing their schemes of work and perhaps researching new courses and better resources for your lessons.

1. List each of the functional areas that exist in your school/college.
2. Explain the purpose of each of these functional areas to the successful running of your school/college.

## 2A.P1 Links between functional areas

For a business to achieve its goals, everybody within the organisation needs to work together to help achieve its aims and objectives and be in regular communication. Communication needs to take place regarding problems, customers' needs, costs, sales, budgets and products. There is a natural flow of goods and services throughout organisations, as shown below:

**Figure 8.3 The flow of goods and services through the business**

This flow chart shows how goods and services flow through a business from one functional area to another. At each stage functional areas need to communicate and information needs to be passed on efficiently to ensure a business can meet its overall aims and objectives.

There are many reasons why there are links between the different functional areas. Some of these are outlined in Figure 8.4.

### Key terms

***Invoices:*** *a list of goods supplied or services given, issued by the seller to the buyer*

***Profit:*** *the difference between the amount earned from selling a good and the amount spent making it*

### Discuss

*Discuss what information is needed to be communicated between each of the functional areas in order to ensure that:*

1. *the business makes money*
2. *the business develops new products*
3. *the business deals with customer complaints.*

### Research

*Choose two different businesses and research what their functional areas are. Find out the purpose of each of these departments and how they link together.*

**Figure 8.4 The links between the functional areas of a business**

| Functional areas | Links/information flow between the functional areas |
|---|---|
| Finance and all other functional areas | Finance needs to share information with all other functional areas as it is responsible for collecting information on sales and costs and communicating which functional areas are on, below or exceeding their targets to meet their objectives. |
| Finance and sales | Finance needs to keep track of the amount of money made from sales, such as the selling price and any discounts given on products. Finance also needs customer details from the sales department so that it can send out invoices. |
| Finance, purchasing and production | Finance needs to keep track of the costs of purchasing the raw materials and how much it is costing the production department to make the products. This is to ensure that the business is still making a profit. It also needs to make sure that it has all of the supplier details from purchasing so that it can check the invoices it has received from suppliers are correct. |
| Finance and HR | HR needs to communicate changes in staffing and salaries to the finance department so that it can make changes to the payroll. |
| ICT and all other functional areas | ICT is responsible for computer-related equipment, for example computers, computer programs, networks, etc. All functional areas need this equipment to communicate effectively with each other in order to meet their objectives. |
| Sales, marketing and customer service | Information about customers should be passed between these three functional areas so that the marketing can be altered to suit changing customer needs and customer service problems can be addressed. |
| Sales, production and purchasing | Production and purchasing need the sales team to tell them which products are selling well so that the necessary quantities of raw materials can be bought and more of the product can be made. Production also needs to tell the sales team when there are problems with meeting customer orders. |
| Sales, production and distribution | Sales must tell the production and distribution team when a customer is expecting to receive a product so that they can ensure it is produced and delivered on time. Similarly, the sales team may have to check with production and distribution before a delivery time is agreed. |
| Sales, R&D and production | Sales needs to communicate with R&D so that it is aware of what customers want and need in terms of products and services. R&D then needs to communicate with production to ensure what it wants to develop can be made. |
| HR | HR is responsible for all of the staffing within a business. To do this it needs to be in constant communication with all functional areas in relation to their staffing issues. |

# Job roles and responsibilities

## 2A.P2 Job roles

Everyone who works for a business has a specified role that is explained in their job title and job description. Job roles differ within organisations and can vary greatly. In smaller businesses, employees often have many different roles whereas in larger organisations staff have very defined job roles and are limited in the tasks for which they are responsible. As the UK's largest employer, the NHS has thousands of different job roles (have a look: www.jobs.nhs.com). Each job is different from the others and the tasks that need to be carried out differ hugely too. You will also notice the pay for each job role changes with the level of responsibility i.e. where they are in the **hierarchy** of the organisation.

The main job roles and the responsibilities associated with them are described below:

- Directors: they are responsible for looking after the interests of shareholders. To do this they ensure that the aims and objectives of the organisation are being met by making decisions about what a business is going to do and how they are going to achieve it.
- Senior managers: largely deal with the everyday problems of a business. They are responsible for motivating staff to achieve the objectives of the business, for setting targets to achieve the objectives set by directors, for making sure that suitable staff are recruited and dismissed when necessary, and ensuring that work is allocated fairly to staff.
- Supervisors or team leaders: they are responsible for managing small teams of junior staff to complete specific tasks. They need to be able to motivate people by building effective relationships and respect within their teams. Supervisors also have the responsibility of allocating tasks to the different staff and, if someone is absent, of reallocating the tasks to other trained employees.
- Operational and support staff/assistants: they are responsible for carrying out everyday administrative work or basic tasks, for example cashier at the supermarket. They have no responsibility for any other members of staff within the organisation and normally report to a supervisor.

Your assessment criteria:

**2A.P2** Describe the responsibilities of two different job roles in two contrasting businesses

**2A.M1** Compare two job roles and responsibilities from different functional areas in two contrasting businesses

**2A.D1** Analyse the impact of organisational structure on job roles and functional areas in a selected business, using appropriate examples

**Key term**

***Hierarchy:*** *the layers of management within an organisation*

**A receptionist's responsibilities are to support the organisation by carrying out administrative duties**

## Job roles, responsibilities and functional areas

In order to achieve 2A.M1, you will need to compare two job roles and responsibilities that exist from different functional areas in two contrasting businesses. For example, a small business with a simple, flat organisational structure could be compared to a large business with a hierarchical structure. In order to do this, you will first need to choose two similar job roles in two very different companies. The differences in the companies need to be explained in terms of their size, structure and so on. In order to make these comparisons, you will need to explain what is similar in the job roles and responsibilities, size and structure and what is different. Although the job titles in the two different organisations may look the same, you will need to research the roles and responsibilities to explain what the differences are between them.

## The impact of different organisational structures on job roles

After completing 2A.M1, you will need to analyse the impact of the organisational structure in which the two businesses operate on the job roles, responsibilities and functional areas. You will need to consider:

- how their place in the organisational structure changes
- what and who they are responsible for
- how the functional area they work in and the people they report to impacts on their job role.

### Research

*For a company of your choice, research the different job roles that exist within the organisation. Explain what the responsibilities are of the different job roles.*

### Research

*Research two different businesses where you can compare two similar job roles and responsibilities. For example, a small business with a simple, flat organisational structure and a large business that has a hierarchical structure.*

**Figure 8.5 Organisational chart for Chester Zoo**

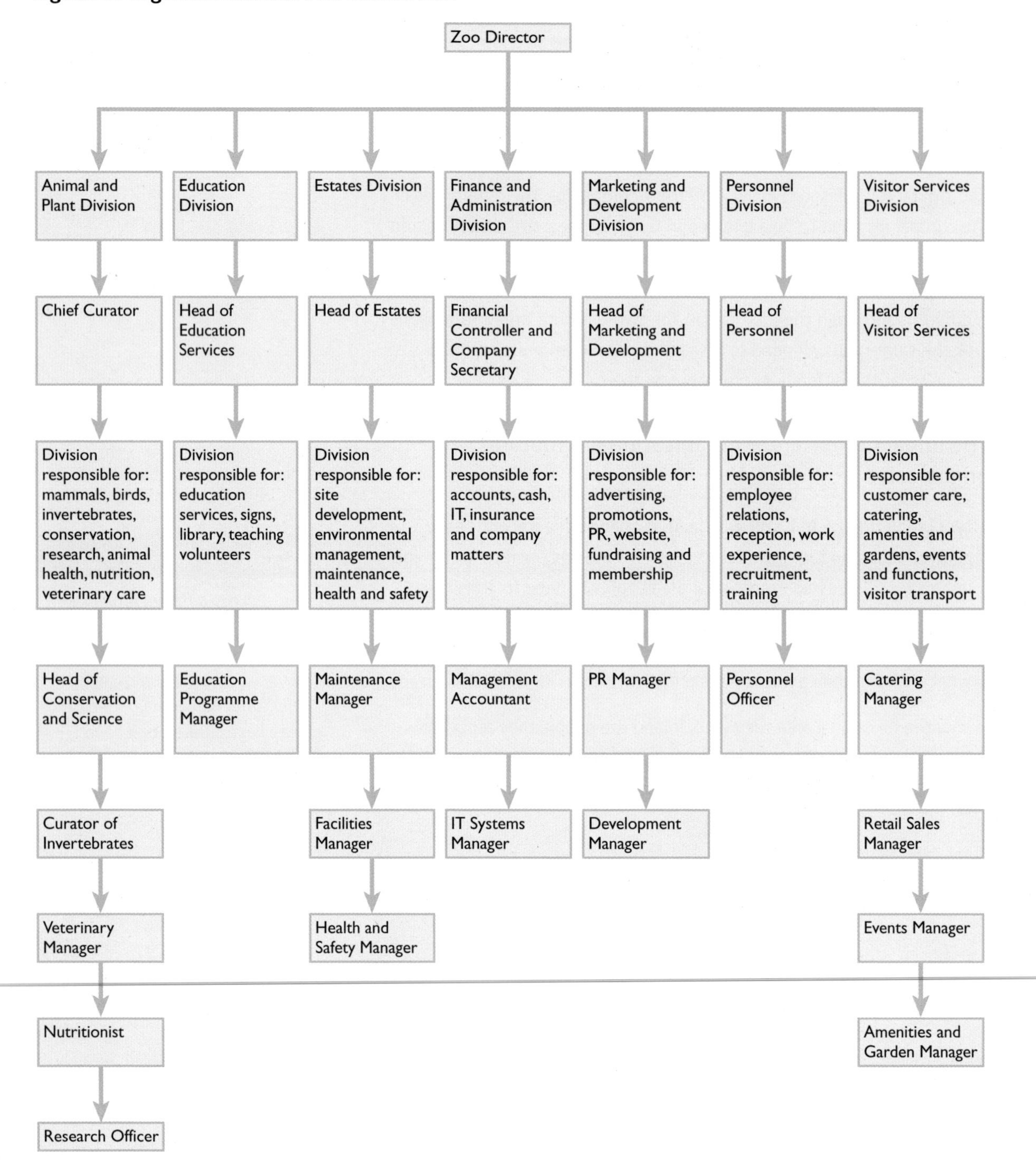

**Case study**

John Williams runs a newsagents. He works with his wife, Debbie, and between them all the day-to-day jobs of the business are carried out. John is responsible for keeping the accounts in order and paying the girl who works for them on a Saturday. He also interviews any new staff. Debbie ensures that all of the in-store promotions are up to date and deals with all of the deliveries and contacts with the suppliers.

Chester Zoo is a charitable organisation that specialises in the conservation of animals and their habitats. There are many functional areas that exist within the business in order for it to be run successfully. The functional areas and job roles are shown in the organisational chart opposite.

1. Describe and explain the purpose of two functional areas in Chester Zoo and John Williams' newsagent. (2A.P1)
2. Identify the responsibilities of two different job roles in Chester Zoo.
3. Describe the responsibilities of two different job roles in both Chester Zoo and John William's newsagent (2A.P2)
4. Compare two job roles and responsibilities from different functional areas in Chester Zoo and John Williams' newsagent. (2A.M1)
5. Analyse the impact of Chester Zoo's organisational structure on the different job roles and the functional areas. Use examples from the organisational chart in your answer. (2A.D1)

**Discuss**

*Discuss the impact of the organisational structure on the job roles, responsibilities and functional area with a partner. Are any of their views different from yours?*

# Recruitment

## 2B.P3 Vacancies

A job vacancy can arise for different reasons: an existing employee may be leaving the business; the business may be expanding, which means new employees are required; an existing member of staff may be off sick, on maternity or paternity leave; or the business is diversifying and therefore people with different skills need to be recruited.

There are many different options open to a business that needs to recruit new staff. It could advertise with the Job Centre (www.jobcentreonline.com), or it could use a recruitment consultant or agency (for example www.hays.co.uk). It could recruit from within the business itself, that is to say advertise inside the business (for example using the intranet) in the hope that a suitable person already works for the business and is able to take on the new role. Or it could advertise the job vacancy in the local or national press, on notice boards or on its website.

Internal recruitment means that the business has decided to recruit from its existing staff as therefore it does not advertise the post to anybody who does not already work for the company. This is an attractive option to some businesses if they believe they already have the ideal candidate for the job working for them but in a different role, as they already know the quality of the candidate's work. It is also cheaper to advertise internally, and the employee will already know how the business operates and can usually start straight away.

There are, however, issues with internal recruitment:

- There is less choice if only internal people are considered. This may affect the quality of the employees.
- It may slow down change. New ideas from outside the business are not brought in.
- Other parts of the organisation may suffer if their best people are taken to work elsewhere.

External recruitment is used when a business does not have the ideal candidate already working for it. Therefore it has to advertise the job outside the organisation, to the general public. This means that the business has a bigger choice of candidates to select for interview and more chance of finding the ideal person. However, it often costs a lot to advertise jobs externally as the company has to pay for advertising and training the new employee.

Your assessment criteria:

**2B.P3** Produce an appropriate and detailed job description and person specification for a specific job

**Key terms**

***Job vacancy:*** *a job that a business needs to recruit someone to perform*

***Recruitment consultant or agency:*** *a person or company that tries to find suitable candidates who meet the requirements of a job vacancy*

***Staff turnover:*** *the rate at which employees leave and are hired by a business*

***Statutory rights:*** *basic rights of employees as set out by law*

When a company is considering recruiting new staff, there are cost and legal implications that employers have to take into account. All employees have **statutory rights** in the workplace, for example, paid holiday time and maternity pay. An employer must also ensure that it has effective anti-discrimination policies. All individuals employed by the business should be treated fairly and be valued equally whatever their race, gender, physical ability, health, religion, nationality or age. Breaking employment laws can result in huge fines for a business. It may also give the business bad publicity, which may stop other talented people from applying for jobs with the company.

Businesses usually have an equal opportunities statement that is available for all staff to read. Laws on discrimination and equality were all brought together within the Equality Act 2006. This includes:

- Equal pay: men and women doing work of equal value must receive the same pay.
- Sex discrimination : both sexes must be treated equally at work, with regard to pay, selection, training, promotion, redundancies and benefits.
- Race discrimination: there should be no discrimination against employees because of their ethnic background.
- People with disabilities: there should be no discrimination against anyone with a disability and businesses should employ a quota of registered disabled people.

### Discuss

*A large company needs to appoint the following staff:*

1. *head of a major department*
2. *trainee manager*
3. *factory worker*
4. *canteen staff.*

*Discuss the most appropriate way to recruit each of the four people. Explain your answers.*

**The Job Centre is a government-run organisation that advertises jobs**

# Developing a job description

## 2B.P3 Developing a job description

Once a business has decided its organisational structure, it needs to set out the responsibilities of each job role. Also, as businesses develop, new job roles will be created all the time. First, an analysis of each job role needs to be completed, and the first question that the organisation should ask itself is 'What do we want the new employee to do?' This can lead to improvements in the organisational structure by making job roles and workloads clearer. It does this by producing a **job description** for each job role. This needs to be done before the job is advertised, so that all potential job applicants know what will be required of them. The job description is usually developed by staff in the department where the vacancy has arisen as they normally have the best understanding of what is required, providing a list of duties and responsibilities for that particular job. The employee who is leaving the post may also be involved in developing the job description and may be interviewed to find out what is involved in the job and the qualities required in the new recruit.

### Contents of a job description

A job description includes the following common elements:

- Job title
- Location of the job
- Description of the organisation's business
- Purpose of the job
- Main tasks of the job
- Lines of reporting – the position in the business including the job title of the person the employee reports to and of those who report to them, if any
- Pay and benefits
- Promotion prospects
- Start date
- Standards required
- Basis of the work – part-time or full-time, secondment, maternity cover or fixed-term contract

Your assessment criteria:

**2B.P3** Produce an appropriate and detailed job description and person specification for a specific job

**Key term**

***Job description:*** *a detailed breakdown of what a job consists of*

The job specification should describe the job succinctly, indicate the role of the employee within the team, and any relationship with other teams; specify the responsibilities of the job; and indicate the typical activities of the employee.

## The importance of the job description for effective recruitment

If a job description is not produced, the organisation would not be aware of the ideal candidate for the job, which means it could end up employing someone who cannot do the job. This would cost the firm money in the long run as extra training may be needed. A good job description should be flexible and dynamic and allow for the employee to grow with the job. A poor job description will keep an organisation and an employee away from trying anything new and learning how to perform their job more productively.

**Research**

*Research a job that you are interested in applying for. This could involve you arranging discussions with people in an organisation of your choice. Try designing your own job description for that job.*

**Figure 8.6 A sample job description**

**Job Description** – *Branning Brothers Car Dealership*

**Business:** Branning Brothers is a small car dealership specialising in good quality secondhand cars, based in Walford, East London.
Approximately five staff are employed at the office.

**Job Title:** Junior car showroom salesperson

**Hours of Work:** 40 hours per week, 9am–6pm, Wednesday–Sunday

**Holidays:** 20 days per year plus bank holidays

**Salary Scale:** £8000 plus 1.5% commission on sales

**Benefits:** Company car

**Responsible to:** Senior salesperson

**Responsible for:** N/A

**Job Purpose:** Deal with customer enquiries; give test drives; explain features of cars. Liaise with customer to arrange finance and collection of vehicles.

**Duties and Responsibilities:**
- Demonstrating features of secondhand cars to prospective buyers
- Negotiating value of trade-in cars
- Arranging finance for purchaser
- Keeping car and showroom looking smart

# Contents of a person specification

## 2B.P3 Contents of a person specification

A person specification describes who would be the perfect person for a particular job and is an extension of the job description. It lists the essential and desirable qualities of the ideal employee, such as:

- attainments and qualifications – the level of education and any industry qualifications essential or desirable for the job
- competency profiles – what the candidate should be able to do and experience of the type of work involved
- special aptitudes or skills – for example numeracy, practical, interpersonal, managerial skills
- interests – for example social activities
- disposition – for example leadership qualities
- circumstances – whether the person is able to move to different locations.

Your assessment criteria:

**2B.P3** Produce an appropriate and detailed job description and person specification for a specific job

**2B.M2** Produce an appropriate and detailed job description and person specification for a specific job, justifying why the documents will encourage effective recruitment

**Key term**

***Person specification:*** *the qualifications, experience and qualities required from the job applicant*

**Figure 8.7 Sample person specification**

**Person specification** – *Branning Brothers Car Dealership*

**Department:** Branning Brothers head office, Walford, East London

**Job Title:** Junior car showroom salesperson

| | **Essential** | **Desirable** |
|---|---|---|
| **Qualifications:** | 5 GCSEs grades C or above including Maths and English | ICT related qualification<br>Full driving licence |
| **Experience:** | Experience of dealing with customers | Previous experience of selling cars and finance |
| **Skills:** | Excellent verbal communication and numerical skills | Use of Microsoft Office |
| **Personal Attributes:** | Professional appearance, outgoing; customer-focused; self-motivated and friendly | Team player |

The person specification must not include any requirements that are not necessary for the job. It should also specify a range of ways that the employee could demonstrate the requirements for the job and should not be confined to conventional qualifications and experience.

The person specification has to be drawn up based on the job description. Figure 8.7 is an example of the person specification for the job description for Branning Brothers.

## The importance of the person specification and job description for effective recruitment

Producing detailed job descriptions and person specifications are essential for ensuring a business recruits the right people and therefore improves the quality of the workforce.

- They make expectations clear to a potential employee.
- They give candidates a clear description of the role.
- They provide a structure and discipline for the company to understand where one job ends and another begins.
- They allow wages and salaries to be structured fairly and logically.
- They provide important reference points for training and development.

If a job description is not produced, the organisation would not be aware of the ideal candidate for the job, which means it could end up employing someone who cannot do the job. This would cost the firm money in the long run as extra training may be needed.

Person specifications assist in the recruitment of new staff by:

- helping a company to focus on the type of person it really wants to do the job
- providing a consistent set of standards for all applicants that can be observed or measured objectively and therefore making it easier to shortlist potential interview candidates, as these are the criteria by which it selects candidates for interview
- providing a structured way of comparing and assessing the applicants
- making sure that everybody in the company knows the criteria by which candidates will be selected for interview.

The requirements set out in the person specification should be specific and, where possible, measurable. To ensure equality of opportunity all criteria on the person specification should be derived from the requirements set by the job description.

**Research**

*Research a job that you could be interested in applying for. This could involve you arranging discussions with people in an organisation of your choice. Create a person specification to match the job.*

**Job descriptions and person specifications help businesses recruit the right people for the jobs**

**Discuss**

*Discuss why a job description and a person specification encourage effective recruitment.*

# Applying for jobs

## 2B.P4 Curriculum vitae

Applying for a job can be a scary experience. When you are looking for a job, the job description and person specification are the documents that you receive to help you decide whether you want to apply for the job or not. If you do decide to apply, they help you to prepare for the interview as you will be asked how you fit the requirements of the job as detailed in the job description and person specification during the interview.

Once you have decided to apply for a job, you may be asked to send them your curriculum vitae (CV). Organisations will use this to assess your experience against what is outlined in the person specification. A CV should look professional, it should be word processed and divided into clear sections.

The following details should be included in your CV:

- Personal details – name, address, contact details (you can also include age, marital status and nationality but it is entirely up to you).
- Personal profile – this should include details of your skills and qualities, work background and achievements and career aims. Your CV should only cover at the most two A4 pages of size 12 font. It should grab the reader's attention and needs to be tailored to the job that you are applying for. For example, if the job involves you being an effective communicator, you could describe how you are a good team worker and are good at working with people.
- Employment history and work experience – if you haven't had much work experience, you may want to highlight your education and training. You should start with your present or most recent job and work backwards in time. You should include employer details, the dates you have worked for them, job title and main duties or responsibilities. You should explain in more detail those jobs that you have had that are relevant to the job that you are applying for, and give examples of skills you used and what these helped you to achieve. It is acceptable to use bullet pointed lists. Try to relate your experience and training to the job description and don't forget to include any voluntary and temporary work. You must also explain any gaps in your employment history, for example if you have been travelling, caring for a relative and so on.

**Your assessment criteria:**

**2B.P4** Produce a curriculum vitae, letter of application and completed application form to apply for a suitable job role

**Key term**

***Curriculum vitae (CV):*** *a document that sets out your work experience, achievements and qualifications*

- Education and training – you must start with your most recent qualifications and go back in time. Use bullet points and include:
  - college/school you attended
  - dates and the qualifications you were awarded and the grades you achieved
  - any work-related courses, if relevant, for example first aid, health and safety.
- Interests and achievements – include hobbies, interests and achievements in this section that are relevant to the job. For example, if you are a member of any clubs, explain how this has helped you to meet new people and gain new skills. Try to avoid putting hobbies such as reading or cooking as these are too general and will not really be of interest to an employer.
- Additional Information – include in this section anything else that you think is relevant, for example explaining in more detail any gaps in your employment history or other relevant skills such as holding a driving licence or your ability to speak other languages.
- References – you normally provide two references when applying for a job. At least one of these should be work-related, or someone who has known you for a while and you must state the relationship of each referee to you, for example Carol Jackson, Store Manager. You may want to list their details on your CV. Alternatively you can just write 'references available on request'.

### Research

*Research a job that you would be interested in applying for. Design your CV in order to apply for the job.*

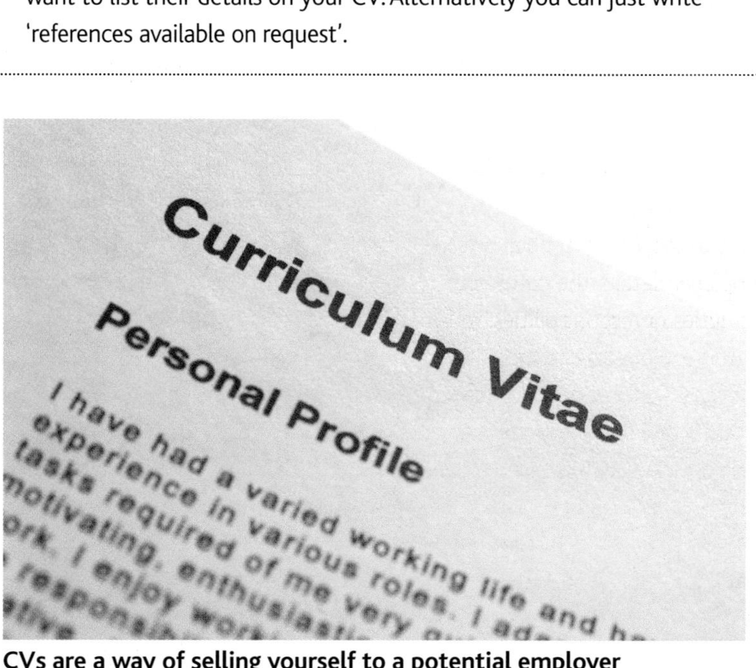

**CVs are a way of selling yourself to a potential employer**

## 2B.P4 Letters of application

When you send a CV to an organisation to apply for a job, you also have to send in a letter of application. You should ensure that this is word processed and should look like a professional business letter.

A letter of application explains why you are sending your CV and why you are applying for the job. In the letter, you should sell yourself and explain why you are the best candidate for the job. Your letter of application should be no more than two sides of A4 and it should be written in line with the job description and person specification. Therefore, the content of the letter should change depending on what job you are applying for.

Structuring your letter of application:

- Paragraph 1: You should state what job you are applying for and where you saw the job advertised.
- Paragraph 2: Introduce yourself and state that you have enclosed your CV. You need to explain in detail your skills, qualifications and relevant work experience.
- Paragraph 3: Explain why you want the job and why you are the best person for it. Explain why you want to work for that particular organisation and what qualities you could bring to that organisation. Ensure you refer to the person specification to highlight how you fit their essential and desirable characteristics.
- Paragraph 4: Thank them for considering your application and state that you look forward to hearing from them.

### 2B.P4 Application forms

When applying to some organisations, they do not ask you to send in your CV with a letter of application. Instead, they ask you to complete an application form. Nowadays, this is usually completed on line. However, if it is a paper application form ensure that you complete it in either blue or black ink and use capital letters. Application forms can take a long time to complete, so take your time and complete the form carefully ensuring there are no spelling and grammatical mistakes.

 **Key terms**

***Application form:*** *a form that is completed when applying for a job at a specific organisation*

***Assessment centre:*** *a place that job applicants are invited to attend where they are given a set of tasks that check their managerial potential*

***Criminal Records Bureau (CRB) check:*** *a check used by employers to identify candidates who may be unsuitable for certain work*

***Letter of application:*** *a letter sent to a potential employer with a CV explaining your additional skills and experience and why you are the best person for the job*

**A sample application form**

## Other requirements when applying for jobs

When you apply for a job, the organisation may want you to send them copies of your qualifications. This could include GCSE, BTEC, A-level and degree certificates and any other relevant qualifications you may have. They usually want to see the originals. If you are applying for a job that involves working with children, it is necessary for you to have a **Criminal Records Bureau (CRB) check** but the employer usually sorts this out for you.

You may also be asked to complete pre-application tests. These are tests that measure your intelligence, memory and personality and sometimes your physical attributes. For example, a physical fitness test is required when applying for the police and armed forces, and your sight is tested when applying to be a pilot.

## Next steps

Once you have completed the application and any tests that need to be done, you will then have to wait to hear if you have been shortlisted. This means that the organisation has considered your application and compared it with their person specification and other applicants. If you have been shortlisted, you will be invited to an interview or an **assessment centre** where an organisation will make a final decision on who they want to employ. If you are not successful at your interview or assessment centre, ensure that you ask for feedback from the organisation so that you can improve your next application.

### Discuss

*In groups, discuss the benefits to organisations of asking job applicants to complete an application form rather than sending in a CV and letter of application.*

# Knowledge and skills

## 2B.M3 Knowledge and skills

In order to achieve 2B.M3, you will need to look at the person specification and job description of a job that you are interested in applying for. When applying for jobs and preparing for interviews it is important that you identify the **skills** and knowledge you already have and more importantly the skills and knowledge that you need to develop.

You will need to justify how your knowledge and skills meet the requirements of the job description and person specification for the role you are applying for.

To help you do this, it is a good idea to complete a skills and knowledge audit, where you identify the knowledge and skills you have that meet those required for the job.

Parmdeep is looking to apply for a job in a large retailer as a customer service assistant. To apply for the job, she needs to know exactly what skills she has and check that these match what is required. She completes a skills/knowledge audit by comparing the skills and knowledge from the job description and person specification and comparing these with her own:

Your assessment criteria:

**2B.M3** Justify how current knowledge and skills meet those required in a given person specification and job description

**2B.D2** Analyse gaps in knowledge and skills that might require further training or development to match the requirements of a given person specification and job description

**Key terms**

***Skill:*** *the ability to do something well*

**It is important to discuss your skills and knowledge with your friends or teacher as they know you best**

**Research and discuss**

*Research a job that you would like to apply for and ensure that you get a copy of the job description and person specification. In pairs, discuss the skills and knowledge that are needed for the job and make notes on whether you have those skills and knowledge. Ask your partner's opinions on your own skills and knowledge.*

**Figure 8.8 Parmdeep's skills/knowledge audit**

| Skills/knowledge required for the job (taken from the job description/ person specification) | Do I have these skills/knowledge? If so, where did I gain them and how competent am I? |
|---|---|
| Communication and literacy skills | • Good use of written English gained from producing a range of reports in my BTEC Business.<br>• During my BTEC Business I have completed many presentations. However, I prefer making individual presentations rather than group ones as I feel more in control. |
| Team working skills | • I have played lots of netball for my school team.<br>• I have also completed my Duke of Edinburgh Bronze Award where we had to complete a group expedition. We had to work closely as a group in order to plan and undertake the expedition. In groups I always strive to make a positive contribution. |
| Organisation skills | • I am self-motivated when I am undertaking a task that I enjoy.<br>• However, I am trying to develop my time management skills as I rarely hand my coursework in on time. I therefore need to improve the preparation that I do. |
| Knowledge of Microsoft Office | • I am very confident using Word and Excel as I use them on a regular basis.<br>• I am also very confident using e-mail (Outlook) as I use it to keep in touch with friends and family. |

## Analysing the gaps

If you want to achieve a distinction, you need to identify where you are lacking some of the skills and knowledge that are set out in the job description and person specification for a particular job role. Once you have done this, you then need to identify what you could do to gain the necessary skills and knowledge. For example, you could go on training courses or do some voluntary work.

Parmdeep now wants to analyse what gaps she has in her skills and knowledge in order to apply for the job. She adds to her knowledge and skills audit:

**Figure 8.9 Parmdeep's knowledge and skills audit showing gaps in her knowledge and skills**

| Skills/knowledge required for the job (taken from the job description/person specification) | Do I have these skills/knowledge? If so, where did I gain them and how competent am I? | Gaps in my skills/knowledge and how I will fill these gaps |
|---|---|---|
| Communication and literacy skills | • Good use of written English gained from producing a range of reports in my BTEC Business.<br>• During my BTEC Business I have completed many presentations. However, I prefer making individual presentations rather than group ones as I feel more in control. | • I always have corrections to the structure of my work and therefore I will make arrangements to talk to the teacher about how this can be improved.<br>• I plan to organise groups better and practise beforehand. |
| Team working skills | • I have played lots of netball for my school team.<br>• I have also completed my Duke of Edinburgh Bronze Award where we had to complete a group expedition. We had to work closely as a group in order to plan and undertake the expedition. In groups I always strive to make a positive contribution. | • I need to develop my leadership and organisation skills. I may organise an event within my college. |
| Organisation skills | • I am self-motivated when I am undertaking a task that I enjoy. | • I am trying to develop my time management skills as I rarely hand my coursework in on time. I therefore need to improve the preparation that I do. |
| Knowledge of Microsoft Office | • I am very confident using Word and Excel as I use them on a regular basis.<br>• I am also very confident using e-mail (Outlook) as I use it to keep in touch with friends and family. | • I am not so confident with Access, PowerPoint or Publisher.<br>• I am planning to sign up to a free computer class after school in order to improve these skills. |

**Case study**

Read the job vacancy below:

Role-based actor, Chester Zoo

We have an exciting vacancy to join our Presenter Team in our exhibition, Dinosaurs Bite Back!

You will be surrounded by lifelike robotic dinosaurs and your role will be to help make them even more thrilling to our visitors. You will be working with the public so, if you have a confident and outgoing personality, you could be the 'Presentersaurus' we're looking for! You will be responsible for helping to develop stories and activities and deliver them to our audience on a daily basis and be involved in our educational public events.

The successful candidate will have a creative and enthusiastic approach to acting and storytelling and have excellent communication skills. He/she will be able to work individually and as part of a small team and maintain effective working relationships. He/she must provide excellent customer care at all times. This post is subject to an enhanced CRB check. Work is 5 days in 7 including Bank Holidays and every weekend. Hours are 9.30 a.m. to 5 p.m. daily, rate of pay is £7.07 per hour and the contract is to run from 31 March to 4 November 2013. Closing date is 1 March 2013.

1. Produce an appropriate and detailed job description and person specification for the above job (2B.P3)
2. Why do a job description and a person specification encourage effective recruitment? (2B.M2)
3. Produce a curriculum vitae, letter of application and an application form for the above job. (2B.P4)
4. Justify how your current knowledge and skills meet the requirements of the person specification and job description that you have produced for question 1. (2B.M3)
5. Analyse any gaps in your knowledge and skills that may require further training or development so that you match the requirements of the person specification and job description completed in question 1. (2B.D2)

**Discuss**

*In pairs, discuss what gaps you may have in your skills and knowledge when comparing them with the requirements of your chosen job description and person specification. How are you going to fill these gaps?*

# Job interviews

## 2C.P5 Job interviews

The interview is a chance for you and the employer to meet one another and for the employer to decide if you are the right person for the job.

### Preparing for the interview

Doing your research is essential before every interview you go to. Whatever organisation you have applied to, there is always some general research you can undertake:

- Its general organisational structure
- Its history and how long it has been operating
- Career progression within the organisation
- The state of the industry
- The location of the interview
- The size of the organisation
- The major competitors
- The job role, what it involves and responsibilities

### Question preparation and anticipation

Use the internet to look at possible questions for the sort of job that you are applying for and prepare some answers. Also, use the job description and person specification to prepare examples of when you have displayed the skills necessary for the job. At the end of your interview, you will also be asked if you have any questions for the interviewers. Make sure you prepare some questions to ask so that you appear enthusiastic and interested.

### Other things to prepare

- Ensure you are dressed appropriately: it is important to look smart so that you give a good first impression. For example wearing a suit makes you look professional.
- Good personal hygiene: ensuring you are well groomed and clean shows your prospective employer that you care about the way you look. Do not chew gum or smell of cigarettes as this can be off-putting for the interviewer.

Your assessment criteria:

**2C.P5** Provide appropriate responses to interview questions for a specific job role

**2C.M4** Demonstrate prior research and preparation when providing appropriate responses to interview questions for a specific job role

**Key term**

***Body language:*** *a type of non-verbal communication that relies on body movements (for example gestures, posture and facial expressions) to convey messages*

**Research**

*Research some possible questions that you may be asked in your interview.*

**Preparing possible questions for an interview**

- Location and travel arrangements: make sure that you know where the interview is going to be, not only the address, but also the room. Also, look at how you are going to get there and make sure you plan the timings so that you are not late. Arrive in plenty of time: make sure that you arrive early. It gives a good impression and allows you a bit of preparation and calm time before your interview. Plan your travel arrangements so that you arrive around 20 minutes early.

## During the interview

Your behaviour during the interview is very important as this is when the interviewer is going to be making important judgments about your suitability for the role. It is the only time they get to meet you before they offer you the job and therefore you need to make a good impression.

Be confident: even though you may not feel like it, looking confident is very important. Be conscious of your body language and your voice. You need to give a good impression of yourself from the minute you walk through the door. As part of your interview preparations:

- brush up on your knowledge and application of body language, for example practise giving and maintaining eye contact with people
- practise displaying confidence, for example your posture and your handshake and the way you sit
- practise an appropriate tone of voice and make sure you are clear when you speak
- practise your active listening skills, ensuring that you do not 'switch off' when people are talking to you, and show interest in what they are saying.

**Research**

*Research and prepare for the job you are going to apply for, ensuring that you prepare appropriate responses to some possible interview questions.*

**Looking smart for an interview**

**Case study**

You applied for the job of role-based actor at Chester Zoo and have been asked to attend the interview.

1. Research and prepare for an interview for the job of role-based actor at Chester Zoo. (2C.M4)
2. Answer the following interview questions (2C.P5):
   **(a)** Why are you interested in applying for this job?
   **(b)** Why do you want to work for Chester Zoo?
   **(c)** Why do you think you are the best person for this job?
   **(d)** What qualities can you bring to the role?

# Personal audit and career development

## 2C.P6 Personal audit

A personal audit can help you to improve your chances of being successful when applying for jobs by identifying the skills and qualifications you have that employers may be looking for. It will help you plan how you are going to get the skills and qualifications that you require. Completing an audit will help you to see whether you meet the criteria outlined in person specifications.

A personal audit may include an assessment of your own:

- knowledge – including qualifications such as GCSEs, BTECs and so on
- skills – including technical, practical, communication and numeracy skills
- interests – including hobbies and activities you do outside school, for example playing sport.

Georgie needs to complete a personal audit as she is unsure what sort of jobs she wants to apply for. She talks to her teachers and works with them to complete her personal audit (Figure 8.10).

**Completing a personal audit can take a lot of thought**

Your assessment criteria:

**2C.P6** Produce a realistic personal career development plan

**Key terms**

***Apprenticeship:*** *a programme that combines on-the-job training with some academic instruction*

***Personal audit:*** *checking that your skills and qualifications match what the employers want*

**Design**

Design and complete your own personal audit. Discuss in pairs types of careers that may suit your skills set and interests.

**Figure 8.10 An example of a personal audit**

## Personal Audit – Georgina Williams

| Qualifications | Predicted Grade |
|---|---|
| GCSE Maths | C |
| GCSE English Language | C |
| BTEC Science | Pass |
| BTEC Business | Merit |
| BTEC Sport | Distinction |

### Skills

**Oral communication** 1
I regularly give presentations in my BTEC Business lessons and I am on the student council where I speak to the other councillors during the meetings. I have also completed some work experience in an office where I had to answer the phone and be polite and clear to customers.

**IT and technical skills** 3
I am very good at using Microsoft Word and PowerPoint as I use these nearly every day for my coursework. I also use Microsoft Outlook to send emails to my friends and family. I have used Excel and Access in ICT lessons.

**Organisational and time management skills** 1
I am a very organised person, I ensure I always make a timetable of when my coursework needs to be handed in and try my best to stick to it and therefore do not miss my deadlines. I have also had to organise my classmates doing tasks for the Student Council.

**Problem solving and practical skills** 2
I am good at problem solving, I try not to panic and try to think of a solution. During my Duke of Edinburgh expedition we came across problems as a group and individually that needed solving. I therefore have a good knowledge of the processes you need to undertake in order to solve a problem.

**Independent working** 3
During my work experience I was expected to take responsibility and act on my own initiative.

**Team working** 2
I have played netball for my school since year 8. This has meant that I work very well in teams as you have to constantly think about the other players. I also work well in group work when I am doing experiments in Science. I make sure I listen to peoples' opinions and share the workload equally.

**Numeracy skills** 3
I am predicted a GCSE Maths grade C and I am confident using basic maths skills including graphs and charts and some statistical techniques such as mean, mode and median. I am not so confident however with mental arithmetic and this could cause a few problems in the future if I need to add up customers orders.

**Skills score:**
I have rated myself out of 5 for each skill.
1: I am very good at this skill
2: I am good but could improve
3: I have to improve this skill
4: It is going to take a lot of hard work to develop this skill
5: I have never used this skill

## 2C.P6 Getting the right careers information and advice

There are so many different careers to choose from that it can be difficult to know where to start. There are lots of services out there to help you get the right information and point you towards careers that you may have never even thought about.

### Developing a career plan

A career development plan sets out your own ambitions and how you are going to achieve them. Every successful career plan will include continuous training and development to ensure you keep up with the current trends.

### Academic or vocational pathway

You need to ensure that you are completing courses that will qualify you for any further or higher education courses you want to study. Every employer will want to see that you have at least a C in both Maths and English GCSE.

You will need to research which educational path will enable you to succeed in your chosen career. The academic pathway means gaining qualifications such as GCSEs and A-levels and then usually completing a degree. There are also career-specific qualifications that you may need to complete. For example, accountants have to complete career specific qualifications such as CIMA (Chartered Institute of Management Accounting); teachers also need to complete a PGCE (Post Graduate Certificate in Education).

The vocational pathway means completing courses such as BTECs that equip you with the skills to do certain jobs. There are also options such as **apprenticeships** and NVQs, which are work-based learning and teach the skills required to do a particular job. For example, all firefighters have to complete an NVQ in Emergency Fire Services. You may also need to consider the type of employment you want, including whether this is on a full-time or a part-time basis. Full-time workers are generally considered to be people who are employed for between 35 and 42 hours per week. Part-time worker are generally employed for up to 20 hours per week. Some people use part-time work as a stepping stone that will lead to a full-time post while others, such as young parents, enjoy the flexibility it gives them.

### Research

*Research some courses that you think may be of interest to you when you finish school or college. What qualifications do you need? How long are the courses for? What job opportunities will the course lead to?*

**Figure 8.11 Sources of information and advice**

| Sources of information and advice | Description |
|---|---|
| Careers advice services | If you are under 19, the government's Connexions services will provide you with free careers advice. |
| Advertisements | There are many websites and newspapers that advertise jobs. Most newspapers publish their job advertisements on a particular day of the week as well as advertising them online. |
| Word of mouth | Someone you know may tell you about a job that has become available. |
| Careers fairs | Many employers have stalls and they can give you the information you need about their industry and business. |
| Friends and family | They can offer some excellent advice as they know you best. |
| Teachers | Teachers can often point you in the right direction to help you. |
| Previous employers | These can provide you with information about careers in a certain area and indicate what training you may need to undertake. |
| Network connections | You may know people who also know people in the industry that you are interested in. |
| Employment and government agencies | Check online to find your local agency. Some may also offer services to help you complete your CV. |

**All firefighters have to complete an NVQ in Emergency Fire Services**

## 2C.M5 Training and targets

Once you have completed your research on your career path you need to look at your **training needs** and to start making development plans and setting personal targets. This will help you to reflect on what you need to do and to stay on track to achieve your career goals.

First, write down any development needs that you have identified from your skills and personal audit, for example enhancing your computer skills by completing a course at college. You then need to write in detail how you are going to acquire these skills either via training or experience. For example, if you need to maintain good levels of oral communication, you may need to start practising speaking in front of audiences and could offer to do a presentation at college.

You should also plan how and when you are going to review your development plan. This means setting yourself personal targets with **timescales** of when you are planning to develop your skills and deadlines for when they need to be achieved.

### A career development plan

A career development plan should be an action plan for the future. It should specify particular areas for development over the next few months and identify how you will achieve your goals, for example training courses to attend. It should include:

- your name
- your proposed job role
- the date
- your career aspirations (short-term and long-term)
- your strengths
- your weaknesses
- your areas for development and target dates
- when you are going to review your career development plan again
- where you expect to be by your next review.

Your assessment criteria:

**2C.M5** Produce a realistic personal career development plan showing independent research and planning

**2C.D3** Evaluate the suitability of a realistic career development plan using interview performance feedback and own reflection

**Key terms**

***Timescales:*** *periods of time in your development plan in which you aim to complete certain qualifications or learn new skills*

***Training needs:*** *any training you need to complete in order to meet your development plan*

**Discuss**

*In pairs:*

1. *Reflect on your performances at your interviews for 2C.P5. What did you do well? What did you do not so well? How could you improve your performance next time?*
2. *Evaluate the suitability of each of your career development plans. Identify areas where they could be improved.*

## The suitability of your career development plan

In order to achieve a distinction, you will first need to reflect on your own performance in the interview that you undertook in 2C.P5. You should use the comments and feedback that you gained from the interviewer to help you to do this. Using this information and the research you have conducted into your career for 2C.P6 and 2C.M5, evaluate the suitability of your career development plan. How realistic is it? You will need to identify areas where you can improve your plan and how it will be updated.

**Case study**

Following your interview for the role-based actor job at Chester Zoo, you decide to complete a career development plan. Complete the following:

1. Research and plan all of the necessary elements for a personal career development plan. (2C.M5)
2. Produce a realistic personal career development plan. (2C.P6)
3. Evaluate the suitability of your career development plan using the feedback you have gained from your interview for the role-based actor post and your own reflection. (2C.D3)

**Planning your career effectively leads to success**

**Discuss**

*In pairs, review your own performance. Record the following information:*

1. *How well are you performing at school or college? Are you achieving good grades, completing work, meeting deadlines?*
2. *Ask your partner how well they think you are doing. Ask them to give reasons for their opinions.*
3. *Complete a career development plan.*

# Assessment checklist

**To achieve level 1, my portfolio of evidence must show that I can:**

| Assessment criteria | Description | ✓ |
|---|---|---|
| 1A.1 | Describe the purpose of two functional areas in two contrasting businesses | ☐ |
| 1A.2 | Identify the responsibilities of two different job roles in a selected business | ☐ |
| 1B.3 | Produce a job description for a specific job | ☐ |
| 1B.4 | Produce, with guidance, a curriculum vitae and letter of application to apply for a suitable job role | ☐ |
| 1C.5 | Provide some appropriate responses to interview questions for a specific job role | ☐ |
| 1C.6 | Produce, with guidance, a personal career development plan | ☐ |

**To achieve a pass grade, my portfolio of evidence must show that I can:**

| Assessment criteria | Description | ✓ |
|---|---|---|
| 2A.P1 | Explain the purpose of different functional areas in two contrasting businesses | ☐ |
| 2A.P2 | Describe the responsibilities of two different job roles in two contrasting businesses | ☐ |
| 2B.P3 | Produce an appropriate and detailed job description and person specification for a specific job | ☐ |
| 2B.P4 | Produce a curriculum vitae, letter of application and completed application form to apply for a suitable job role | ☐ |
| 2C.P5 | Provide appropriate responses to interview questions for a specific job role | ☐ |
| 2C.P6 | Produce a realistic personal career development plan | ☐ |

**To achieve a merit grade, my portfolio of evidence must show that I can:**

| Assessment criteria | Description | ✓ |
|---|---|---|
| 2A.M1 | Compare two job roles and responsibilities from different functional areas in two contrasting businesses | ☐ |
| 2B.M2 | Produce an appropriate and detailed job description and person specification for a specific job, justifying why the documents will encourage effective recruitment | ☐ |
| 2B.M3 | Justify how current knowledge and skills meet those required in a given person specification and job description | ☐ |
| 2C.M4 | Demonstrate prior research and preparation when providing appropriate responses to interview questions for a specific job role | ☐ |
| 2C.M5 | Produce a realistic personal career development plan showing independent research and planning | ☐ |

**To achieve a distinction grade, my portfolio of evidence must show that I can:**

| Assessment criteria | Description | ✓ |
|---|---|---|
| 2A.D1 | Analyse the impact of organisational structure on job roles and functional areas in a selected business, using appropriate examples | ☐ |
| 2B.D2 | Analyse gaps in knowledge and skills that might require further training or development to match the requirements of a given person specification and job description | ☐ |
| 2C.D3 | Evaluate the suitability of a realistic career development plan using interview performance feedback and own reflection | ☐ |

# INDEX

# Photo acknowledgements

Alamy: 5, 7, 19, 21, 25, 35, 43, 49, 50, 51, 55, 57, 75, 77, 87, 89, 90, 91, 92, 93, 95, 96, 97, 98, 101, 103, 104, 105, 111, 119, 127, 129, 130, 135, 137, 139, 144, 152, 154, 158, 159, 181, 185, 195, 197, 198, 200, 203, 214, 215, 218, 223, 231, 241, 249, 259, 261

Competition Commission: 199

Facebook: 110

Getty Images: 3, 15, 17, 23, 30, 32, 33, 36, 37, 39, 64, 88, 103, 105, 118, 127, 141, 145, 149, 156, 171, 173, 175, 177, 179, 182, 191, 193, 197

Ros Horton: 13, 198

Jeff Moore: 187

Shutterstock: 7, 11, 26, 27, 34, 41, 46, 56, 58, 63, 67, 71, 72, 81, 83, 94, 100, 113, 116, 121, 125, 132, 136, 147, 149, 151, 160, 163, 164, 167, 189, 191, 201, 206, 208, 210, 211, 213, 217, 219, 226, 233, 236, 239, 245, 247, 248, 250, 253, 254

Social Enterprise: 34